Africa and the Third Millennium

AFRICA AND THE THIRD MILLENNIUM

Edited By
GEORGE KLAY KIEH, JR.

Africa World Press, Inc.

P.O. Box 1892
Trenton, NJ 08607

P.O. Box 48
Asmara, ERITREA

Africa World Press, Inc.

P.O. Box 1892
Trenton, NJ 08607

P.O. Box 48
Asmara, ERITREA

First Printing 2008

Book and cover design: Saverance Publishing Services
(www.saverancepublishing.com)

Library of Congress Cataloging-in-Publication Data

Africa and the third millennium / edited by George Klay Kieh, Jr.
p. cm.
Includes bibliographical references and index.
Includes index.
ISBN 1-59221-604-8 (hbk.) -- ISBN 1-59221-605-6 (pbk.)
1. Africa--Politics and government--21st century. 2. Africa--Economic conditions--21st century. I. Kieh, George Klay, 1956-
JQ1875.A7235 2007
960.3'3--dc22

2007035380

TABLE OF CONTENTS

LIST OF TABLES

PREFACE

There is a general consensus among scholars, practitioners and Africans from all works of live, irrespective of their ideological persuasions, that the previous millennia forced the continent into a disadvantageous position vis a vis the other regions of the world, especially the metropolis. However, there are divergent explanations for the specific causes of the adverse impact of the old millennia on Africa. In addition, there are various competing pathways that have been proffered as the terra firma for lifting Africa from the dungeon of underdevelopment. There is the emergent agreement that the new millennium provides another opportunity for African states to rethink their peripheral status in the international "balance of power," and to fashion policies that would enable them to address their respective perennial development challenges.

It is against this background that this book was conceived. But, in view of the fact that the challenges facing African states and the continent are numerous, the determination was made to identify and address some of the "frontier issues" such as the state, the overarching architecture; economic development; democratization; urbanization and social development; the environment, the most crucial sector; and stability as reflected in the incidence of civil wars. Although the various chapters in the book are not linked by a shared Weltanschauung, the shared orientation is that suggestions need to be devised to help address the region's myriad problems. In other words, it is not enough to analyze the continent's various problems. Instead, the diagnosis of the problems must be linked to the formulation of ideas that would help to address the many challenges. Moreover, in the age of the "new globalization," it is imperative to reposition Africa. If this is not done, the continent would be saddled with the various negative effects of the phenomenon. Ultimately, this would worsen its development woes and further marginalize it in the global power calculus.

Several persons made the writing of this book possible. First, I would like to thank the contributors for agreeing to participate in the project, especially for the patience they showed as the drafts of their chapters were reviewed, and for their prompt responses to the various editorial queries.

Second, I would like to thank my dear wife, Doris, for providing assistance with the reformatting and word processing of some of the chapters to ensure uniformity. Beyond that, she demonstrated the usual understanding as I devoted substantial amount of time to the editorial chores that are associated with edited volumes.

Finally, it is our hope that this volume will contribute to the on going debate about the African predicament. Especially, it is our desire that the various suggestions offered would be useful as Africa and its constituent states design modalities for tackling the various development challenges. As in the 1960s during the "wave of independence," Africa is again at another critical juncture. If the ruling classes refused to provide leadership in tackling the continent's plethora of problems, and the subaltern classes are complacent in pressing for change, the continent would be finally doomed! For the sake of Africa's children, it is our hope that serious and sustained efforts would be made to reverse the African predicament for the better.

- George Klay Kieh, Jr.

PART I

BACKGROUND

Chapter 1

Introduction: Africa and the Old Millennia

George Klay Kieh, Jr.

INTRODUCTION

The previous two millennia for Africa, to paraphrase the legendary African musician Fela Anikulapo-Kuti, were marked by the shedding of "tears and blood."[1] Since its initial contact with Europe, the continent's relationship with the metropolis has been marked by exploitation and marginalization. To make matter worse, the continent's local ruling classes have failed to provide the critical leadership that is exigent and imperative for exiting the neo-colonial state and ushering in a new pro-people, pro-democracy and pro-development construct that is reflective of the historical and cultural experiences of Africans. Consequently, Africa entered the 21st century, among other things, as the most underdeveloped region in the world in terms of all of the economic and social indicators. The World Bank (2000, p.1) provides a stark description of the African predicament:

> Despite gains in the second half of the 1990s,… [Africa] enters the 21st century with many of the world's poorest countries. Average per capita is lower than at the end of the 1960s. incomes, assets and access to essential services are unequally distributed. And the region contains a growing share of the world's absolute poor, who have little power to influence the allocation of resources…

Against this background, the purpose of this chapter is three fold. First, the chapter will survey the African predicament during the previous two millennia. Second, it will discuss the focus of the book. Third, it will summarize the major arguments of the various chapters of the book.

THE OLD MILLENNIA

The Phases

The impact of the two previous millennia on Africa can be gauged by examining four epochal phases. The first one is Africa's initial incorporation into the evolving global capital system through the establishment of formal contacts with various European powers beginning in the 16th century. Pressed by the imperatives of their domestic economies and those of the international capitalist system, the European imperialist powers saw Africa as a region from which they could acquire critical goods. Accordingly, various imperialist surrogates traveled to Africa and engaged the region's peoples in a system of predatory trade. Under the system, the imperialist agents brought goods that were outdated and inferior and thus unmarketable in Europe and sold them to unsuspecting African traders. In exchange, the imperialist economic agents received valuable commodities that were important for the development of their respective countries and the emerging global capitalist system. The resultant "system of unequal exchange" (Wallerstein, 2004; Arrighi, 1994; Frank, 1971) laid the foundation for Africa's eventual incorporation into the international capitalist system.

Exhilarated by the successes of predatory trade, and pressured by the exigencies of their respective capitalist economies particularly the need for labor, the imperialist powers made the determination that Africa could satisfy their critical need. Hence, slavery, the most venal, dehumanizing and exploitative system ever known the human- kind was devised. Under this nefarious scheme, the imperialist powers took thousands of Africans in shackles to work on their various plantations in Europe and the Americas. These enslaved Africans provided the labor power for helping to build the foundation for European economic power and prosperity.

Convinced that Africa was an "economic bonanza" that could serve as a permanent plantation for supplying the commodities that would help feed their industrial-manufacturing complexes, the imperialists decided to formally colonize Africa. Thus, the imperialist powers convened the infamous "Berlin Conference" in 1884. The crux of the conference was to militate against the occurrence of the disorder that usually accompanies imperialist competition. So, the imperialist powers formulated and implemented a "formula of dividing the spoils." Based on this arrangement, each imperialist power was allocated several territories.

The emergent colonial order was based on an interlocking web consisting of various elements—cultural, economic, political, religious and social—designed to establish and consolidate the imperialist stranglehold on Africa. In the cultural realm, the imperialist powers made concerted efforts to obliterate Africa's indigenous cultures. The dominant instrument was the demonization of indigenous African cultures as "paganistic, barbaric and uncivilized." This was then followed by the imposition of the culture of the colonial power on their respective colonies. Specifically, this involved the wholesale replacement of indigenous African cultural values, norms and mores by European ones. Economically, each colonial power designed a "division of labor" for its colonies under which the latter produced assigned products, thereby laying the basis for the development of monocrop-based peripheral capitalist economies. Among other things, each economy was based on the venal exploitation of labor and farmers, and the dominance of the European ruling classes. At the political level, state terrorism became the mainstay of the relationship between the colonial state and the colonized society. Under this tapestry, the imperialist powers, among other things, denied African their fundamental political rights and civil liberties. Each time Africans protested against the cruelty of the colonial state, they were pummeled by the full battery of the coercive arsenal. In the religious domain, the various traditional African religions were vilified as the embodiment of savagery and sorcery. In their stead, the imperialist powers imposed their brands of Christianity. The shared distinguishing feature of these brands in practice was the glaring absence of the Christ-like Christianity's core commitment to social justice and human dignity.

Saddled with various challenges and problems, the imperialist powers reluctantly made the determination to dismantle their respective colonial empires, and to grant the various African colonies political independence. Accordingly, the 1960s were considered "Africa's golden age," evidenced by the wave of "flag independence" that swept across the continent. As Ramsay (1993, p.3) observes, "Times were electric...Hopes were high." The collective hope of the African peoples was that with the end of colonialism the continent would be able to realize its fullest potentials. Specifically, with its rich and fertile soil, vast natural resources and industrious peoples, the mass hope was that each independent African state would replace the European authoritarian multiplex with a pro-people, pro-democracy and pro-development one.

However, the African peoples did not take cognizance of the fact that the imperialists had devised another insidious scheme ostensibly intended to keep their control over Africa fully in tact. So, neo-colonialism replaced colonialism as the new framework of metropolitan domination over Africa. According to Babu (1992, p.15),

> Neo-colonialism is the off-shoot of colonial ideologies and economics, conditioned by the needs of the cold war and the reconstruction of European economies devastated by World War II. Africa had to supply cheap raw materials to hasten Europe's economic recovery.

Neo-colonialism was established and maintained by an array of interrelated instruments. Overall, the post-colonial state was a replica of the colonial one in terms of its nature, character, mission, values, institutions, rules, processes and policies (see chapter 3). So, as the overarching framework, the post-colonial state became the principal conduit for the maintenance of Africa's subordination to the interests of the imperialist powers. Accordingly, several instruments were fashioned by the portrait of the post-colonial state. First, the imperialist powers facilitated the establishment of malleable African ruling classes that were subservient to the former's interests. For example, during the "Cold War," the two dominant imperialist blocs—"American" and "Soviet"—provided their respective client regimes with political, economic and military assistance as the payments for the latter's subservience. In those African countries where there were anti-imperialist regimes in power, steps were taken to depose them. For example on January 17, 1961, American and Belgian imperialism spearheaded the overthrow and subsequent murder of

Patrice Lumumba, the Prime Minister of the Congo (now the Democratic Republic of the Congo). Lumumba's "major crime" was his determination to democratically reconstitute the Congolese state so that it could serve the interests of the majority of the people. Realizing that Lumumba's agenda was antithetical to their imperialist agendas of political and military domination and economic exploitation, the United States, through its Central Intelligence Agency (CIA), and the Belgian intelligence agency planned and executed the coup that deposed the Lumumba regime. Vann (2002, p.1) provides the empirical evidence about Belgian and American complicity in deposing the democratically elected government of the Congo thus:

> In November 2001, an all-party commission of inquiry formed by the Belgian government released a report acknowledging that Belgium played a role in the murder of the Congolese leader. In fact earlier investigations have uncovered ample proof that the the assassination of Lumumba was the direct result of order given by the Belgium government and the Eisenhower administration acting through the Central Intelligence Agency (CIA) and local clients financed and "advised" by Brussels and Washington.

After an appreciable period of instability, in 1965, General Joseph Mobutu (his name was later changed to Mobutu Sese Seko), the Chief of Staff of the Congolese Armed Forces staged a military coup under American directives (Blum, 1995). Thereafter, for more than three decades, the Mobutu regime allowed the United States and its allies to, *inter alia*, exploit the Congo's vast economic resources. Again, one year later, American and British imperialism collaborated in ousting Ghanaian President Kwame Nkrumah from power (Baptiste, 2005; Blum, 1995; Stockwell, 1978).

The reason was that the two imperialist powers and their allies were terrified by Nkrumah's pan-Africanist agenda that called for, among other things, the establishment of a single sovereign entity "The United States of Africa." Clearly, the realization of such a project would have dealt a major blow to the economic, political and military interests of the American-led bloc. The Nkrumah regime was replaced by a military junta led by General Joseph Ankrah, a stooge, who served as an instrument for supporting Western imperialism. Furthermore, throughout the "Cold War" the United States and its allies supported some of the most repressive regimes on the African continent, including Arap Moi in Kenya; Barre in Somalia; Doe in Liberia; and Mubarak in Egypt. Not to be outperformed in terms of the support for authoritarian regimes, Soviet imperialism initially supported Barre in Somalia, prior to his defection to the competing American imperialist bloc, and the murderous regime of Mengistu Hailemariam in Ethiopia.

Second, the imperialist capitalist powers consolidated Africa's subordinate position in the international capitalist system through the use of several mechanisms. Within the context of predatory trade, Africa retained its position as the supplier of raw materials to feed the industrial and manufacturing machines in the United States, Europe and Japan. In addition, foreign aid was used to essentially compensate the various client regimes as rewards for their subservience to imperialism. Also, foreign private investment provided the imperialist powers with conduits through which to exploit Africa's labor and natural resources. In turn, this allowed metropolitan-based businesses, especially multinational corporations, to siphon off billions of dollars in profits. Another imperialist tool used for the maintenance of neo-colonial domination in Africa was debt. Given the fact that Africa's ruling classes lacked a people-centered vision of national development, they plundered and pillaged the various African states' resources for their personal benefits. Additionally, the ruling classes mismanaged state resources by, among other things, wasting resources on frivolous non-revenue generating projects. Strapped for money, African states turned to the imperialist powers, international financial institutions and commercial banks for loans. Being cognizant that loan giving would help consolidate their stranglehold over Africa, the imperialist powers and their banks and global financial institutions doled out loans to various African states. By 1992, African states' external debt stood at $194.3 billion (World Bank, 2005). In order to service the debt, African states collectively spent $15.2 billion per annum throughout the 1990s (Owusu et al, 2000). One of the major resultant effects was that by 1995, African was engulfed, to paraphrase Payer (1974) in a "debt trap."

Third, the imperialist powers foisted on African states peripheral capitalist domestic political economies that mirror the portrait of the global one. As I have previously argued, the neo-colonial state was the foundation of the system. Characteristically, the neo-colonial state lacked autonomy—both relative and otherwise—and was non-hegemonic. Accordingly, the neo-colonial state was an instrument for serving the interests of the global ruling classes and the local African surrogates. For example, the coercive instruments of the neo-colonial states were used recurrently by various African states to cow the subaltern classes into submission. In order to manage the state, the imperialist powers supported plaint compradors who had no commitment to the development of their various countries; instead, these African compradors were wedded to serving the interests of the imperialist powers at the expense of helping provide jobs, education, health care, housing, clean drinking water and acceptable sanitation for their citizens and protecting their political rights and civil liberties. Organizationally, Africa's various peripheral capitalist economies lacked industrial bases. This meant they did not have the technological capacity to manufacture goods. Instead, they simply served as plantations for the production of raw materials—agricultural commodities, minerals and oil. So, in effect, African states produced what they did not consume and consumed what they did not produce. Similarly, the economies were disarticulated. That is, there were no relationships between and among the various sectors of the economy. Thus, even the introduction of minimum technology in one sector did not spill over into the other sectors. The other dimension was that the ruling classes failed to provide the required leadership that was exigent for domestic capital formation. Instead, the former used their control over state power to engage in predatory private accumulation of wealth. Accordingly, while the masses of the African peoples were relegated to the abyss of abject poverty and human deprivation, the members of the ruling classes and their relations enjoyed very high standard of living.

ON THE EVE OF THE NEW MILLENNIUM: THE AFRICAN PREDICAMENT

What was the predicament of Africa in 1999, the eve of the new millennium? This critical question will be addressed by examining some of the aspects of the state of environmental, economic, political and social development. In terms of the environment, the African ecology was saddled with several problems, including land degradation, desertification, declining soil productivity, growing imbalances in terms of biodiversity, pollution—land, water and air—and the depletion of fresh water sources. As the United Nations Economic Commission for Africa (2001, p. 5) notes, "The cumulative impact of the [pressures] on the environment [was] extensive degradation of land and other natural resources."

Economically, the various indicators showed that Africans were living precariously at the margins. For example, in terms of income inequality, the Gini coefficient for Africa was 44.4 % (United Nations Economic Commission for Africa, 1999, p.9). There was a similar outcome in terms of poverty: 44% of the total population of Africa lived below the region-wide poverty line of $39 per capita per month (United Nations Economic Commission for Africa, 1999, p.6). To make matters worse, Africa was engulfed in the dungeon of indebtedness. The region's total external debt stood at about $350 billion (Panafrica News Agency, 1999, p.1). In addition, the per annual cost of servicing the debt was about $15.2 billion (Owusu et al, 2000). Overall, Africa had 34 of the world's 48 poorest countries (World Bank, 2005, p.xx).

In terms of political development, there were some successes and failures. In the case of the former, the "third wave of democratization" precipitated the liberalization of the political space and consequent improvement in the respect for, and promotion of political rights and civil liberties. According to Freedom House (1999), nine countries in Africa were considered "free." That meant these countries were making progress in terms of political democratization—the promotion of the freedoms of association, assembly, the press, speech, thought, movement, religion, etc. Another success was that one-partyism was replaced by multi-partyism. Furthermore, this development opened up the political space for the legalization of opposition political parties. Yet, another favorable outcome was that it became possible for incumbents to lose free and fair elections. For example, two well entrenched autocrats—Kamuzu Banda, the President of Malawi and Kenneth Kaunda, the President of Zambia—, who had governed their respective countries since they gained independence in the 1960s, lost in competitive elections held during the early 1990s. Also, the liberalized political space provided the opportunity for the emergence of several non-governmental organizations in various sectors of the society. These private groups contributed to the development of emerging robust civil societies throughout the continent. However, there were myriad failures. For example, 44 countries remained in the shackles of authoritarianism. Of the number, 19 countries were considered "partially free" (Freedom House, 1999). This meant that they had made some progress toward political liberalization; however, they still had authoritarian proclivities. Even more, 25 states, the majority, remained in the abyss of authoritarianism (Freedom House, 1999). As for overall stability, Africa was plagued with 12 civil wars, including five on going ones in Angola, Senegal, Somalia, Sudan and Uganda (Conflict Watch,1999). These civil wars had broad and expansive ramifications, including refugee crises; the problem of internally displaced persons; economic dislocation and the decline of production; the exacerbation of environmental degradation; destruction and wanton killings, especially of civilians.

Socially, the various markers pointed to growing deterioration of the quality of life for the majority of Africans. Hence, it was no surprise that the average life expectancy on the continent was 48.8 years (United Nations Development Program, 2001). In terms of the broader human development context, no African state attained the highest level. Instead, 18 countries made some progress in terms of the provision of the basic human needs of their citizens. However, the preponderant majority, 35 African countries, made very little progress.

On balance, the negative impact of the two previous millennia was more than the positive. In fact, the only sector that showed some positive results was the political one. And these outcomes were quite recent—post-1990. So, the negative political consequences combined with those from the other sectors painted quite a bleak picture for the continent on the eve of the third millennium. Particularly, the post-independence era has exacerbated the continent's plethora of problems. Unfortunately, the opportunities for Africa to break from its sordid state have been squandered by the ruling classes. Hence, as Ramsay (1993, p.3), posits, "For most Africans, independence has been more of a desperate struggle for survival rather than an exhilarating path to development."

THE FOCUS OF THE BOOK

The book has two major interrelated objectives. First, the book is designed to examine the nature and the dynamics of some of the frontier issues—the post-colonial state, economic development, democratization, social development, the environment and political instability— that faced Africa during the previous two millennia. The purpose is to place these issues and their associated dynamics in context.

Second, the book is intended to offer some policy suggestions for addressing the challenges posed by these issues. In other words, the purpose is to contribute to the effort of addressing the critical question of what needs to be done? The book takes cognizance of the fact that is not enough to simply chronicle and analyze the myriad problems that have confronted Africa and its constituent states during the two previous millennia, especially since the inception of the post-independence era. Instead, Africanist scholarship must offer alternative trajectories for helping to promote stability, holistic democracy and development on the continent.

THE ORGANIZATION OF THE BOOK

The book consists of nine (9) chapters. In chapter 1, George Klay Kieh, Jr. provides the context for the book. He begins by discussing the impact of the old millennia on Africa. Specifically, he examines the roles of the predatory trading system that constituted the basis for the formalization of contacts between Africa and Europe; slavery and colonialism. He then focuses on the final half of the previous millennium by discussing the African condition since the post-colonial era.

Julius Ihonvbere provides the framework for the book in chapter 2. Based on the previous millennium, he identifies and examines several issues—debt, investment, aid, unemployment, hunger, poverty, diseases and information technology—that are pivotal to Africa's ability to address the various frontier issues that are the loci of this book. In other words, according to Ihonvbere, addressing the aforementioned issues well is the prerequisite for Africa's capacity to deal with the frontier issues, especially in this age of the "new globalization." In policy terms, he suggests various interlocking options that would help enable Africa to address the prerequisites and the frontier issues— those addressed in the book as well as others: 1) The exigency of deconstructing and reconstituting the repressive neo-colonial state; 2) the opening up of the political space through constitutional engineering; 3) the re-invigoration of regional and sub-regional integration frameworks; and 4) rethinking state sovereignty.

In chapter 3, George Klay Kieh, Jr. tackles the critical issues of the state in Africa. His central argument is that the *sine qua non* for examining the nature and dynamics of the African predicament rests on an understanding of the African state. Accordingly, he explores the development of the state in pre-colonial African societies and the imposition of the colonial and neo-colonial ones. He then assesses the impact of the state on development in the continent. Kieh concludes by suggesting that African cannot overcome its multifaceted crises of underdevelopment, unless the neo-colonial state is deconstructed, rethought and democratically reconstituted.

The seemingly unending cycle of economic crisis in Africa is the focus of chapter 4. John Mukum Mbaku begins by examining the internal and external causes of the economic problems confronting the continent. At the internal level, he blames, among other things, the corrupt and inefficient elites for formulating and implementing poor policies and plundering and pillaging the resources of their respective countries for personal gains. Externally, Mbaku lays the responsibility at the doorsteps of the colonial powers, multinational corporations and the strangulating "Structural Adjustment Programs" (SAPs) imposed on African states by the International Monetary Fund. As the panacea, Mbaku proposes the undertaking of institutional reforms, the creation of wealth, the development and enforcement of effective property rights laws and efficiency in the public sector.

In chapter 5, George Klay Kieh, Jr. addresses the state of the democratization project on the continent. He commences by discussing the "first" (anti-colonial) and "second" (anti-post-colonial authoritarianism) waves of democratization on the continent. He then focuses the chapter on the successes and failures of the "third wave." According to Kieh, the greatest success of the "third wave" has been the liberalization of the political space in several African countries. However, he argues that political democratization has failed to both encompass the totality of the continent and to be consolidated in the most of the states. Also, he maintains the "third wave" has not occasioned fundamental changes in the material conditions of the continent's subaltern classes. He concludes by suggesting various ways for invigorating the project, including the democratic reconstitution of the state.

Ebenezer O. Aka, Jr. examines the critical issue of urbanization. Specifically, he discusses issues such as population and urban change; the nature and dynamics of stress on social services; and the forces of urban growth. Among other things, Aka posits that Africa's urban morphology reflects one of the major consequences of the challenges facing the region. That is, Africa's largest cities exhibit what he terms "urban internal dualism"—the co-existence of formal and informal sectors. Aka then suggest several policy remedies, including the decentralization of urban activities; job creation; the integration of the informal sector into the orbit of state regulations; the improvement of the infrastructure; the improvement of public transportation services; the need to pay attention to the environmental effects; and the exigency for the restructuring of the continent's major urban centers.

In chapter 7, Wafula Okumu discusses the sordid state of the environment in Africa. He addresses three major interrelated issues. First, he provides the historical context of the problems by examining the role of colonialism in creating the conditions for degradation on the continent. Second, he identifies and discusses some of the major environmental challenges facing the region, including degradation; desertification of the land; the lack of the protection and sustainable use of the forests; pollution; and urban waste disposal. Third, he proposes ways for tackling the problems: 1) The change of attitude toward the environment; 2) the waging of a serious campaign against poverty; 3) the prudent management of population growth; 4) improvement in communication and access to information about the environment; and 5) a broader project of democratization and state restructuring.

In chapter 8, Augustine Konneh explores the roots of civil conflicts, including wars, on the continent. He identifies several general factors as the culprits—-the colonial legacy; the nature of the post-colonial state; regionalism; inequalities in income and wealth; and external interference and intervention. Konneh then applies this causal framework to the specificities of seven case studies—Sierra Leone, Liberia, the Democratic Republic of the Congo, Rwanda, the Sudan, Somalia and Mozambique. Drawing from the findings of the cases studies, he argues that civil wars have adversely affected the continent in several major ways: 1) The weakening of state control; 2) the creation of an anarchical environment; 3) the exaction of death and destruction; 4) the instability contagion; 5) the termination of productive economic activities; and 6) capital flight. Against this background, he suggest that African states need, to *inter alia,* develop new and inclusive development-oriented national agendas; address the problems of economic inequalities; tackle the issue of gender inequality; invest in education and human resource development; and promote a culture based on tolerance and peaceful co-existence.

George Klay Kieh, Jr. attempts to pull together the common threads of the various contributions in chapter 9. First, he summarizes the major findings of the various contributions. Second, he draws some lessons that could be used to tackle the labyrinthine of issues confronting the continent. He concludes by arguing that the very neo-colonial state that has been responsible for Africa's crises of underdevelopment cannot preside over its renewal. Hence, he posits that the neo-colonial state must deconstructed because the repository of evidence shows that it has performed dismally. Alternatively, he proposes the establishment of a new state construct that would make the peoples of African the centerpiece of the state-building project.

CONCLUSION

In this chapter, four related issues were examined. First, the chapter discussed the phases of the two old millennia, especially their impact on Africa. The discussion commenced with the establishment of formal contact between Africa and the various imperialist powers in the 16th century. The basic finding is that the resultant relationship was an asymmetrical one in which the Europeans exploited and cheated the Africans within the framework of the evolving system of predatory trade. Also, the initial formal contact laid the foundation for the incorporation of African states into the international capitalist system as peripheral actors. The slavery phase deprived Africa of its critical human resource pool, which was indispensable to the continent's development. Through the most brutal system every designed by human beings, the European imperialist powers took Africans from their homes as cargos and forced them to work as slaves on European plantations in the Americas and Europe. Colonization then ensued anchored on the formal annexation and control of African states by various European powers. Colonialism adversely affected Africa in every facet of live—from cultural to social. The independence phase did not, and has not fundamentally changed the conditions on the continent. In fact, colonialism was replaced with neo-colonialism. In the latter phase, the imperialist powers broaden the scope of their domination of Africa and maintained their stranglehold over the continent through various mechanisms, including the neo-colonial state and plaint ruling classes.

Second, the chapter assessed the impact of the two millennia on Africa. Using 1999, the eve of the third millennium as the threshold, the chapter argued that while some progress was made in the political realm in terms of liberalization, the overall situation on the continent remained bleak. That is, the composite of factors showed that the two millennia, especially during the post-colonial phase of the second one, adversely affected the continent in myriad ways.

Third, the chapter discussed the focus of the book. The base objective is to provide some suggestions for improving the African predicament in some of the critical areas. Each of the chapters in the volume begins with an evaluation of the African predicament in the particular sector—the travails of the state, economic development, social development, etc. In short, the overarching goal is to use the assessment of the challenges facing the continent in the selected sectors as the context for fashioning suggestions for ameliorating them. In other words, there was sensitivity to the fact that the book needed to transcend simply cataloguing the continent's pantomimes, and engage in efforts to come up with some suggestions for helping to lift the continent from the abyss of the multifaceted crises of underdevelopment.

Fourth, the various chapters in the book were summarized. This involved the presentation of the research problems and the findings. In each chapter, the attempt was made to raise the questions and issues that are germane to the core of each of the sectors addressed.

Note

1. The characterization "tears and blood" is derived from Fela Anikulapo-Kuti's famous song "Tears, Sorrow and Blood."

References

Anikulapo-Kuti, Fela (1977). Song: "Tears, Sorrow and Blood."

Arrighi, Giovanni (1994). *The Long Twentieth Century: Money, Power and the Origins of Times*. London: Verso.

Babu, A.M. (1992). "The Struggle for Post-Uhuru Africa." In Peter Anyang' Nyong'o (ed.). *Thirty Years of Independence: The Lost Decades?* Nairobi: Academy Science Publishers.

Baptiste, Fitzroy Andre (2005). "The United States, the Caribbean and Africa: from the Cold War to the War on International Terrorism." *Africa Update*. Vol. XII. Issue 1, pp. 2-10.

Blum, William (1995). *Killing Hope: U.S. Military and CIA Intervention Since World* War II. Monroe: Common Courage Press.

Conflict Watch (1999). "Conflict Watch and Renaissance Barometer." Issue 4, pp. 40-42.

Frank, Andre Gunder (1971). *Capitalism and Underdevelopment in Latin America*. London: Penguin.

Freedom House (1999). *Freedom in the World, 1998-1999*. New York: Freedom House.

Kuti, Fela (2000). *Tears and Sorrow*. Musical CD.

Owusu, Kwesi et al (2000). *Through The Eye of a Needle: The African Debt Report*. London: Jubilee2000 Coalition.

Panafrican News Agency (1999). "Botswana Wants New Approach Toward Africa's Debt." August 30, p.1.

Payer, Cheryl (1974). *The Debt Trap: The IMF and the Third World.* New York: Monthly Review Press.

Ramsay, Jeffress (1993). *Africa.* 8th ed. Guilford, CT: Dushkin Publishing Group, Inc.

Stockwell, John (1978). *In Search of Enemies: A CIA Story.* New York: W.W. Norton.

United Nations Development Program (2001). *Human Development Report, 2001.* New York: Oxford University Press.

United Nations Economic Commission for Africa (2001). *The State of the Environment in Africa.* New York: United Nations Economic and Social Council.

United Nations Economic Commission for Africa (1999). *Economic Report on Africa, 1999: The Challenges of Poverty Reduction and Sustainability.* Addis Ababa, Ethiopia: UNECA.

Vann, Bill (2002). "The Unquiet Death of Patrice Lumumba." *World Socialist Website.* January 16, pp. 1-2.

Wallerstein, Immanuel (2004). *World Systems Analysis: An Introduction.* Durham, NC: Duke University Press.

World Bank (2005)*African Development Indicators, 2005.* Washington D.C.: The World Bank.

World Bank (2000). *Can Africa Claim The 21st Century?* Washington D.C.: The World Bank.

Chapter 2

Africa and the New Millennium: Issues and Challenges

Julius O. Ihonvbere

INTRODUCTION

There is a growing consensus that in spite of the emerging sites of hope on the African political landscape, the region still faces daunting obstacles to growth, development and peace (Camdessus, 1995, p.218). From the World Bank (World Bank, 1995, p.122), through prominent scholars (Lancaster, 1993, p.19) and other international organizations, it is readily acknowledged that the region is backward in several respects. Statistical indictors of progress are hardly reflective of the conditions of living, and the challenges from structural distortions and contradictions remain formidable. The end of the "Cold War" and the increasing integration of the global economy have generated new dynamics, pressures, expectations, and fears in Africa. As well, the triumph of the market and the demise of communism have not only increased the power and influence of donors, lenders, and the multilaterals, but have also posed severe challenges and opportunities for the African continent. On the one hand, there is the opportunity to fully integrate into the emerging global capitalist order to exploit the developments in science and technology, the new information revolution, and the expansion of the global market. Such an integration, it is argued, will open up extensive opportunities for trade, investment, foreign aid, and support for other developmental objectives (IMF, 1995). On the other hand, the changes in the global market hold out the risks of further marginalization, and the redirection of investments and aid to other parts of the world, for a variety of reasons.

The complaints about aid and compassion fatigue by the donors are evidence of increasing frustration with the intractable and complex problems and contradictions of the continent. It is contended by those who see the deepening crisis of the region as an inhibition to full and effective participation in the new global order that the legacies of colonial and neo-colonial exploitation and mismanagement, the crisis of the state and society, and conditions of poverty, foreign domination, instability, and institutional and infrastructural decay and dislocation make effective participation in the global order almost impossible (Lancaster, 1993, p.19; Wright, 1992). Even the World Bank is of the view that Africa's future, in the increasingly complex and competitive global order is at best, bleak and uncertain, that it is "falling further behind the rest of the world," and that current projections point at a "depressed per capita income level" for the future (Chinery-Hesse, 1993, p. 145). This sort of projection raises several questions not just about the future of Africa, but also about its "post-Cold War" relations with other regions of the world. What sort of internal transformations are needed to empower the region to take advantage of current and future changes in the global order? Is the global system structured in such a way as to make it possible for a debt-ridden, crisis-ridden, and poverty-stricken region to effectively and profitably participate in the emerging global dispensation? How will on-going implementation of orthodox structural adjustment packages as well as difficult political liberalization programs in the context of deepening crisis and global marginalization facilitate or mediate Africa's participation in the new globalization? This chapter will attempt to answer some of these questions by highlighting some of the issues and challenges facing the continent.

A CHANGING GLOBAL ORDER?

Is the global system really changing? What exactly do we mean by *change*? These questions might appear simplistic, even mundane. But they are important to a holistic appreciation of the depth and implications of current movements in the global system. Until the recent explosion of the Asian myth evidenced in the near total economic breakdown of the so-called "Asian Tigers," as well as the crisis in Latin America, Japan and parts of Europe, it was almost considered a sin to be critical of the new globalization given its numerous promised benefits. The Asian crisis brought the world to a new reality and encouraged a re-examination of not just the role of the multilaterals but also the value of orthodox economic theory, especially in a developing country's context. Without doubt, the global system is entering a new era. The end of the twentieth century is ushering in unprecedented and largely unanticipated changes, especially in the context of the rapidity and decisiveness with which the changes are occurring (Farrell, 1994): the reunification of Germany with the collapse of the Berlin Wall; the peace talks between Israel and Palestine; the end of apartheid in South Africa and the election of Nelson Mandela as the first black president of that country; the collapse of the Soviet Union as a super power and nation; the widespread adoption of market reform programs as dictated and supervised by the World Bank and the International Monetary Fund (IMF); and the emergence of the United States as the hegemonic military and economic power in the world (Jackson, 1995). As well, we can add a renewed role for the United Nations especially in the areas of humanitarian relief, peacekeeping, and peace-making; the preponderance of micro-nationalism; and efforts by the United States to sell the "American way of life" as the only credible alternative left for the entire world in the face of the assumed victory of the bourgeoisie over communism and totalitarianism (Taiwo, 1995). To this already impressive list of novel developments, we can also add the deluge of struggles for multi-partyism which have altered the political landscape of many nations especially in Africa.

These changes have precipitated a near redundancy of non-alignment as a political/ideological posture in global power relations; the drastic alteration of "Cold War"-based foreign policy platforms; and promoted the emergence of new economic alignments or trade blocs. Of course, we are also beginning to witness new immigration restrictions which "display more racist tendencies toward minorities, particularly of African descent" (Wright, 1992, p. 26). Interestingly, the end of the "Cold War" and the triumph of the market and the United States have received intellectual support and rationalization from scholars like Francis Fukuyama in his "End of History" thesis, and Samuel P. Huntington in his "Clash of Civilizations" postulations (Fukuyama, 1998; Huntington, 1993).

The changes outlined above have completely altered the content and direction of global social, economic, and political relations. As the World Bank jubilantly declared in its *World Development Report* of *1995*, "These are revolutionary times in the global economy. The embrace of market-based development by many developing and former centrally-planned economies, the opening of international markets, and great advances in the ease with which goods, capital and ideas flow around the world are bringing new opportunities, as well as risks, to billions of people" (World Bank, 1995,p. 1). One can hardly disagree with this new euphoria: communications are faster, cheaper and more open; the activities of governments are increasingly more open to external scrutiny; and there are more discussions of economic cooperation and integration beyond ideological and political lines. Even Cuba and communist China are doing more business with capitalist economies and carrying out internal reforms along market lines, even if they refuse to admit to such ideological somersaults. A crisis-ridden continent like Africa, with most of the least developed nations of the world, is increasingly caught in the unpredictable and highly sophisticated and competitive vortex of this emerging global order. Unfortunately, Africa was not quite ready for these changes and so, was caught unaware.

One can ask the question: was Africa prepared for this new "revolution"? Are there institutions and structures on ground to receive, mediate, resist, reject, or recompose the products of on-going changes? What are the ideological platforms on which Africa will be participating in the new globalization and engaging the powerful forces of monopoly capitalism? Finally, how will the plethora of contradictions, conflicts and suspicions all over the region, within and between nations, condition Africa's location and role in the emerging order? One would be really stretching the limits of generosity to claim that Africa was ready for the numerous developments within the continent much less in other parts of the world. Africa was not even prepared for the dramatic changes that took place in South Africa that culminated in the election of Mandela as president and the vigorous and aggressive expansion of South African businesses into other African economies. Beyond these however, the new globalization is marked by other critical features that further demonstrate the weakness and vulnerability of the African economy (Rasheed, 1993).

One major feature of the new globalization is the increasing powerlessness of the state, at least, as far as regulating the movement of information, ideas, capital, even skills is concerned. As the World Bank admits, "Governments are increasingly seeking to improve the international competitiveness of their economies rather than shield them behind protective walls" (World Bank, 1995, p. 51). The implication is that governments are taking steps to give more autonomy to private initiatives and to cede some political ground to powerful corporations. Rapid changes in information technology have greatly impacted on the autonomy, capabilities, and spheres of action open to the nation state. Boutros-Ghali (1995, p. 12) has observed that " (t) he time of absolute and exclusive sovereignty has passed and states must find a balance between the needs of good internal governance and the requirements of an ever more interdependent world." As well, as is evident in Africa, the state is increasingly under pressure and attack, and quite a handful have become stagnant, exhausted or have collapsed out rightly (Kaplan, 1994). The developments in the "post-Cold War era" have opened the way for articulating new patterns of responses to deepening political problems around the world, especially in Africa. This is evidenced in the responses to Somalia, Liberia, The Sudan, Burundi, Rwanda, South Africa, Sierra Leone, the Democratic Republic of Congo, Lesotho, Nigeria, and other spots of crisis (Mendez, 1995). Though these responses have been bedeviled by inconsistencies and other financial and logistical problems, the fact remains that the United Nations is becoming "a central point of constance in the midst of flux" (Perez de Cuellar, 1990, p.4). According to Perez de Cuellar (1990, p. 4), this renewed interest in and role of the UN is clearly evidenced in intensification of activities emanating from the Security Council, the office of the secretary general, as well as from the numerous specialized agencies of the UN.

The renewed interest (especially by the United States) in the UN is equally the reasoning behind an emerging global moral and political responsibility that has encouraged interventions not only in the states mentioned above, but also in other crisis locations like Haiti and Bosnia at great financial and other costs (Atwood, 1995). The increasing interest in human rights and peacekeeping at the global level has opened up new debates on the issues of sovereignty and autonomy (Carlsson, 1995).To be sure, in some instances, as is the case with China, economic interests have frequently overshadowed human rights issues for Western nations especially the United States. However, as the 1995 execution of Nobel Prize nominee, Ken Saro-Wiwa and eight other environmentalists by the military junta in Nigeria showed, the global community can be swift to action in defense of human rights. In fact, Nigeria was not only suspended from the Commonwealth but many Western nations reviewed diplomatic, trade and aid relations and imposed limited sanctions (Wren, 1995; Connors, 1995; Abiola, 1995). Thus in the area of meting out justice within its borders, the contemporary state can no longer claim an absolute degree of sovereignty. Every action against groups, communities, individuals, dissidents, even coup plotters, comes under the very critical scrutiny of international human rights groups and foreign governments. International human rights groups have clearly become powerful advocates of the rights of individuals and communities within nations. As well, the multilaterals have come to command unprecedented influence and power over national governments that they not only influence and determine the nature of economic policy but also political developments and contestations. Developed nations no longer hide behind diplomatic language and culture to express their political interests in their relations with developing states. Their control over information, foreign aid, loans, investment, and military hardware is now easily mobilized to support political agendas for poverty-stricken and debt-ridden states (Great Decisions, 1993). At no time in the post-Westphalian history of the contemporary state system have non-state actors wielded more relevance, influence, and power than at the moment. The break down of ideological orthodoxies and the search for new patterns of socio-economic and power relations have further reduced the relevance of the state in favor of less formal and private structures and institutions. The singular influence and power of election monitors in the current global order attest to the ever growing significance of non-state actors as newly elected or re-elected governments often require their stamps of approval for international acceptability and legitimacy.

On balance, it would appear that scientific, economic, and social factors, rather than political developments, have contributed more significantly to the erosion of state sovereignty and in shaping the character of the new globalization in recent times. As the nations of the world came to depend more on each other, as transportation narrowed distances, as communications made it possible for people to interact and exchange information and ideas, and as nations became readily permeable to the power of new communications systems, the ability of the state to lay claim to some higher level of authority gradually weakened. Of course, since the 1980s with the crisis in the former Soviet Union, and more so since the emergence of the independent republics, the triumph of the market has not only narrowed ideological positions but has also drawn nations together in the struggle to permeate markets, attract foreign aid and investments, and attract new technologies (Business Week, 1994). What is instructive however, is that in most of the on-going discussions about the new globalization Africa is hardly considered or taken seriously. This is in spite of the "encouraging progress made in transforming sub-Saharan Africa," and the far-reaching socio-economic and political reforms that governments have been forced to adopt to please lenders, donors and international pressure groups (Ihonvbere, 1991). These reform packages, often imposed from abroad and supervised by the multilateral agencies and credit clubs, have served in no small measure to erode the autonomy and sovereignty of African states. The combination of externally designed, imposed, and supervised political and economic conditionalities-structural adjustment and political pluralism-is part of the conditions determining Africa's integration into the emerging global order, as a dependent, vulnerable, weak, dominated, and almost helpless peripheral actor in the new divisions of labor and power (Lancaster, 1990).There is no doubting the fact that in a world relatively liberated from hard ideological constraints, "new technology is rewriting old concepts of sovereignty and over time will also change national objectives" (Wriston, 1989, p. 73). Recent struggles for democracy in developing countries have benefited significantly from the cellular phone and fax machines which despotic and repressive governments could not control: "Ideas transmitted by satellite broadcasts, fax machines, and Internet ports are prying open even authoritarian regimes" (Wriston, 1989, p. 73). Most of these major technological contraptions are not produced or even assembled in Africa, save perhaps, South Africa. Yet, this is world that is increasingly being run and conditioned by technology, in particular, information technology. In Africa, except for a handful of countries like South Africa, business is still performed mostly manually, relying on outdated information, completely oblivious of new possibilities opened up by new technology. From banking to insurance, through import-export activities to information collection, processing, and dissemination, Africa is still decades behind parts of Asia and Latin America, not to mention Europe and North America.

What has been referred to as the "digital age" with "powerful data networks" is drawing developing nations "into the borderless information economy" (Wriston, 1989, p. 73). Nations of the world really have no choice about joining or opting out of the new information age. To opt out is to be isolated and cut off from the massive flow of ideas and information badly needed to cope with the developments of the twenty-first century. On the other hand, participating in the information age requires a high degree of political openness, administrative flexibility, rapid changes in science and technology, even a revolutionary transformation of the educational system of the country. Internet connections are expanding by 16% every month, fiber optics are transmitting 40 billion bits of data per second. Governments have practically lost the capacity to keep pace with the generation, processing, manipulation, and dissemination of information around the world (UNRISD, 1995, p.9). The World Bank further supports these claims when it notes that in line with the new global emphasis on the market as the prime mover of growth and development, "technological changes have made the world easier to navigate—goods, capital, people, and ideas travel faster and cheaper today than ever before. Underlying these changes have been huge reductions in transport and communications costs" (World Bank, 1995, p. 51). So far, African states are not poised to move in the direction of exploiting these new developments. Yet, as African nations wallow in confusion, poverty, superstition, the recycling of outdated information and ideas, and continue to rely on old and already discarded technology, around the world, medical practices, experiments in science and technology, banking services, academic research and so on are being undertaken in cooperation, by persons separated by hundreds of thousands of miles. The use of computers, even by faculty members in the sciences is still a rarity at most African universities, after more than seven years after the advent of the twenty-first century!

All over the world, even in the most developed market economies, governments are rapidly losing control over the flow of money. As the IMF itself has admitted, "this integration of financial markets is not only irreversible, but it can only broaden and intensify in the future. Let us not make the mistake of believing that the answer to financial crises lies in reviewing this globalization through exchange controls and less open markets" (Camdessus, 1995, p. 218). The most efficient Central Bank cannot boast of having full knowledge of, or control over domestic financial transactions. The computer has put within the reach of average citizens the power to execute complex banking transactions within the confines of their homes. Geographical location or currency denominations now mean almost nothing to the new financial market place (Wriston, 1989, p. 72). Where does Africa stand in this new globalization of the financial market place? The answer is; "nowhere": the currencies are either worthless (for examples, Democratic Republic of the Congo and Somalia), excessively devalued (Ghana and Zambia as good examples) or generally inconvertible. Most of the countries are so poor that their central banks simply exist in name. Others can no longer control inflation, while several countries only do business in the weekly auctioning of foreign exchange in the name of rationalizing the financial market as part of a usually poorly implemented adjustment package. Businesses are not going into Africa because the near worthlessness of the currencies is depressing the market and there are practically no buyers for non-essential commodities and services. Banks are yet to be computerized, and transactions still take forever.

The most powerful actors in the new globalization are transnational corporations. They are rapidly streamlining technology, labor training, utilization, and exploitation; regulations, and production processes. This also includes a strategy to as much as possible, streamline and rationalize consumption around the world to facilitate the production and marketing of goods and services without frequent retooling, investments in fixed capital or skill development. The end of the "Cold War" is strengthening the power and influence of the corporations and encouraging them to move into untested waters. The end of apartheid encouraged MacDonald's into South Africa, and encouraged South African corporations to move rapidly into neighboring countries (Farrell, 1994). While Western business interests have not been deterred by the uncertainties in the Middle East and Eastern Europe, "the foreign direct investment response has been, at best, hesitant and weak in Africa" (Johnson-Sirleaf, 1994, p. 9). As Johnson-Sirleaf (1994, p.9) has noted, though most African states have developed "new investment codes, the number of sectors previously reserved for nationals has been sharply reduced; screening procedures have been simplified and one-stop investment centers have been established; the relative equity share that foreigners are allowed to hold in enterprises has been raised; and tax holidays of up to ten years or more are now common, the annual average flow of foreign direct investment to Africa over the 1985-89 period was $2.6 billion." In the same period, Latin America and the Caribbean received $6.0 billion, East, South and South-East Asia received $13.6 billion, North America received $55.8 billion, and Western Europe received $60.8 billion. In fact, of the "23 Sub-Saharan African countries with more than 2 million people, ten had no foreign direct investment inflows and only six had inflows of more than two dollars per capita" (Johnson-Sirleaf, 1994, p. 9).

It is clear therefore, that the new globalization is not redirecting resources towards Africa in any credible or substantial sense. Rather, unlike other developing regions, and in spite of the rapidly expanding global financial market, Africa has not expanded its "exports of manufactures," it remains a producer of "primary commodities and terms of trade have continued to fall" (World Bank, 1995, p. 52). Increasingly lacking the capacity to generate foreign exchange, and without an appreciable inflow of investments, even to those countries which have clearly decided for open markets and liberal democracy like Zambia, Africa cannot be an effective actor in the new globalization.

THE LIMITS OF THE NEW GLOBALIZATION

Africa entered the twentieth century as a dependent, foreign-dominated, technologically backward, politically unstable, vulnerable, and marginal actor in the global system. Decades of foreign aid, albeit informed by "Cold War" considerations and calculations, political support for ideological client states, and investments, even if in enclave sectors, produced no appreciable change in the region's unprecedented deterioration, dislocation, and decay. The reasons for this unenviable situation are not lost to observers and scholars of Africa. According to Yaker (1993, p.132), "Africa, potentially the richest continent, with the poorest people, having been exploited for a long time, can and must become a dynamic developing region if there is to be a common future for mankind." Yet, decades of mismanagement, coups and counter-coups, environmental degradation, the exploitation and marginalization of women, misplaced priorities, and the neglect of basic human needs have precipitated distortions and disarticulations in Africa's political economy. As well, unbridled corruption, the privatization of the state and its resources, the suffocation of civil society, the manipulation of primordial loyalties, and criminal abuse of power have also eroded opportunities for creativity, innovation, growth and development. Furthermore, the reproduction and rationalization of neo-colonial economic relations and unequal exchange relations with powerful profit and hegemony-seeking transnational corporations have hampered the overall economic environment. Consequently, limited or no investments in science and technology, the neglect and exploitation of the rural areas and rural producers, an urban-based investment pattern and extroverted consumption patterns have precipitated a huge foreign debt profile and discouraged investment and external support (Ihonvbere,1994). According to Rasheed (1993, p. 41), the net result has been that:

> Economic growth proved to be elusive, managing an average rate of only 2.1 per cent per annum (in the 1980s, and much less in the 1990s). This translated into a fall in per capita incomes at the average rate of about 1 per cent per annum. The human and social conditions of the majority of the African people worsened considerably. Poverty increased in both the rural and urban areas; real earnings fell drastically; unemployment and underemployment rose sharply; hunger and famine became endemic; dependence on food aid and food imports intensified; diseases, including the added scourge of AIDS, decimated populations and became a real threat to the very process of growth and development; and the attendant social evils-crime, delinquency, family disintegration-intensified with a vengeance.

It is precisely these conditions of desperation and weakness that have constrained the ability of Africa to be effectively part of the changing global order in a positive sense. What this means is that Africa will likely remain in the backwaters of the new globalization, reaping most of the negative outcomes and being unable to influence on-going changes. The negative consequences of the new globalization have more implications for Africa's survival, than on-going positive developments: how can Africa protect itself from further manipulation, exploitation, marginalization, and vulnerability?

Clearly, the move towards a globalized political economy is not flawless or without conflict. Only those economies with goods and services to sell, and which can attract investors because of viable political structures, high credit rating, good infrastructure, and an aggressive global agenda will benefit from the emerging global economy. Only those nations with the ability to harness and process information, link up with or develop new technology, and those with the level of skills development relevant for a growing competitive globalized economy will benefit from the emerging order. Africa can hardly make a stake on any of the grounds above. Even Nigeria with its estimated huge population of over a hundred million is in total disarray, bedeviled by tyranny of military rule, corruption, infrastructural decay, violence, and political uncertainty. As well, "approximately 180 million of sub-Saharan Africa's 500 million people can be classified as poor, of whom 66.7 percent, or 120 million, are desperately poor. By every international measure, be it per capita income ($330), life expectancy (51 years), or the United Nation's Index of Human Development (.225 compared to .317 for South Asia, the next poorest region), Africa is the poorest region in the world" (USAID, 1993, p. 20) The region's sovereignty is under greater pressure and as the state loses the capacity to perform, it also loses credibility abroad and legitimacy internally (Ihonvbere, 1992).

The rapid growth which is accompanying the new globalization is generating severe environmental pressures and problems. As transnational corporations compete for market hegemony in Africa (and other parts of the developing world), they are stretching regulations, and utilizing several extra-legal mechanisms to gain one advantage or the other. This has increased corruption and further eroded the already weak ability of these states to regulate the corporations. Because the developed markets offer better pay and conditions of work, and in the context of deepening systemic crisis in Africa, the brain drain has intensified as hundreds of thousands of the most educated and experienced professionals flee the continent for other parts of the world. In countries like Nigeria, Ghana, Zambia, and Kenya, this has extended to unskilled labor. The new globalization has not stemmed the deepening employment crisis, spiraling inflation, the lack of international confidence in African economies, and the weak structures of state and society which impede creativity and productivity. Automation, the use of robots, reliance on synthetics, stock-piling, and other cost-cutting production and marketing techniques are actually stifling the expansion of the labor force and creating antagonistic stratification within the ranks of the working classes. International negotiations on trade and tariff, intellectual property, labor relations, immigration, use of local resources, pollution, and technology transfer hardly take Africa into consideration (Farrell, 1994).

Given the desperate conditions of African economies, the new globalization, rather than alleviate the region's poverty, is actually consolidating and deepening it. As social and cultural specificities become more pronounced and politicized, African nations increasingly become ineligible for most forms of support from the developed economies. Admittedly, programs sponsored by donors and aid agencies "have achieved negligible or limited results" (USAID, 1993, p. 5) over the decades; but such poor results have only made it almost impossible for Africa to capitalize on current developments, innovations, and opportunities in the global system. In any case, donors are cutting aid to the poorest nations and expanding investment and support for the more vibrant or promising economies like South Africa, Indonesia, and Malaysia. The contradictions, negative coalitions, and weaknesses of state and society have been compounded by ethnic, religious, regional, and other primordial contradictions and conflicts which scare away investors and force regimes to divert scarce resources to security, survival, and conflict containment. No serious investor, new globalization or not, would seriously think of investing new capital in locations of crisis and conflict in the region. As the IMF has warned:

> Many others, especially in Africa, are still mired in poverty. What is more, while globalization is a monumental force of economic integration that can benefit the poor countries by speeding their devel-

> opment, it may also lead to the marginalization of those countries that refuse to undertake, or are prevented from undertaking, the necessary structural adjustment effort (Camdessus, 1995, p.194).

Of course, even if one were to subscribe to the orthodox stabilization and structural adjustment packages of the IMF and the World Bank, African states have failed woefully to put in place successful and sustainable reform programs in the last two decades. In fact the World Bank has identified only one successful case of adjustment in Africa, Ghana. This claim remains questionable even among Ghanaians (Ghana Drum, 1995). According to the World Bank (1991, p. 18),

> Despite the efforts to improve the macroeconomic environment, open up markets and strengthen the public and financial sectors, most African countries still lack policies that are sound by international standards. Even Africa's best performers have worse macroeconomic policies than the newly industrializing economies in Asia. Few besides Ghana come close to having adequate monetary, fiscal, and exchange rate policies. And Ghana lags behind other adjusting countries elsewhere-Chile and Mexico for example-in trade and public enterprise reform.

Rather than reduce government expenditure, cut waste, rationalize financial obligations, promote self-reliance, attract investors, control inflation, and encourage productivity among other promised goals of adjustment, African states have been rent by riots, increased state intervention, corruption, economic dislocation, rising unemployment, and general deterioration on all economic and social indicators. While governments in other parts of the world are responding to the new globalization by constructing what has been referred to as the "competitive state," (World Bank, 1991, p.33) the beleaguered African state is merely struggling for legitimacy, hegemony, and survival in the face of severe challenges from non-bourgeois communities and constituencies. Based on current socio-economic and political balances, location and role in the global division of labor and power, the underdeveloped level of science and technology development, and the nature of contestations for power, it is doubtful if the new globalization will have much to offer Africa.

BEYOND THE NEW GLOBALIZATION: SOME PRESCRIPTIONS

Africa has been a victim of too many negative developments in the global system. The continent has been attacked, exploited, colonized, and neo-colonized by powerful external interests for centuries. It was also a victim of the slave trade, and no matter how generous we might wish to be, the continent had not recovered from the ravages, distortion, deformations, and other consequences of the colonial experience (Rodney, 1972; Ake, 1981). In spite of post-colonial alignment and realignment of political forces, the drastic reconstruction of the political terrain, and changes in the continent's relations with the outside world, it is yet to overcome structural impediments to growth, peace, development and democracy implanted in the colonial era. To be sure, local elites and interest groups which benefit from the existing dependent and unequal arrangements continue to rationalize and legitimize the status quo to the detriment of the region (Rodney, 1972; Mazrui, 1986, Ayittey, 1992). Political independence was not accompanied by socio-economic and cultural liberation, and since the 1960s, Africa has remained the weakest region in the global system, totally incapable of influencing or determining the content and context of global affairs, and dependent on the productive capacities of other nations (Ayittey, 1992, p. 8). As the saying goes, the continent consumes what it does not produce, and produces what it does not consume; it does not set the prices for what it imports and has not control over the prices of what it exports. This is hardly the profile of as region that can enter, find a comfortable location, and participate or compete in the new globalization (Jaycox, 1992, p. 11). Yet, all is not lost. As Atwood (1995, p. 6) has correctly noted, "Africa's future holds both immense potential and enormous difficulties."

For Africa to be an effective actor in the new globalization therefore, some major structural changes must take place. First, a drastic deconstruction and reconstruction of the repressive and exploitative neo-colonial state. Since this state has been identified with all the ills of the region and has been unable to serve as a fountain of protection and inspiration to the people, it becomes rather evident that until this state is restructured to serve the interest of the majority, intervene less in the economy, facilitate an enabling environment for creativity and productivity, Africa will remain mired in the sea of confusion, hopelessness, waste, domination, and instability. A state that has no legitimacy cannot be expected to serve as the motor for growth, development, and transparency much less good governance. Clearly, the state in Africa has not been constituted and has not operated as a *state* in Africa; it has operated more like a zig-zag and confused structure with no sense of direction and no sense of mission. It has historically embarked on a project of destruction rather than one of construction; it has squandered rather than generated resources; it has asphyxiated rather than build and reinvigorate civil society; and it has mortgaged rather than liberate the African economy. Unable to legitimately organize an agenda for growth and development, the African state, its institutions and custodians have relied on the manipulation of primordial loyalties, the politics of defensive radicalism and diversion, repression, and asphyxiation of civil society to maintain control. Organizing development in the interest of the people and promoting an agenda that would facilitate participation in the global system has hardly featured in the overall program of the African state. Reconstructing this state to make it efficient, effective, responsible, stable, legitimate, accountable, would be a monumental challenge if not impossible (Ihonvbere, 1994). The reconstruction of the state to reflect and serve the interests of the majority can only come about through the mobilization, education, and full involvement of the people in the on-going struggles to restructure Africa's political landscape (Sandbrook and Halfani, 1993).

The second major challenge is the opening up of political spaces. This is directly linked to the recomposition of the repressive neo-colonial state. It would require not just the termination of military and one-party dictatorships, but also the drawing up of viable constitutional arrangements guaranteed by the active role of popular organizations in civil society. There is no alternative to a genuine democratic process in Africa (Ihonvbere,1995).Conditions of repression, uncertainty, instability, and constant harassment of popular forces only drain already scarce resources, discourage investors and donors, and force desperate and insecure governments to divert resources to survival and so-called security. Only a genuine democratic agenda can bring out the best of the people and their communities, promote popular mobilization, encourage creativity, and redirect resources to critical and productive sectors of society. Decades of irresponsible governance, presidents-for-life, one-man rule, one-party states, confused ideological systems, and military dictatorships have set Africa back and consolidated its marginalization in the global system.

The only platform on which this new idea is being articulated or could be effectively articulated is in the on-going struggles for democracy, accountability, social justice, popular participation, gender equality, and the empowerment of the people, their constituencies and communities. Grinding poverty, the failure of adjustment programs, the end of the "Cold War" and reduced external support for dictators, and the emergence of new pro democracy movements and leaders have played significant roles in promoting the new upsurge of struggles for democracy. Though there are many problems and most of the new victories are still tentative and unconsolidated, it is increasingly being realized that only a truly democratic agenda can move the region away from the decades of neglect, decay, deterioration, and dislocation.

A third challenge relates to regional integration. If the developed economies are taking regionalism very seriously as evidenced in the establishment of the North American Free Trade Area (NAFTA) and the European Union, then Africa should take it even more seriously. To date, the record of regionalism in the region has been very poor: characterized by excessive politicization, lack of political will, disrespect for protocols, weak currencies, petty jealousies, colonial legacies, and pressures from conditions of underdevelopment and dependence. The 1991 adoption of the African Economic Treaty in Abuja, Nigeria equally reflects a high degree of unseriousness. Though it is expected to culminate in the establishment of a common market and the election of an African parliament in 2025, the long time span and current emphasis on nationalistic policies show that the goals might never be attained. In fact, African leaders have not demonstrated an acknowledgement of the deepening crisis of the region, and the fact that regionalism requires the mobilization of all productive sectors and citizens. As well, a collective regional agenda will make no head way until African states open up the political landscape internally, and establish new national orders based on genuine democracy, accountability, and the mobilization of the people for increased productivity (Obasanjo and Mosha, 1993; Ihonvbere, 1993).

A fourth issue that African states must contend with in the contemporary era is the revision of traditional notions of "autonomy" or "independence." True, many of the states are young, at least when compared to nations in other parts of the world. But this is no excuse not to learn from past experiences and to avoid past mistakes. Old notions of sovereignty and nationalistic economic policies will only serve, in the context of the changing global order, to consolidate the region's peripheralization in the global division of labor. Regionalism requires that some degree of sovereignty be ceded to larger organizations or institutions of collective action aimed at growth, development, peace and stability. For poor and underdeveloped nations that have failed to attract sufficient foreign investments and are clearly hundreds of years behind in the new technologies, the essence of regionalism, and the voluntary surrender of substantial degrees of sovereignty cannot be overstated. If African states fail to exploit the current global momentum towards regionalism, the region's marginal location and role in the global order might just become permanent. In Europe, nation-states have demonstrated some desire and resolve to give up a degree of sovereignty in order to enjoy the benefits of regionalism. It is amazing that African governments that willingly (or unwillingly) accepted economic, and later political conditionalities which were openly designed and are supervised by foreign interests still spend much time protecting claims to absolute sovereignty. The truth is that with the embarrassing record of most African governments, they have practically no legitimate ground on which to exercise sovereign rule over their peoples. Decades of repression, human rights abuses, and the squandering of national riches have eroded the tenuous legitimacy they inherited from colonial rule. In the new globalization, with the rapid integration of information networks and the unprecedented improvements in communications, traditional notions of sovereignty, beyond its legal articulation to capture the sanctity of recognized boundaries, will mean very little. Africa must realize that only through the collective mobilization of resources, planning, design of a viable and interconnected future, can the small, weak, distorted, and marginalized economies survive the on-going competition in the global system.

Finally, the policies outlined above: restructuring of the state, political openness, regionalism, and a revised understanding of the importance of sovereignty, can only enable African states to take national planning, plan discipline, accountability, and the provision of basic needs more seriously. Essentially, this will involve a grand agenda to re-attract qualified citizens who now dot every nook and corner of the globe, re-attract donors and investors, and strengthen local currencies. It would also require an agenda to promote local accumulation through investment in productive activities, rehabilitate decaying infrastructure, and revitalize the dying educational system. This sort of agenda, anchored on the principles of good governance and an openly democratic system, will encourage the people to become more creative, productive, and supportive of government policies thus reversing the current conditions of anger, alienation, withdrawal, and overt/covert resistance to the state, its institutions, and custodians. Though, clearly, the market is not enough, and the state, strengthened and more efficient will continue to play a critical role in Africa's quest for development, the need for very deep-rooted internal restructuring cannot be understated. In order words, a far-reaching and comprehensive new national order must precede any effort to find a new location and role in the new global division of labor and power.

CONCLUSION

The chapter has attempted to examine the major challenges that will confront Africa in the twenty-first century as consequences of changes in the international system, and to suggest some ways in which the challenges could be addressed. Since the advent of the "new globalization" in the 1990s, the global system has undergone cultural, economic, political, security, social and technological changes. For example, in the cultural sphere, new consumption habits have been introduced in efforts to occasion "homogenization." Economically, trade, private investments and the flow of capital have expanded. In the political realm, state sovereignty, the cornerstone of the "Westphalian international system" is under stress. In the security sphere, since the attacks on the United States on September 11, 2001, "international terrorism" has become a major issue. Socially, the outbreak of various diseases such as the "bird flu" has necessitated international cooperation. Undoubtedly, technological advances constitute the motor forces of the monumental changes the global system has, and continue to experience.

In the case of Africa, given the fact that the region is weak and dependent, it is not well positioned to address these monumental global changes, especially to derive benefits from them. Instead, overall these global changes are leading to the further marginalization of Africa. For example, the African Continent is not deriving dividends from the explosion in investments and international finance. Clearly, the underlying reason for Africa's incapacity to deal with the global changes is that the region failed to develop the requisite internal structures, programs and policies for dealing with the challenges of the "new globalization."

Finally, with the first decade of the third millennium more than midway, it is imperative for African states to develop the requisite modalities for dealing with the imperatives of the new millennium. If the region fails to do so, its full integration into the global economic system would only lead to more adverse consequences, including its further peripherilization. Against this backdrop, the chapter suggests that the post-colonial state needs to be reconstituted; the political space needs to be expanded so that Africans can have greater freedoms to innovate; serious attention needs to be given to both subregional and regional integration across the continent; and African states need to rethink their dogmatic approach to sovereignty. Alternatively, a new approach to sovereignty needs to be based, among other things, on the surrender of domestic authority over policy areas that can be better managed at the sub-regional and regional levels rather than at the state level.

References

Abiola, Hafsat (1995)."Words are not Enough." *The New York Times*. December 4.

Ake, Claude (1981). *A Political Economy of Africa*. London: Longman.

Atwood, J. Brian (1995). "Sustainable Development and Crisis Prevention: The U.S. Agenda for International Development." *International Politics and Society*. Vol. 1 No. 1, pp.1-20.

Ayittey, George (1992). *Africa Betrayed*. New York: St. Martin's Press.

Business Week (1994)."Introduction: 21st Century Capitalism." November.

Camdessus, Michel (1995). *Closer Integration in Global Economy Vital for Africa*. Excerpts from Address at the High-Level Meeting of the United Nations' Economic and Social Council (ECOSOC) held in Geneva, Switzerland. July 6. Reproduced in International Monetary Fund Survey. Washington D.C.: IMF. July 17, 1995.

Carlsson, Ingvar (1995). "The U.N. at 50: A Time for Reform." *Foreign Policy*, Issue 100, pp. 3-18.

Chinery-Hesse, Mary (1993)."Divergence and Convergence in the New World Order." In Adebayo Adedeji. *Africa Within the World: Beyond Dispossession and Dependence*. London: Zed Books.

Connors, Cathy (1995). "Bishop Tutu Ask Stringent Sanctions Against Nigeria." *The New York Amsterdam News*. December 2.

Farrell, Christopher (1994). "The Triple Revolution." *Business Week*. November.

Fukuyama, Francis (1998). "The End of History?" *The National Interest*. Vol. 16, pp. 3-18.

Ghali, Butros-Butros (1995). *An Agenda for Change*. New York: United Nations.

Ghana Drum (1995). "Happy 38th Mother Ghana, But Where Are We Heading To?" Vol.4. No. 3.

Great Decisions (1993). "The End of Sovereignty." Itacha, New York: Foreign Policy Association.

Huntington, Samuel (1993). "The Clash of Civilizations?" *Foreign Affairs*. Vol. 72. No. 5, pp. 22-49.

Ihonvbere, Julius O (1995). "Beyond Governance: The State and Democratization in Sub-Saharan Africa." Journal of Asian and African Studies. Vol.31. No.50, pp. 141-158.

Ihonvbere, Julius O (1994). "Between Debt and Disaster: The Politics of Africa's Debt Crisis." *Indepth: A Journal of Values and Public Policy*. Vol. 4. No. 1, pp.108-132.

Ihonvbere, Julius O (1993). "The African Crisis, Regionalism and Prospects for Recovery in the 1990s." In Bruce Berman and Piotor Dutkiewicz (eds.). *Africa and Eastern Europe: Crisis and Transformations*. Kingston, Ontario: Queens University Press, pp. 121-132.

Ihonvbere, Julius O (1992). "Surviving at the Margins: Africa and the New Global Order." *Current World Leaders*. Vol. 35. Vol.6, pp. 1053-1072.

Ihonvbere, Julius O (1991). "The Economic Crisis is Sub-Saharan Africa: Depth, Dimensions and Prospects for Recovery." *The Journal of International Studies*. Vol. 27, pp. 41-69.

International Monetary Fund (1995). "Sub-Saharan Africa: Route to Success Lies in Sound Economic Policies." *IMF Survey*. February 20.

Jackson, Robert (1995). "International Community Beyond the Cold War." In Gene Lyons and Michael Mastanduno (eds.). *Beyond Westphalia? State Sovereignty and International Intervention*. Baltimore, MD: Johns Hopkins University Press.

Jaycox, Edward (1992). *The Challenges of African Development*. Washington D.C.: The World Bank.

Johnson-Sirleaf, Ellen (1994). "Some Reflections on Africa and the Global Economy." In William Minter (ed.). *U.S. Foreign Policy: An Africa Agenda*. Washington D.C.: Africa Policy Information Center.

Kaplan, Robert (1994). "The Coming Anarchy." *Atlantic Monthly*. February, pp.44-76.

Lancaster, Carol (1993). *United States and Africa: Into the Twenty-First Century*. Policy Essay No.7. Washington D.C.: Overseas Development Council.

Lancaster, Carol (1990). "Governance in Africa: Should Foreign Aid Be Linked to Political Reform? In *Africa Program. Africa Governance in the 1990s: Objectives, Resources and Constraints*. Atlanta, GA: The Carter Presidential Center.

Mazrui, Ali (1986). *The Africans*. London: BBC Publications.

Mendez, Ruben (1995). "Paying for Peace and Development." *Foreign Policy*. No. 100, pp. 19-32.

Obasanjo, Olusegun and Felix Mosha (eds.) (1993).*Africa: Rise to Challenge*. New York: Africa Leadership Forum.

Pẹrez de Cuellar, Javier (1990). *Report of the Secretary-General on the Work of the Organization, 1990*. New York: United Nations.

Rasheed, Sadig (1993). "Africa at the Door of the Twenty-First Century: Can Crisis Turn to Opportunity?" In Adebayo Adedeji (ed.). *Africa Within the World: Beyond Dispossession and Dependence*. London: Zed Books.

Rodney, Walter (1972). *How Europe Underdeveloped Africa*. London: Bogle L'Ouverture.

Sandbrook, Richard and Mohamed Halfani (eds.) (1993). *Empowering People: Building Community, Civil Associations, and Legality in Africa*. Toronto: Center for Urban and Community Studies, University of Toronto.

Taiwo, Olufemi (1995). *The Be-Like Mike Syndrome*. Unpublished Paper. Department of Philosophy, Loyola University.

UNRISD (1995). *States of Disarray: The Social Effects of Globalization*. Geneva: UNRISD).

United States Agency for International Development (1993). *Africa: Growth Renewed, Hope Rekindled: A Report on the*

Performance of the Development Fund for Africa, 1988-1992. Washington D.C.: USAID.

World Bank (1995). *World Development Report, 1995: Workers in an Integrating World.* Washington D.C.: World Bank.

World Bank (1991). *World Development Report, 1991.* Washington D.C.: World Bank.

Wren, Christopher (1995). "U.S. Is Seeking Further Ways to Punish Nigeria for Executions." *New York Times.* December 17.

Wright, Stephen (1992). "Africa in the Post-Cold War World." *TransAfrica Forum.* Vol.9. No. 2, pp. 25-37.

Wriston, Walter (1989). "Technology and Sovereignty." *Foreign Affairs.* Vol. 67. No. 2, pp. 63-75.

Yaker, Layashi (1993). "The Case for Solidarity in the South." In Adebayo Adedeji (ed.). *African Within the World: Beyond Dispossession and Dependence.* London: Zed Books.

PART II

THE MILLENNIAL ISSUES

Chapter 3

The State in Africa

George Klay Kieh, Jr.

INTRODUCTION

Historically, Africans have experienced three major genres of states: pre-colonial, colonial and post-colonial (the current type). Each state type was, and is being shaped and conditioned by various forces and factors and their associated dynamics. However, there were, and are variations in the specificities of the state constructs that were either developed by Africans within the contexts of the objective conditions of their divergent local realities (the various pre-colonial states) or those imposed on them by the imperialist powers (Britain, France, Portugal, Belgium, Spain, Germany and the United States) during the colonial and post-colonial eras. The various state formations—both independently developed by Africans and those imposed on them by external powers—were essentially reflections of the worldviews and interests of the dominant classes. This is because as Mutua (2001, p.208) aptly notes, the state is an "empty vessel and a construct with which groups hold political power in a society to pursue their goals...The dominant class or political interests that capture the state make it the public expression of their particular...vision." Accordingly, the resultant features of the state—nature, mission, character, values, institutions, rules, processes and policies—were designed to promote the interests of the dominant forces. The state thus became antagonistic to alternative visions and interests, while being a vigorous prosecutor of the dominant social vision (Oculi, 2007, p.89).

Against this background, the purpose of this chapter is four-fold. First, it will examine the historical development of the pre-colonial and colonial state genres in Africa, including the forces and factors that shaped and conditioned their evolution. Second, using the post-colonial state in Africa as its focus, the chapter will assess the emergence of this state type and its features. Third, it will assess the impact of the neo-colonial state on development. Fourth, the chapter will suggest some ways for democratically reconstituting the neo-colonial state in Africa so that it can serve the interests of the majority of Africans.

THE HISTORICAL DEVELOPMENT OF THE STATE IN AFRICA

Background

The state in Africa has evolved through two major stages: the pre-colonial and the colonial. However, the development of the two state genres were decoupled: The imposition of the colonial state truncated and distorted indigenous state formation in Africa, and imposed an alien and externally determined construct on the African peoples. Thus, the pre-colonial state was not the progenitor of the colonial and post-colonial ones. Instead, the historical links are between the colonial and the post-colonial states; the former laid the foundation for the development of the latter.

In this vein, this section of the chapter will focus on the development of the pre-colonial state genre, its truncation and distortion, and the imposition of the colonial construct. This will provide the context for the examination of the development of the post-colonial state, including its features and the ramifications for national development.

The Pre-Colonial States

Prior to the onslaught of colonialism, Africans were able to build large and complex states in different times and places (Khapoya, 1998, p.68). In East Africa, there were the Axum and Kush Kingdoms. North Africa had various state systems, including the Egyptian Kingdom. Also, in West Africa, there were the Ashanti, Igbo, Malian, Songhay and Yoruba Kingdoms, among others. Significantly, as Wepman (1993, p.5) asserts, "Contrary to the racist characterization of Africa as the 'dark continent,' Africa had governments as organized and stable, and laws as clearly defined, as any in Europe or Asia."

The nature, institutions, rules and processes of the pre-colonial states reflected the historical and cultural experiences of the various groups and the objective conditions prevailing in them. Accordingly, the various states had diverse general overarching missions, including serving the interests of the majority of the citizens. So, there was a typology of pre-colonial African states based on the complexion and operation of the political economy—democratic states, authoritarian states, hybrid states, etc.

Africa's formal contact with Europe commenced in the 16th century initially with Portuguese imperial agents. The European incursion into Africa was the extension of piracy that was going on along the Mediterranean coasts (Palmberg, 1983, p.5). This began the process of integrating the region into the global capitalist system. Trade was the principal vector for Africa's initial incorporation into the European-dominated system. The trade was based on what Martin (2002, pp.1-2) calls a "system of unequal exchange." That is, Africans traded their comparatively expensive goods for inferior European ones.

Pressed by the need for labor imperative of the evolving capitalist political economy, the European imperialists made the determination that Africa would address the need. In this vein, the Europeans embarked upon the quest for labor in Africa to work on their plantations in Europe and the Americas. The resultant was the establishment of the most dehumanizing, exploitative, repressive and nefarious system in the annals of humankind—the slave trade. The Europeans used various insidious devices, including kidnapping and "purchasing" to get African labor. Moreover, the Europeans encouraged and orchestrated wars between various African states as vehicles for taking "prisoners of war." In turn, these so-called "prisoners of war" were then "sold" to European slave traders. The European slave traders loaded Africans like cargo onto various ships bound for European plantations located in Europe and the Americas. The African slaves were chained like animals and subjected to various dehumanizing conditions. One of the major consequences was that thousands of Africans died while en route to slavery. Life on the various slave plantations was brutish and perilous. For example, African slaves worked under horrendous conditions and were subjected to unmitigated violence and myriad actions by the slave over lords. In the process, thousands of Africans died from hunger, malnutrition, disease and wounds suffered from the sundry acts of brutality meted out against their persons.

Over the course of the slave trade, Africa lost 20-30 million human beings (Palmberg, 1983, p. 8). These were mainly the cream of the human resource pools of the various African societies. This was because the exigency of plantation-based capitalism required a labor force that was young and healthy. Clearly, the forced transfer of the cream of the African labor pool deprived the continent of a critical resource that was indispensable to its development. Thus, the slave trade represented the second phase of the emerging dialectical tension between Europe and the United States, on the one hand, and Africa, on the other: The development of Europe and the United States occasioned the underdevelopment of Africa.

The Colonial State

Buoyed by the dividends reaped from the "system of unequal exchange" and slavery, the European imperialists made the bold determination to colonize Africa. The colonial appetite was developed as a consequence of the recognition by the European imperialists that by annexing and controlling Africa they would have the continent's vast economic resources at their disposal. These resources could be used to further the socio-economic development of Europe. However, the imperialists were quite concerned that an unregulated and uncoordinated fight for the continent among the various European powers would have been chaotic. Consequently, the European imperialist powers—Belgium, Britain, France, Germany, Italy, the Netherlands, Portugal and Spain—convened a meeting in Berlin, Germany, from 1884-1885, ostensibly to develop a systematic process for the continuation of the project of pillage and plunder in Africa. Interestingly, having surveyed the landscape of Africa, the imperialist powers were fully cognizant of the continent's economic topography. This information coupled with the dynamics of the global "balance of power" provided the *terra firma* for each imperialist power's "bargaining strategy and position." In the end, as Oliver and Atmore (1994, p.100) aptly observe, "The European powers partitioned Africa among themselves with such haste, like players in a rough game, that the process has been called the 'scramble for Africa'."

The next step in the colonization project was to translate the decisions of the Berlin Conference into territorial realities in Africa. Hence, like all invaders, the imperialist powers marshaled their respective coercive apparati and dispatched them to Africa. Birmingham (1995, p.3) exposes the venality of colonization project thus:

> ...Indeed [the imperialists] sent armies to Africa in order to turn the boundaries on their maps into frontiers on the ground.Owners of the land who resisted the arrival of the self-styled forces of "civilization" were to be "pacified" by conquest.

Several African states challenged and resisted the imposition of European colonialism. In some cases, this resulted in prolonged wars with the European invaders. However, ultimately, the European imperialist powers prevailed because of their superior military capacities. So, by the early 1900s, the imperialist powers had established their suzerainty over Africa. The consequences for Africa were numerous—cultural, economic, environmental, political, religious, security and social—and devastating. For example, hitherfore sovereign and independent African states lost their autonomy and became colonies in the respective empires of the various imperialist powers. Overall, the phenomenon truncated and aborted the process of autonomous development in Africa.

Significantly, colonialism established a "Berlinist state" as the overarching architecture for prosecuting the colonial project. Although the "Berlinist state" had variants—Belgian, British, French, etc. —, it had shared features—nature, mission, character, values, institutions, rules, processes and policies. In terms of its nature, the colonial state was a construct conceived and designed in an external environment devoid of the cultural and historical experiences of African societies. Instead, it was the embodiment of the European vision of conquest, pillage and plunder.

The mission of the colonial state was twofold. First, the state was an instrument for fostering the plunder and pillage of Africa's resources to help promote the socio-economic development of the various imperialist powers. Operationally, each imperialist power formulated and implemented a "colonial division of labor" under which each African colony was assigned the role of producing a particular product—coffee, cocoa, cotton, etc.—to feed the industrial and manufacturing complexes based in the metropolis. Also, the colonial powers prevented and debarred their colonies from engaging in economic relations such as trade with their rivals. Hence, the direction of the economic relations was colonies to the colonial power. Second, the state was a vehicle for fostering the process of the private accumulation of capital by the marauding nationals of the various colonial powers who were resident in the colonies. This was done in various ways, including the seizure of indigenous lands and their transfer to the respective citizens of the colonial powers.

The colonial state had a multidimensional character—absolutist, repressive, exploitative, and negligent, among others. As an absolutist construct, the colonial state controlled virtually every aspect of life—cultural, economic, political, religious and social. Berman (1998, p.313) provides an excellent summation of the totalitarian orientation of the "Berlinist state:"

> The state in colonial Africa, within the broader context of the intrusion of capitalist modernity was the central institutional force in the organization, production and distribution of social resources. It also shaped the accompanying changes in the social criteria for access to those resources; and the resulting social differentiation

> between individuals and communities. By authoritatively defining rules of behavior that specified for Africans what was required, prohibited and permitted, the colonial state structured the choice of individuals by constructing social, economic and political situations; assigning individual rules, identities; and defining the choice of goals, strategies and behaviors.

In the cultural realm, the state superintended the campaign for the denigration of traditional African values and the consequent imposition of European ones. Economically, the colonial state redistributed land and determined who should produce what and how (Ake, 1996, p.2). In the political domain, it ensured, *inter alia*, the maintenance of "control." Religiously, the state led the assault on traditional African religions, and masterminded the imposition of the Western version of Christianity on Africans. In the social sector, the state, for example, went into the business of education to ensure that workers could do the jobs they were required to perform and would remain steadfast in the performance of their often tedious and disagreeable tasks (Ake, 1996, p.2). Another dimension of the colonial state's character was its propensity to use repression as the foundation for the conduct of state-society relations. This was poignantly demonstrated in the state's reaction to protest by Africans against various acts of suppression. Instead of engaging the aggrieved Africans in dialogues with the goal of addressing their legitimate concerns, the colonial state consistently and recurrently responded with brute force. Usually, this resulted in visiting destruction and death on Africans. As Crowder (1987, p.11) notes, "[The colonial state engaged] in burning of villages, destruction of crops, killing of women and children and the execution of leaders." Similarly, as a negligent construct, the colonial state refused to, among other things, provide for the basic needs of the African peoples. Hence, the state was absent from the lives of the people, providing little in the way of welfare, protection, education, justice, health and national identity (Reddy, 2001, p.299).

The "Berlinist state" propagated sets of values that provided the norms for the various sectors of the society. For example, Africans were socialized to believe in the mythology of the "superior-inferior cultures" dichotomy both in terms of the relationships between European and indigenous African cultures, and between and among the various indigenous African cultures. Specifically, the Europeans peddled the preposterous notion that their "cultures were inherently superior to those of the traditional African ones." Thus, Europeans were the so-called "civilized peoples," while Africans were the so-called "primitive peoples." Similarly, within the pantheon of indigenous African ethnic groups, the Europeans anointed the so-called "superior groups" and vilified the so-called "inferior groups." Operationally, the full battery of the colonial state's ideological machinery was mobilized to inculcate these values into the minds of colonized Africans. Also, in the economic sector, capitalist values such as private ownership, the profit motive and rugged individualism became the *regles de jeu.*

Characteristically, the colonial powers designed various bureaucracies as the institutional tapestries. Although, there were variations in the complexions and nomenclatures of these colonial institutions, they performed the common major twin functions of the subjugation and exploitation of Africans. In other words, irrespective of their divergent European national origins—Belgian, British, Dutch, French, German, Italian, Portuguese and Spanish—, the various sets of colonial institutions were all designed to keep Africans under imperial control and to create the enabling conditions for the exploitation and robbery of Africa's vast natural and other resources on behalf of the metropolis.

In terms of the rules, the colonial state in collaboration with the metropolitan powers formulated and implemented plethora of regulations without any consultation with the colonized Africans. The various rules were expansive in terms of their sectoral scope—there were rules for virtually every aspect of the colonial polity. Clearly, the rules were designed to provide the legal justification for the immoral colonial construct and its pedigree.

Linked to the corpus of rules in the various sectors of the colonial society were myriad processes. The latter served as the vehicles for implementing the latter. For example, the "kangaroo trial" served as a major legal vehicle through which the various anti-people and anti-human rights laws were enforced. Similarly, in the economic realm, the "purchasing processes" operated by the various marketing boards served as the conduits for implementing the regulations regarding the pricing of various commodities produced by African peasants.

Correspondingly, the colonial state formulated and implemented various policies governing all of the sectors of the society. For example, the land policy revolved around the expropriation of the indigenous Africans' land for use by the colonial state and the citizens from the metropolis, who were resident in the various colonies. For example, the British colonial state's land policy in Southern Rhodesia (now Zimbabwe) was anchored on inequity. The British colonial state divided the 96,000,000 acres of the territory as follows: 47,176,000 acres of the best land were given to Europeans (who numbered about 60,000), while the native population (about 1,300,000) were assigned 21,600,000 acres of settlement (Jaja, 1998, p.13).

THE POST-COLONIAL STATE

Background

The post-colonial state in Africa is the by-product of its colonial progenitor. The former was bequeathed by the latter beginning in the 1960s, as the colonial state exhausted the course of its historical development. Several major factors contributed to this outcome. First, the colonial state was battered and bruised by the anti-colonial struggle that was waged in each colony by an amalgam of Africans representing divergent class, ethnic, regional, religious and gender backgrounds. In cases such as Algeria, an armed struggle was waged against the illegitimate colonial state. Second, the devastation wrought on the economic multiplexes of the various colonial powers by World War Two severely undermined their base. Third and related, there were domestic pressures within the metropolis for the various colonial powers to focus their attention on the imperatives of internal reconstruction. Fourth, the end of the Second World War witnessed a shift in the global "balance of power:" The European states lost their positions as the dominant global powers; they were replaced by the United States and the Soviet Union. Fifth, colonialism was an anathema to the emergent global capitalist system. Hence, there was pressure from the United States, the new dominant capitalist power, for its European allies to dismantle their respective colonial empires.

The end of the colonial state was greeted with profound joy by Africans across the region, who had suffered from its excesses. So, the dawn of the post-independence era triggered a sense of optimism among Africans. Ramsay (1993, p.3) captures the state of ecstasy thus:

> The times were electric. In country after country, the flags of Britain, Belgium and France were replaced by the banners of the new states, whose leaders offered idealistic promises to, remake the continent and the world. Hopes were high, and the most ambitious of goals seem obtainable. Even non-Africans spoke of the resource rich continent as being on the verge of a develop- take-off. Some of the old, racist myths about Africa were at last being questioned.

However, the majority of the African peoples had barely recovered from the post-independence festivities when it became clear to them that the colonial state was in tact. In fact, if anything had changed, it was that Africans had replaced Europeans as the managers of the state. In short, the first generation of African leaders with very few exceptions—Ghana, etc. —simply inherited the colonial state and made no effort to democratically reconstitute it. Hence, the neo-colonial state that emerged basically retained the portrait of its colonial predecessor. Moreover, the subsequent generations of African leaders have made no effort to deconstruct, rethink and democratically reconstitute the post-colonial state. Even the so-called "third wave of democratization" that began sweeping across the continent in the 1990s, has failed to transform the neo-colonial state (see chapter 5 for a full discussion).

The Portrait of the Neo-Colonial State in Africa

Like it colonial progenitor, the neo-colonial state has several basic features—nature, mission, character, values, institutions, rules, processes and policies. Although, there are nuances among the various neo-colonial states in the continent, they all have shared features—a common portrait. This will be the focus of this section of the chapter. The nature of the neo-colonial state reflects the vision of the various colonial and imperialist powers. Devoid of the historical and cultural experiences of the African peoples, the neo-colonial state was conceived in the bowels of the imperialist project. The neo-colonial state was designed and shaped to continue overseeing and promoting the asymmetrical, dependent and patron-client relationship between Africa and the metropolis.

Relatedly, the mission of the neo-colonial state is to continue from where its colonial predecessor left off. At the vortex is the imperative of fostering imperialist domination and its resultant plunder and pillage. The derivative is to create an enabling environment within each neo-colonial African state for the imperialist powers and their multinational corporations to exploit, plunder and pillage the various states' vast resources for the benefit of the metropolis and to the detriment of the continent—the continuation of the dialectical relationship between the development of the metropolis and the underdevelopment of African states. An ancilliary function of the neo-colonial state is to facilitate the private accumulation of capital by African state managers and their coterie of clients. Interestingly, the mission is reflective of the fact that the neo-colonial African state is "Janus-faced:" On the one hand, it creates wealth for the imperialist powers and their multinational corporations and their African surrogates, but on the other hand, it creates impoverishment and deprivation for the masses of Africans.

The character of the neo-colonial state is multidimensional—dependent, repressive, exploitative, predatory, negligent, etc. In other words, as Agbese (2007, p.36) correctly notes, "The African state is a composite of several tendencies. The ascendancy of any particular tendency is a function of numerous conjunctural factors." As a dependent formation, the neo-colonial state and its managers rely on the metropolitan states and their bourgeois classes for their survival. For example, as export enclaves, the neo-colonial economies of African states primarily rely on their export earnings as the life blood. The fate of their export earnings is decided by the whims and caprices of the metropolitan powers that control and dominate the global marketplace. Hence, when there is a demand in the metropolis for a particular raw material, then the peripheral capitalist economy concerned experiences a period of "economic boom." Conversely, when the demand is low, then the affected African peripheral capitalist state experiences a bust. Also, as a repressive construct, the neo-colonial state, *inter alia*, violates human rights; undermines the viability of multipartyism and uses force as the foundation of state-society relations. As Ake (2001, p.3) asserts, "[The post-colonial state] presented itself as an apparatus of violence, had a narrow social base, and relied for compliance on coercion rather than authority." Another dimension of the character of the neo-colonial state in Africa is that it is the engine of exploitation. That is, it creates the enabling environment for the metropolitan powers and their multinational corporations to exploit the labor of African workers and pillage and plunder the natural resources of African states. Similarly, it allows state managers and the other members of the local ruling classes to engage in the private accumulation of capital from the public coffers. In essence, as Nzongola-Ntalaja (1992, p.13) argues, "Since the state is the major avenue of wealth accumulation for those who control it, a major pre-occupation of the African ruling class has been to expand and consolidate the state's role in the economy." The related character flaw is the neo-colonial state's predatory impulse. In this case, the state allows the use of its resources, including state enterprises, not to promote the public good but to serve private interest (Nzongola-Ntalaja, 1992, p.13). Essentially, the state becomes a buffet service, where state managers and other members of the ruling class and their surrogates can "eat all they can eat." Also, the state promotes the profit-seeking agenda of the metropolitan-based businesses. As a negligent social formation, the neo-colonial state does to attend to the needs of the majority of the African peoples. That is, the state does not, among other things, help to create jobs to talk much more about decent and well paying ones, and provide health care, education, housing and other basic needs of its citizens. Instead, as Kieh and Agbese (2007, p.4) note, "For the masses of the African people, the state merely acts an extractor of resources and the dispenser of misery and injustice."

The neo-colonial state has several values, which are reflective of the dynamics of the peripheral capitalist mode of production and its relations of production. For example, the overarching value that undergirds the search for jobs in the public sector is not to provide public goods for the benefits of the masses of the citizens, but to foster the personal private accumulation of wealth. Hence, the expectation is that public officials would accumulate money and other material assets at the expense of the state, while they are in office. The related value is that those who control state power must marshal the coercive resources of the state to repress, marginalize and contain those who either want to dislodge or criticize them. This is why the struggle for the control of state power has become an epic "life and death battle" in Africa's various neo-colonial formations.

Understandably, state institutions are designed to serve the interests of the dominant classes. Even if these institutions appear democratic on the surface or in theory, functionally they are authoritarian entities. This is because the logic of the peripheral capitalist state in Africa requires, among other things, that the state apparatus provides the institutional framework for supporting the ruling classes' agenda of private accumulation amid mass impoverishment. And when the poverty-stricken subaltern classes protest and resist, the state institutions have the collective role of keeping them in check and eventually cowing them into submission.

Similarly, the rules that provide the parameters for conducting the affairs of the state are subordinated to the acquisitive impulse of the metropolitan-based multinational corporations and the local compradorial classes. Again, even, if the rules appear democratic in letter, their implementation is conditioned and shaped by the imperatives of the peripheral capitalist political economy. For example, it has now become fashionable for neo-colonial African states to establish environmental protection regimes. Ostensibly, these regimes are designed to halt the rising tides of environmental degradation by, among other things, regulating the behavior of businesses, especially metropolitan-based ones. However, in reality, these environmental regimes are never enforced. The most vivid evidence is the general state of environmental decay across the continent—water, air and land pollution, etc.

State-based processes are clearly designed to foster the interests of the ruling classes. In the current age of the so-called "third wave of democratization," the various processes are ultimately designed to convey the façade of transparency and mass participation, while ultimately ensuring the service of the interests of the ruling classes. One of the interesting contemporary processes is privatization. Under the "new" development regime established by neo-liberalism, peripheral capitalist African states are required to, *inter alia*, sell public corporations to private interests. This is based on the "legendary" caveat that the private sector is more efficient than the public sector in the management of economic resources. In reality, the process of privatization ensures that state holdings in the public sector are transferred to capitalists, who, in turn, use them to foster the private accumulation of wealth. So, in effect, the process of privatization has, and continues to serve the interests of capitalists not the masses. For example, private capitalist firms are selling water at prices that the members of the subaltern classes cannot afford; hence, the African masses continue to rely on polluted waterways as the sources for the water needs.

Basically, the policies of the various peripheral capitalist states on the continent—cultural, economic, environmental, political, religious, security and social—are not designed to improve the conditions of the subaltern classes. Instead, like the other elements of the portrait of the neo-colonial state, they are intended to serve the interests of the members of the local ruling classes and the metropolitan-based external patrons. For example, cultural policies are designed to make the state the captive of one particular ethnic group to the exclusion of the others. In effect, the state becomes an "ethnic state" in which the dominant ethnic group receives a disproportionate share of the public resources. Clearly, this is a deliberate strategy by the ruling classes to use ethnicity as an instrument to drive a wedge between and among the members of the subaltern classes. So, instead of viewing themselves as members of the exploited classes, the masses divide themselves along ethnic lines as a consequence of state policies. In the economic domain, as I have already mentioned, privatization has become the developmental fetish. The economic policies of virtually all of the peripheral capitalist states in Africa are anchored on "rolling back the state" from the economy. Alternatively, the public's wealth is being transferred to private capitalists, who have no interests in the welfare of the subaltern classes. Politically, the liberalization policies—the promotion of political rights and civil liberties—are not designed to fundamentally alter the nature and dynamics of the peripheral capitalist political economy. Instead, they are intended to bamboozle the masses into believing that they are major stakeholders in the polity, and that their views are pivotal to the shaping of public policies. Also, the religious policies are designed to privilege one faith over the other. That is, it is common for the state in Africa's peripheral formations to elevate a religion or a sect to the pedestal of national pre-eminence usually for opportunistic reasons. In such cases, religion is simply used by the ruling class as a source of support amid the crisis of illegitimacy. In terms of security policies, they are fundamentally designed to protect the regimes from mass uprising and to secure the private properties of the members of the ruling classes and the metropolitan-based multinational corporations. This is reflected in the fact that the neo-colonial states allocate substantial portions of public resources to the military and security apparatus of the state. Socially, the policies on public education, health care, housing and other basic human needs are never designed to improve the material conditions of the members of the subaltern classes. Fundamentally, this can be gauged by examining the amount of state resources that are allocated to these critical areas in the annual budgets of the various neo-colonial states.

THE IMPACT OF THE NEO-COLONIAL STATE ON DEVELOPMENT

What has been, and is the general impact of the neo-colonial state on development in Africa? This critical question will be addressed by examining the various dimensions of development in Africa—cultural, economic, environmental, political, religious, security and social.

Cultural Development

The neo-colonial state has adversely impacted cultural development in the continent in several major ways. First, there is a profound deficit of nationalism. That is, in the preponderant number of African states the citizens do not have shared affinity that organically linked them to the state. Instead, by and large, citizens have loyalties to other entities other than the state. The primary reason for the disconnect between citizenship and nationalism is that the neo-colonial state has woefully failed to make citizens major stakeholders in the body politic. Instead, the state is the handmaid of the faction and/or fraction of the ruling class that controls state power at a given historical juncture. Hence, the neo-colonial state has become distant and irrelevant to the lives of the majority of Africans.

Second, the state and its custodians are the chief architects of ethnic polarization and division. Amidst the crisis of legitimacy in which most African states are engulfed, the manipulation of ethnicity has become a major weapon in the arsenal of the ruling class. Since they are incapable and unwilling to promote a national agenda based on ethnic inclusion, the ruling factions or fractions of the ruling classes divide Africans by, among other things, making the state an ethnic one. Operationally, the ethnic group or groups that are aligned with the ruling faction or fraction are privileged over the others. Ultimately, this leads to needless polarization and tension and at times civil war between the dominant ethnic group, on the one hand, and the subordinated ethnic groups, on the other.

Third, the neo-colonial state has continued the campaign of its predecessor to denigrate traditional African values and to impose and retain the stranglehold of Western cultural imperialism. For example, African languages are still being subordinated to Western languages such as English and French. In several African states, these Western languages are the official *lingua franca*. Accordingly, they are the media through which public affairs and commerce are conducted and learning (education) takes place. As Prah (2002, p.1) laments,

> ...African languages have been constitutionally accorded, rarely, "official "transactions. Only official languages have this position, and in Africa official languages are almost always colonial languages...in all of these [African] states, the colonial forms of speech have reigned supreme and in time entrenched...It is indeed amazing that at the onset of a new millennium, Africa represents today the only major historical and cultural area of the world where despite their indigenous socio-cultural majorities, countries prefer to use the languages of their erstwhile masters...

Economic Development

As I have argued in chapter 1, the post-colonial epoch in Africa has been marked by a debilitating economic crisis that has made the preponderant majority of Africans to live perilously at the margins. Despite the implementation of the sundry so-called "economic recovery plans" by the continent's various neo-colonial state managers and Bretton Woods Institutions—International Monetary Fund (IMF) and the World Bank—, life for the vast majority of Africans remains a daily struggle for survival. Moreover, even the recent repackaging of the neo-liberal economic doctrine and the implementation of the various global "debt forgiveness" plans—Heavily Indebted Poor Countries Initiative and Enhanced Heavily Indebted Poor Countries Initiative—are showing no signs of ending Africa's perennial economic woes. Two major indicators can be used to capture the depth of the unending economic crisis in Africa. At the core, the rate of poverty continues to burgeon. For example, in 2004, the rate stood at an alarming 46% (United Nations Economic Commission for Africa, 2005, p.5). These are the Africans would virtually have no means to provide for their basic needs—food, etc. Accordingly, they barely survive by being dependent upon "handouts."

Another measure is unemployment. In 2004, the combined figure for the unemployed and the working poor was 55% of the continent's population (United Nations Economic Commission for Africa, 2005, pp. 5-7). Of this figure, the former accounted for 10% and the latter 45%. The combined figure captures the magnitude of the unemployment conundrum better because there is no substantial difference between the unemployed (those without jobs) and the working poor (those who are employed but do not earn barely enough to provide for their basic human needs).

Environmental Development

Although African states have established environmental regulatory agencies, much progress has not been made in containing the tides of degradation and unsustainability. The principal reason is that in most cases the various regulatory mechanisms have not enforced the various rules that are designed to promote the good health of the environment.

Three major factors account for this. First, African states have not made the required investment of resources into the development of the human needs-based infrastructure such as public lavatories that would help militate against the continual use of land and water sources for excretion. Second, African states have not helped to create jobs that would help prevent the unemployed from engaging in activities that are harmful to the environment. Third, African states have demonstrated the lack of political will to regulate the economic activities of the metropolitan-based multinational corporations that are polluting the environment.

Against this background, the environment in the continent continues to deteriorate evidenced by, among others, the persistence of air, water and land pollution and deforestation. Clearly, these environmental problems continue to adversely affect the health of millions of Africans in terms of their vulnerability to diseases. Furthermore, these problems are occasioning changes and shifts in climatic conditions. In turn, these could cause erosion, flooding and other disasters.

Political Development

After the collapse of colonialism, the failure of the African ruling classes to set into motion the democratic reconstitution of the neo-colonial state enveloped the continent into the cocoon of multifaceted crises of underdevelopment. The effects of the crises adversely impacted the continent's subaltern classes. This then set the stage for the disintegration of the broad national coalitions that waged the various anti-colonial struggles across the continent. The resultant was the establishment of an antagonistic relationship between the ruling and subaltern classes akin to the colonial era. Over time, the polarizing nature of the lever that anchored state-society relations laid the foundation for instability.

The initial sign of the failure of the post-colonial state building project was the wave of military coups that rocked the continent beginning in the 1950s. Like dominos, various states across the continent fell to the expansive ambit of military intervention and the subsequent military rule. In their various coup broadcasts, the "soldiers in mufti" (Nordlinger, 1970) used the various affected states' crises of underdevelopment as the pretext for their engagement in the political arena as governors (Kieh, 2004). The various military regimes promised to end the crises of underdevelopment and to usher in new democratic orders based on the synergy of cultural, economic, political and social development. However, the horrendous performance of the various military regimes across the continent (in some cases worse than the civilian regimes that they deposed) helped to fuel the flame of instability. This was evidenced by, among other things, the twin phenomena of the increased frustration of the subaltern classes and the inception of a seemingly unending cycle of counter-coups.

Another dimension of the instability conundrum was the outbreak of various civil wars across the continent. Exasperated by the failure of the ruling classes and their civilian and military regimes, various groups resorted to armed violence against the state as the *dues ex machina* for addressing their pathetic conditions. In cases like Nigeria, the civil war ended with the military defeat of the aggrieved groups. Emboldened by the "military victory," the Nigerian ruling class made some cosmetic structural changes, including the creation of new ethnically-based states. However, these "reforms" did not fundamentally impact the material conditions of the aggrieved groups in the eastern region. In other cases like Somalia, civil wars have continued with no apparent end in sight.

By the end of the 1980s, only African few countries—Botswana, the Gambia and Mauritius—had made appreciable efforts to tackle the critical challenge of dismantling the authoritarian governance multiplex that was bequeathed to the continent by colonialism. On the other hand, the overwhelming majority of the continent's constituent states were firmly under the control of various autocratic civilian and military regimes. Although various pro-democracy groups across the continent had made laudable strides to challenge these authoritarian regimes, their efforts were thwarted by the confluence of institutionalized state-sponsored violence and the patronage of the two global power blocs—the Western camp under American leadership and the Soviet orbit under the control of the Kremlin.

The beginning of the decade of the 1990s witnessed the emergence of another opportunity for the continent to exorcise the authoritarian demon. Dubbed the "third wave of democratization," (see chapter 5), there was, *inter alia*, a clamor for the dismantling of the authoritarian state across the continent. On the eve of the new millennium, there was emergent evidence that the continent's political landscape was changing for the better. For example, new constitutions were written and adopted; the political space was being liberalized evidenced by the promotion of political rights and freedoms; and multiparty elections were held in various African states thereby giving the overwhelming majority of Africans the opportunity to freely choose their leaders for the first time in the post-colonial era. Interestingly, in countries like Malawi and Zambia, well entrenched "princes," "autocrats," "prophets" and "tyrants," to use Jackson and Rosberg's (1982) characterization, were ousted in free and fair multiparty elections.

However, after nearly two decades, the "third wave of democratization" has apparently run out of "steam." The overarching obstacle remains the fact that the neo-colonial state has not been deconstructed, rethought and democratically reconstituted. Hence, the democratization project is being pursued in the bowels of the very neo-colonial construct that has visited brutality, exploitation, marginalization and neglect, among other things, on the continent's subaltern classes. Since the neo-colonial state is intrinsically anti-democratic, it has, among other things, set into motion reverses across the continent. For example, in Nigeria, the year 1999 was greeted with optimism by the majority of Nigerians, other Africans and those with interest in the continent. This was because with the "farewell to arms" (Welch, 1987), it was believed that the end of the stranglehold that the military has had on state power for more than three decades would produce a new democratic dispensation. However, after eight years under the so-called "new democratic order" under the presidency of retired General Olusegun Obasanjo, it is clear that Nigerian is still an authoritarian state. The fraud and violence plagued 2007 state and national elections in the country provide further evidence that political democratization cannot succeed under the aegis of a non-reconstituted neo-colonial state. Similarly, the other dimensions of the continent's crises of underdevelopment—cultural, economic, environmental, security and social—have not been addressed. Even in those African states like Benin and Mali where the "third wave of democratization" has positively impacted the political landscape, there has not been improvement in the material conditions of the majority of the citizens. In these cases, the emerging pattern is based on "political rights and freedoms without socio-economic ones."

Religious Development

As in other regions of the world, religious development in Africa has followed two major trajectories: the fusion of state and religion and the separation of state and religion. In the case of the former, the state is virtually indistinguishable from the hegemonic religion. In fact, state policies are derived from the parameters set by the doctrine of the dominant religion. In light of this, the state is then intolerant of other religions that provide alternative pathways that conflict with the doctrine of the "national religion." For example, in Libya, Islam is considered the "national religion." Hence, other religious groups based on divergent theologies are not permitted to operate in the country. Those who dare to challenge the edict risk incurring the wrath of the state. In the latter case, the state is not wedded to a particular religion; and thus, state policies are not based on the doctrinal pillars of a religion. In short, the state is secular. Also, the state allows various religions to organize and proselytize.

Another outcome of religious development on the continent is the marginalization of traditional African religions. Given its colonial origins, the state in Africa has continued the practice of not according recognition to the plethora of indigenous African religions, even in the so-called secular countries where religious pluralism is supposedly practiced. As their colonial progenitors did, African post-colonial state managers have continued to demonize indigenous African religions as paganistic. For example, in Nigeria, the federal government constructed a national mosque for Muslims and a national cathedral for Christians. But, there is no national shrine for the traditional African religions.

In some African states, religion has become a source of conflict and instability. One dimension of the problem is the growing tension between Christians and Muslims. In countries like Nigeria, there have been various religious-based violent conflicts between Christians and Muslims as part of the epic battle revolving around the issue of "their God versus ours." Another side of the conundrum has been conflicts between the state and various Islamic sects. For example, in Egypt, there has been an on going conflict between the government and the Islamic Brotherhood over the issue of the relationship between the state and religion. The former wants to keep Egypt as a secular state, while the latter wants to Islamize the country.

Security Development

With very few exceptions, the mainstay of security in Africa is the primacy of regime security. This is reflected in the fact that substantial amounts of state resources are devoted to the military and security sectors as the kernels of the protective tapestry of the regime in power. Some of these resources are used to establish, train and maintain various elite military and security units that have primary responsibilities for the protection of the regime. For example, in Liberia under the Doe regime, large sums of money and logistics were allocated to the Special Anti-Terrorist Unit, the elite military force that had the principal responsibility for protecting the president. Given the primacy of authoritarianism on the continent, most of the regimes therefore lack popular support among the members of the subaltern classes. Moreover, in light of the fact that these regimes have formulated and implemented public policies that have repressed and impoverished the members of the subaltern classes, state managers are fearful of mass retribution. Hence, the military-security apparatus has become the instrument for protecting the state managers from the wrath of the masses.

The primary consequence of the regime security orientation has, and continues to be the failure of the state to provide for the basic needs of the majority of its citizens. As I argue in the next section, state neglect is reflected in the sordid state of human development on the continent. As the annual Human Development Report published by the United Nations Development Program has recurrently shown, with few exceptions, the state in Africa has done a very poor job, *inter alia*, in providing public education, employment opportunities, public health, access to clean drinking water and access to acceptable sanitation. Consequently, Africa is engulfed by a "human security crisis" that has contributed, among other things, to mass hunger, malnutrition, vulnerability to diseases and short life expectancies.

Social Development

The failure of the neo-colonial state to promote meaningful social development since the post-colonial era has been one of the major contributing factors to the larger "human security crisis" that has engulfed the continent. State failure in the social sector can be captured by various indices. Public education has never been a major national priority. And this has been reflected in various ways, including the general small size of state financial allocations and the lack of adequate logistical support. Particularly, in the current epoch of neo-liberal orthodoxy as is being enforced by the "Bretton Woods Institutions"—International Monetary Fund (IMF) and the World Bank—, the neo-colonial state in Africa is shrinking its already meager support for public education. The major outcome is that African states lack the requisite pool of trained and skilled human resources to power their development. Thus, African states have become increasing reliant on so-called "foreign experts" to provide the skills and professional and technical skills that are imperative for their development. According to the United Nations Development Program, African states spend over $4 billion per year to employ 150,000 expatriate professionals (Editorial Board, 2007, p.1).

Likewise, African state managers have not adequately invested in the public health infrastructure. For example, during the 1980s, the average state allocation for public health was 4% of annual government expenditures (Rodino, 2005, p.1). This attitude of neglect had profound adverse effects on the lives of the African peoples. The overarching adverse consequence was the increased vulnerability of the masses of African to diseases. Particularly, thousands of Africans died from curable diseases, due to the pathetic state of the public health system.

In the related areas of access to clean drinking water and acceptable sanitation, the neo-colonial state has not given the required attention to these twin critical areas. According to the United Nations Development Program (2001, p.171), from 1990-1998, only 46% of the population of Africa had access to safe drinking water. Faced with the inadequacy of cleaning drinking water, millions of Africans rely on sources that are often polluted by human waste and other contaminants. This practice increases their vulnerability to various water borne diseases. In terms of sanitation, from 1990-1998, 300 million or 48% of the population of Africa had access to acceptable sanitation (United Nations Development Program, 2001, p. 171). There are several dimensions to the sanitation problem. A major one is that the inadequacy of public and private lavatory facilities forces scores of Africans to use various waterways (some which also serve as sources of drinking water), vacant lots and the beaches to dispose of their excreta.

Adequate housing is another major casualty of the crisis of social underdevelopment that has afflicted Africa during the post-colonial period. With increasing urbanization (see chapter 6), the population has outstripped the availability of adequate housing. Regrettably, the neo-colonial state in Africa has failed to make this critical human need area a priority. Accordingly, there have been two major consequences. At one level, homelessness has become a national tragedy as reflected by the fact that thousands of Africans are sleeping on the streets, in abandoned buildings and other dehumanizing areas. On the other, there is an increase in the ghettoization of Africa's major urban centers.

TOWARD THE RECONSTITUTION OF THE NEO-COLONIAL STATE IN AFRICA: SOME SUGGESTIONS

Clearly, the neo-colonial state in Africa has failed to cater to the aspirations and needs of the majority of the African peoples. Hence, its failure, as Samatar and Samatar (2002,

p. 5) observe, "Is uncontested." Hence, Africa needs a new pro-people, pro-democratic and pro-development state as the replacement for the current neo-colonial construct and its associated pedigree.

Against this backdrop, two major steps are proposed as the bedrocks of the democratic reconstitution of the state. First, there is the exigency of convening national conferences in the various African states at which all of the major stakeholders in the respective countries would be represented. The agenda should consist of two major items: the rejection and dismantling of the neo-colonial state and the formulation of the elements of a new state. I would contend that it is in the best interest of Africans to develop a social democratic state instead of a liberal democratic one. This is because social democracy is a holistic architecture that embodies cultural, environmental, economic, political and social democracy. On the other hand, liberal democracy places emphasis on political rights and freedoms.

Second, the portrait of the new state should reflect its social democratic core. At the base, the nature of the state should reflect the shared cultural and historical experiences of all of the ethnic groups in the various African states. The character should be pro-people, pro-democracy and pro-development. In terms of the mission, it should revolve around the use of the state's resources to ensure that all of the citizens have decent standard of living so that they can fulfill their human potentials. The new national values should promote, among other things, pan-Africanism, ethnic, regional and religious pluralism, the respect for elders, gender equality, and a good work ethic. Also, the various public institutions should be designed to promote social democracy. Accountability, transparency and the due process of law should anchor the web of democratic rules and processes. Finally, public policies in all of the sectors should make the welfare of the citizens the paramount pre-occupation.

CONCLUSION

The chapter has attempted to examine the development and the attendant dynamics of state-building in Africa—pre-colonial, colonial and post-colonial. The discussion was guided by four major arguments. First, during the pre-colonial era, there were various states in Africa. Each state was developing independently based on its objective realities. Colonialism aborted the process of autonomous indigenous state-building on the continent.

Second, colonialism imposed an authoritarian state construct on Africa. The construct was driven by the imperatives of European imperialism. Hence, its institutions, rules, processes and policies were guided by the overarching purpose of promoting the interests of the European imperialists. Specifically, this required, among other things, the use of state terror as the centerpiece of relations with the colonized Africans; economic exploitation and marginalization; and social neglect.

Third, the portrait of the post-colonial African state is a replica of its colonial progenitor. The first generation and subsequent generations of the African ruling classes made no effort to deconstruct and democratically reconstitute the post-colonial or neo-colonial state. Hence, like its colonial predecessor, the neo-colonial state has visited repression, exploitation and neglect on the majority of the peoples of Africa.

Fourth, African needs to dismantle the neo-colonial state and to replace it with a new social democratic one. The portrait of the new state must be designed both in form and praxis to serve the interests of all of the peoples of the various African states. In order to do this, the new social democratic state must have a characteristic pro-people, pro-democratic and pro-development orientation.

References

Agbese, Pita Ogaba (2007). "The State in Africa: A Political Economy." In George Klay Kieh, Jr. (ed). *Beyond State Failure and Collapse: Making the State Relevant in Africa*. Lanham, MD: Lexington Books.

Ake, Claude (1996). *Democracy and Development in Africa*. Washington D.C.: The Brookings Institution.

Berman, Bruce (1998). "Ethnicity, Patronage and the African State: The Politics of Uncivil Nationalism." *African Affairs*. Vol. 97. No. 388, pp. 305-341.

Birmingham, David C (1995). *The Decolonization of Africa*. Athens, OH: Ohio University Press.

Crowder, Michael (1987). "Whose Dream Was It Anyway? Twenty-Five Years of African Independence." *African Affairs*. Vol. 86. No. 342, pp. 7-24.

Editorial Board (2007). "African: Brain Drain Costs Continent 4 Billion Dollars Annually." *News*, April 13.

Jackson, Robert and Carl Rosberg (1982). *Personal Rule in Africa: Prince, Autocrat, Prophet, Tyrant*. Berkeley, CA: University of California Press.

Jaja, Cheedy (1998). "Hobbes Theory of Colonialism and the African Colonial Experience: Structural and Programmatic Affinities." *APA Newsletters*. Vol. 97. No. 2, pp. 11-15.

Khapoya, Vincent (1998). *The African Experience: An Introduction*. 2nd ed. Upper Saddle, NJ: Prentice-Hall.

Kieh, George Klay and Pita Ogaba Agbese (2007). "Introduction: The Travails of the Post-Colonial State in Africa." In George Klay Kieh, Jr. and Pita Ogaba Agbese (eds.). *The State in Africa: Issues and Perspectives*. Lagos, Nigeria: Kraft Books.

Kieh, George Klay (2004). "Military Engagement in African Politics." In George Klay Kieh, Jr. and Pita Ogaba Agbesa (eds.) *The Military and Politics in Africa: From Engagement to Constitutional and Democratic Control*. Aldershot: Ashgate Publishing.

Martin, Guy (2002). *Africa in World Politics: A Pan-African Perspective*. Trenton, NJ: Africa World Press.

Mutua, Makau (2001). "Savages, Victims and Saviors: The Metaphor of Human Rights." *Harvard International Law Journal*. Vol. 42. No.1, pp. 201-245.

Mutume, Gumisi (2004). "Rough Road to Sustainable Development." *Africa Renewal*. Vol. 18. No. 2, pp. 19-20.

Nordlinger, Eric (1970). "Soldiers in Mufti: The Impact of Military Rule Upon Economic and Social Change in the Non-Western States." *American Political Science Review*. Vol. 64. No. 4, pp. 1131-1148.

Nzongola-Ntalaja, Georges (1992). *The African Crisis: The Way Out*. SAPES' Seminar Paper Series No. 2. Harare, Zimbabwe: SAPES Books.

Oculi, Okello (2008). "State and Security in Africa." In George Klay Kieh, Jr. and Pita Ogaba Agbese (eds). *The State in Africa: Issues and Perspectives*. Lagos: Kraft Books.

Oliver, Roland and Anthony Atmore (1994). *Africa Since 1800*. Cambridge: Cambridge University Press.

Palmberg, Mai (1983). *The Struggle for Africa*. London: Zed Press.

Prah, Kwesi Kwaa (2002). "Language, Neo-colonialism and the African Development Challenge," *TriContinental*. No. 150, pp. 1-6.

Ramsay, Jeffress (1993). "Introduction." in Jeffress Ramsay (ed.). *Africa*. Guildford, CT: Dushkin Publishing Group, Inc.

Reddy, Movindri (2001). "Ethnic Conflict and Violence: South Africa, Punjab and Sri Lanka." In John Mukum Mbaku et al. *Ethnicity and Governance in the Third World*. Aldershot: Ashgate.

Rodino, Virginia (2005). "African Debt, War and Imperialism are Linked." *Global Research*. August 2, pp. 1-5.

Samatar, Abdi and Ahmed Samatar (2002). "Introduction." In *The African State: Reconsiderations*. Portsmouth, N.H.: Heinemann.

United Nations Development Program (2001). *Human Development Report, 2000*. New York: Oxford University Press.

United Nations Economic Commission for Africa (2005). *Economic Report on Africa, 2005*. Addis Ababa: UNECA.

Welch, Claude (1987). *No Farewell to Arms? Military Disengagement from Politics in Africa and Latin America.* Boulder: Westview Press.

Wepman, Dennis (1993). *Africa: The Struggle for Independence.* New York: Facts on File.

Chapter 4

Economic Development in Africa

John Mukum Mbaku

INTRODUCTION

In the 1960s, as many colonies in Africa gained independence from the Europeans, it was generally believed that capture of governance and economic structures by indigenous elites would provide the wherewithal for rapid economic growth and development. Many Africans were optimistic that the new leaders would provide the enabling institutional environment for (1) wealth creation; (2) peaceful coexistence of each new country's diverse population groups; and (3) generally improve the welfare of historically marginalized and deprived groups and communities (see, e.g., Stepanek, 1999). Unfortunately for Africa's poor, the indigenous elites who captured the evacuated structures of colonial hegemony moved quickly to privatize the state and used the latter's structures as instruments of plunder to extract extralegal benefits for themselves. Although many of the post-independence development programs initiated and implemented by these elites generated significant benefits for state custodians (civil servants and politicians), they imposed enormous costs on the people, increased levels of poverty, and marginalized many groups and communities and pushed them further to the peripheral regions of society. Today, Africa, especially the sub-region called sub-Saharan Africa, is the poorest part of the world (see, e.g., UNDP, 2002; UNDP, 2005).

Despite the tremendous changes that have taken place in the continent since the late 1980s, especially in the political arena, most of the continent's economies are still characterized by relatively high levels of poverty and deprivation, poorly developed infrastructures, excessive and unmanageable external debt, endemic political and bureaucratic corruption, political violence and institutional instability, destructive ethnic mobilization, and several other ills that remain important obstacles to economic growth and poverty alleviation in the continent. In this chapter, we examine the present condition of Africa's economies and make suggestions on how to improve the continent's ability to generate the wealth that it needs to meet its obligations.

ECONOMIC STRUCTURES

Even after more than forty years of independence, many countries in Africa still have economic infrastructures that are poorly developed, do not have the capacity to serve as an anchor for productive economic activities, are incapable of meeting the needs of the entrepreneurial class, and generally do not represent a viable foundation for building an efficient and productive economy. In more than forty years of independence, few African countries have been able to develop and sustain viable economic infrastructures. In several of these countries, the infrastructures inherited from the colonial state have been misused, overexploited, and allowed to "die" from lack of maintenance. As a consequence, infrastructures throughout the region have deteriorated significantly. Hence, as Africans begin their eighth year in the new millennium, they must secure resources to rehabilitate these infrastructures so that they can become positive contributors to economic growth and wealth creation.

One of the most important parts of the national infrastructure is capital, which includes social overhead and physical capital. Physical capital is made up of structures and equipment used in production. Social overhead capital, on the other hand, consists of hospitals, dispensaries and health clinics, educational facilities, and several forms of shelter. In order to avail itself of both forms of capital, each African country must have resources in the form of savings. Unfortunately, most African countries have very low domestic savings rates and as a result, have not been able to contribute significantly to capital formation efforts (World Bank, 2003, 2006; UNDP, 2002, 2005).

While official savings rates and formal measures of capital are quite low across the continent, these, however, tend to overlook hidden forms of wealth among rural farmers, petty traders, artisans, and various other entrepreneurs whose economic activities are often kept deliberately invisible to the state and international organizations. Hence, the relatively large informal sectors and underground economies that exist in many African economies make it very difficult to accurately determine the rate of domestic savings and the actual stock of capital in each economy. It is important to note that in some economies (e.g., Democratic Republic of Congo, Ghana, Nigeria, and Cameroon), which have relatively high rates of corruption, a significant amount of savings in the informal sector has been accumulated through extralegal means—usually by high ranking state custodians. Those who own these illegally accumulated capital resources usually do not invest them locally, for fear that the wealth and its earnings could later be confiscated by the government when the political "entrepreneur" is no longer in good standing with the government. In choosing to invest such ill-gotten resources abroad, the owner also expects to establish a retirement home in the foreign country where he can escape to in case he loses his political influence. For these and other reasons, most owners of resources accumulated through extralegal means do not usually invest in the domestic economy (see, e.g., LeVine, 1975; Jua, 1998; MacGaffey, 1983).

Healthcare Services

A country cannot expect to maintain a healthy and productive workforce if its citizens do not have adequate and effective access to health care services. Access to basic health care represents an important determinant of economic growth and development. Unfortunately, most Africans do not have effective access to health care services. First, as a result of poor economic performance during most of the last forty years, many countries in the continent have not been able to provide their citizens with viable and fully functioning health care systems. Second, in those countries in which health care infrastructures actually exist, they are concentrated in the urban areas, depriving rural inhabitants of access to hospitals, clinics, dispensaries, clean water, and other services that are needed to maintain a healthy and productive work force. Third, as a result of high levels of venality in the public services of many countries in the region, provision of public goods and services to the population is capricious, selective, and designed to benefit primarily politically dominant groups, as well as those who have the resources to pay the bribes required by civil servants before they can be granted access to services. Finally, since the advent of the IMF and World Bank imposed structural adjustment programs (SAPs), many governments have reduced expenditures on health care and other welfare enhancing and life saving public goods and services in favor of debt service, so they can continue to have access to resources from the Bretton Woods institutions (see, e.g., UNDP, 1990) and other international lenders.

The health of Africans, like that of people in other parts of the world, is affected by the environment in which they live. For example, many people get sick because they lack access to clean water, which is used for drinking and cooking. Infants and children are especially susceptible to waterborne diseases. According to the World Bank (1998b, p. 95), consumption of water contaminated by feces causes diseases that make up as much as 10 percent of the total disease burden in developing countries (including those in Africa) today. Contaminated drinking water remains a very severe problem for Africa, especially in many of the informal settlements that litter the urban centers of the continent. Although some efforts have been made to improve the quality of water through improved sanitation and sewage treatment, most citizens still lack adequate access to clean drinking water.

The World Health Organization (WHO) measures the quality of health care in a country by the percent of the population that has access to health care services, improved water sources, and improved sanitation facilities. According to World Bank (2003, 2002a) data, although citizens of a few African countries (Egypt, Libya, Mauritius, and Tunisia) do relatively well, most Africans still do not have access to basic health care services. Between 1980 and 2000 (World Bank, 2002a, pp. 106–109), there seems to have been some improvements in provision. One needs to note, however, that the data only measure the supply of services, without any indication as to actual rate of consumption or the extent of benefits derived by the people. Recent data from the World Bank (2006) and the UNDP (2005) show that most Africans, especially women, infants and children and rural inhabitants are still severely disadvantaged when it comes to access to basic health care.

As mentioned earlier, most health facilities in the African countries are located in the urban centers, with services available only to those who can afford to bribe the civil servants whose job it is to serve the public. Recent evidence from Cameroon and Nigeria has revealed that physicians and other staff members at public hospitals often withhold treatment from the sick until the latter (or their relatives) can supply requested bribes. In several instances, many corrupt civil servants in these countries are known to openly negotiate the extralegal payment that must be paid to them before certain members of the population are provided with what are essentially free public goods and services (Agbese, 1998; Jua, 1998; Mbaku, 2007). Hence, even in countries that have relatively adequate health care infrastructures, allocation of the services generated by these assets may be so selective and capricious that most citizens are denied access.

Gross neglect of the rural sectors of many African countries by their governments has forced the people who reside in these areas to resort to private provision, mostly through nongovernmental organizations. Many of the voluntary agencies that provide a variety of services to rural inhabitants (e.g., Christian churches) have done so since the colonial period. They provide a variety of services, ranging from prenatal care to expectant mothers to water wells for people in the villages. During most of the post-independence period, when public provision has not been forthcoming or allocation has been capricious, churches and other NGOs have usually stepped in and provided the necessary goods and services. Throughout most of rural sub-Saharan Africa, church-funded dispensaries, clinics, and hospitals are the primary (and often the only) source of health care for most people, including those suffering from HIV/AIDS. Since the mid-1980s, many African villages have formed their own community improvement organizations, which have actually teamed up with NGOs in the United States and other developed countries to secure critical social services (e.g., water, primary education, literacy programs for the adult population, and other welfare enhancing services). The modest improvements in access to health care indicated by World Bank (2002a, pp. 106–109) data may not be due to significant improvements in bureaucratic efficiency but may actually be the result of the replacement of the state by NGOs in many rural parts of the continent (Ihonvbere, 1994).

Data on physicians per 1,000 people are also used to determine access to health care. According to the World Bank (2003, pp. 258–259), the number of physicians per 1,000 people in Africa ranged from a low of 0.0 in Burkina Faso, Central African Republic, Eritrea, Niger, and Tanzania to a high of 1.6 in Egypt during the 1995–2000 period. As the World Bank data show, Africans are among the least likely people in the world to have access to adequate and effective health care services. One needs to note that while Africans in general are severely disadvantaged when it comes to health care, certain groups and communities within the continent are actually worse off—these include children, women, rural peasants, and the urban poor.

Recent data (see, e.g., World Bank, 2006; UNDP, 2005) do not show any significant improvements in the key indicators of health in Africa, especially given the challenges that many national health care systems are facing from the HIV/AIDS pandemic, malaria, the mass exit of nurses, physicians, and other health professionals to the more stable economies of North America and Western Europe and the oil-rich Gulf States, as well as the return of such highly contagious diseases as tuberculosis.

Taxing Africa's Fragile Health Systems: The Role of HIV/AIDS

During most of the post-independence period, few African countries have been able to provide their citizens with adequate access to health care. Instead, most of them have had extremely fragile health care systems, all of which have been incapable of meeting the needs of their respective populations. In addition to the fact that Africa's health care infrastructure has been forced to deal with a significant number of endemic diseases (e.g., malaria, tuberculosis, and yellow fever), it must now face the scourge of a pandemic that appears to have no cure—AIDS. The latter, which first emerged as a major health concern in the late 1970s, has become the greatest challenge to the health of Africans.

According to the Joint United Nations Program on HIV/AIDS (UNAIDS) and the World Health Organization (WHO), the total number of people in the world living with HIV/AIDS in 2003 was 40 million, a significant increase from the previous year. Of that number, most of them can be found in the developing countries. The latest information in HIV/AIDS does not show any improvements in the situation in Africa. In fact, conditions have deteriorated significantly and infection rates continue to rise and the disease remains the single most important determinant of mortality for Africans (UNAIDS, 2003, p. 5). In 2003, of all the people living with HIV/AIDS in the world, as much as 60 percent of these were in Africa. By 2005, that percentage had fallen only slightly, to 58.70 percent (UNAIDS, 2006, p. 505).

The impact of the rapid rise in HIV infection rates on African societies has been quite enormous. The most affected areas include,

- rapidly declining child survival rates;
- falling life expectancy;
- health care systems that are no longer able to deal with even basic ailments;
- an explosion in the rate of orphanhood; and
- significant lost production since the majority of the dead are people in their most productive years.

Today, AIDS is the single most important threat to human and economic development in Africa. In fact, AIDS is threatening to reverse nearly half a century of improvements in the human condition. Given the fact that the health care systems of most African countries, especially those in sub-Saharan Africa, are very fragile, the arrival of AIDS has dealt a significant blow to national efforts to improve existing care systems. In fact, in some countries in the region, the burden placed on the national health care system by AIDS is so enormous that several of them have, for all intents and purposes, collapsed.

Of all the people who were infected with HIV in 2003, nearly 70 percent of them were in sub-Saharan Africa. Perhaps more important is the fact that almost three-quarters of all global deaths from AIDS in 2003 occurred in sub-Saharan Africa. Although Africa has only 10 percent of the world's population, it has a disproportionate share of the global HIV/AIDS deaths. The prevalence of HIV varies significantly across the African continent, ranging from less than 1 percent in Mauritania to nearly 40 percent in Botswana and Swaziland (UNAIDS, 2003, p. 7; also see UNAIDS, 2006). In fact, sub-Saharan Africa has emerged as the epicenter of the AIDS pandemic. Since the disease became a global health problem in the late 1970s, it has killed a lot of people, most of them in Africa. Although Southern Africa accounts for less than 2 percent of the world's population, it is home to about 30 percent of people living with HIV/AIDS worldwide. Of all the people who have died from AIDS so far, more than 80 percent of them have been Africans.

According to UN and WHO data for 1998, 9 out of 10 children (<15 years) infected with HIV were in Africa (UNAIDS, 1998). As much as 95 percent of all AIDS orphans are Africans. At the end of 1999, Africa had a cumulative AIDS-related orphan population of a little over 12 million. Since then, that number has increased significantly—by as much as 1,600,000 by 2005 (UNAIDS, 2006, p. 509). The magnitude of Africans infected, dead, and dying is such that the meager gains in human development during the last forty years are likely to be wiped out completely. In fact, there is fear that the productive populations of some countries in Africa, especially in sub-Saharan Africa, may be totally decimated by the pandemic.

Since HIV began to spread worldwide, more than 30 million sub-Saharan Africans have been affected with the virus. Of these, more than 12 million have died. A little over a quarter of the dead are children. According to some recent estimates (UNAIDS/UNICEF/WHO, 2003; also see UNAIDS, 2006), about 1,000 adults and children are dying from AIDS each day in the worst-affected countries in Africa. In fact, the very people who are expected to rescue Africa from its present development quagmire are being decimated by AIDS.

Unless a cure is found for the disease soon, it promises to wipe out most of the modest gains made by African countries in human development during the post-independence period. Life expectancy at birth is the key indicator of the level of human development in a country. According to WHO (1998, p. 7), "the epidemic will wipe out precious development gains by slashing life expectancy." In a country such as Botswana, which since independence has made significant improvements in the quality of life of its people, the disease is expected to cause significant development regression.

Botswana currently has an infection rate of 40 percent. According to WHO and World Bank (2002b, p. 314) calculations, a child born in Botswana in the new century, ceteris paribus, will expect to live barely past his 39th birthday, as opposed to his 70th, had AIDS not been a health problem for the country. From 1996 to 1997, as measured by the United Nations Development Program's human development index (HDI), Botswana suffered significant regression in development. In fact, it dropped as much as 26 places on the index (UNDP, 1997). Based on WHO and UN data, life expectancy in the nine countries with an adult HIV prevalence rate of 10 percent or more (Botswana, Kenya, Malawi, Mozambique, Namibia, Rwanda, South Africa, Zambia, and Zimbabwe) is expected to decline on the average by about 17 years. In the absence of AIDS, life expectancy in these countries was expected to rise to 64 years by 2010–2015. Instead, as a result of the impact of AIDS, life expectancy is expected to regress on the average to 47 years (WHO, 1998, p. 7). Although Botswana has made significant improvements in the fight against AIDS, as a result of concerted efforts by the government, the country's HIV prevalence rate remains one of the highest in the region (see UNAIDS, 2006).

Part of the deterioration in life expectancy in Africa is expected to come from decreases in child survival rates. HIV has become the most important contributor to falling child survival rates in sub-Saharan Africa, significantly reversing many years of achievement in fighting a variety of childhood diseases. By the end of the first decade of the new millennium, the infant mortality rate in South Africa is expected to rise to 61 (that is, 61 children born in South Africa are expected to die before they reach age one year). Without AIDS, the infant mortality rate in South Africa would have fallen to 38. Other African countries with relatively high HIV infection rates (e.g., Swaziland, Lesotho, Mozambique, Zimbabwe) are expected to suffer similar fates (WHO, 1998; UNAIDS, 2006).

AIDS has already created a lot of orphans in Africa. In Zimbabwe, for example, where more than 25 percent of the country's 5.5 million adults have been infected by HIV, AIDS is having a devastating impact on the country's children. As mentioned earlier, as much as 1,000 people are dying each day from AIDS in the worst affected areas of the continent. A significant portion of these deaths occur among widowed mothers many of whom have been widowed by AIDS, leaving the children without any parents. Unfortunately, many governments in sub-Saharan Africa have not yet devised effective programs to deal with this burgeoning orphan population and the problems (e.g., child abuse, prostitution) that are likely to arise. Recent data on AIDS-related orphans paint a dismal picture for most countries in the southern region of the continent. In Zimbabwe in 1999, for example, there were as many as 900,000 AIDS-related orphans. Ethiopia had 1,200,000; Nigeria, 1,400,000; Tanzania, 1,100,000; and Uganda, 1,700,000 (World Bank, 2002b, p. 315). Since these data were released, conditions have not improved and the number of AIDS orphans in these countries has continued to grow (UNAIDS, 2006, p. 509).

AIDS is killing a significant portion of Africa's trained and skilled human resources. Business managers, university professors, accountants, lawyers, physicians, dentists, carpenters, nurses, and other professionals, have all succumbed to the disease. Skilled labor resources that took many years and enormous amounts of scarce resources to train and educate are being decimated by AIDS. The forgone output, although it has not yet been determined, is enormous. In addition, many business enterprises are finding it very difficult to stay operational because of the relatively large increases in health insurance premiums. In fact, health care costs have become a significant part of the overall operating costs of many firms. In Botswana, it is estimated that within the next few years, AIDS-related costs will rise from less than 1 percent of the wage bill to more than 5 percent as a result of rapid increases in infection rates (WHO, 1998, p. 9).

For all of Africa, AIDS represents one of the most important development problems of the new millennium. Presently, there is no cure for AIDS. Thus, Africans are left with only one option—prevention. Effective prevention calls for grassroots programs designed and executed by the African people themselves. It is incumbent upon the leadership of each African country to engage the people in a national discourse on HIV/AIDS and design appropriate policies to deal with it. If, however, the continent's leaders allow foreign actors to continue to lead the fight against AIDS in Africa, there is not likely to be significant reductions in infection rates. Africans themselves must spearhead the fight against AIDS in order for policy to have any positive impact. Generic programs developed abroad without the full and effective participation of relevant stakeholders in the continent and imposed on the people will most likely not work. Africans should learn from the dismal performance of the structural adjustment programs, which were imposed on them by the IMF and the World Bank. While several reasons have been advanced to explain the failure of SAPs (see, e.g., Ihonvbere, 1994), the most important of them is the fact that relevant stakeholder groups in Africa were not allowed to participate fully and effectively in their design and execution. Instead, the programs were designed abroad and imposed on various African societies, with little attention paid to such specificities as culture, geography, collective historical experience, language, level of economic development, and popular modes of communication.

Conceivably, one can look at an HIV/AIDS education program as consisting of four important components: (1) research and collection of time and place data/information; (2) design of the actual program; (3) implementation; and (4) post-implementation review. How well these processes are handled will determine the program's success or failure. If, as it has been the case with many post-independence development policies in Africa, the program described above is controlled and dominated by external actors (that is, non-stakeholders), the result will be failure to meet the objectives of reducing HIV infection rates.

Consider the following issue: How can abstinence (from sexual relations) be promoted and sustained among school-age children? Allowing citizens at the village level to design and execute programs to educate their children and where necessary, provide them with the facilities to do so, would be more effective than imposing on them programs designed by elites at the center or their foreign benefactors (notably the IMF and the World Bank). As argued by the World Bank (1998c, p. 38), in dealing with the developing countries, "care must be taken not to undermine useful traditional knowledge" whose development was informed and constrained by local realities and often can be more important in solving local problems than imported knowledge. For example, in efforts to treat diarrhea in several developing countries, Western experts vigorously and aggressively promoted a subsidized, ready-made industrial oral re-hydration solution, effectively undercutting the use of well-known and proven traditional remedies. After the subsidies were ended, usage of the foreign-made solutions declined significantly. Unfortunately by this time most households had forgotten how to prepare and apply local remedies and infection rates increased significantly. Thus, it is essential that prevention programs, and indeed, all development programs, involve as much as possible the relevant stakeholder groups in each African country.

During most of the post-independence period in Africa, public policy has been top-down, elite-driven, and non-participatory, with most of the people excluded from participating. The hope is that as more countries adopt democratic systems of governance, citizens will be afforded more opportunities to participate in public policies, especially in those directly affecting their lives.

Education and Capital Formation

Human capital is one of the most important determinants of wealth creation and economic growth. Skills can be developed through formal education and on-the-job training.

According to the World Bank (1998a, 1998b, 2005), Africa lags behind most other regions of the world in enrollment in education and human capital formation. Africa's continued inability to provide its various economies with highly skilled and well-trained labor resources has resulted in (1) poor and highly inefficient utilization of emerging technologies; (2) failure to generate new knowledge domestically and to import only those technologies that complement local ones; and (3) continued dependence on the industrial West for knowledge to be used in economic growth and development.

In Tanzania during the 1994–1997 period, for example, only 5.0 percent of children of secondary school age were attending school, and only 1.0 percent of those of college and university age enrolled in some kind of higher education. Although sub-Saharan Africa performed slightly better than Tanzania (World Bank, 2002a, pp. 323-329), the region continues to lag behind other areas of the world. In fact, in 1998 only 4.0 percent of sub-Saharan Africans of university age were enrolled in higher education compared to 14 percent for the world (World Bank, 2002a). Also detrimental to the capital formation effort is the fact that throughout the region, the few educational facilities that the governments provide are usually located in the urban areas and as a consequence, most of the people who reside in the rural areas do not have effective access to opportunities for capital formation.

Except in rare cases, most African universities are located in the urban areas and as a consequence, most citizens who reside in the rural areas do not have effective access to these important centers for human capital formation (see, e.g., Commonwealth, 1999; Europa, 1998). In addition, instruction in the majority of Africa's universities is undertaken primarily in some European language (e.g., English, French). As a result, most of the people who live in the rural areas, virtually all of whom are fluent only in their own ethnic languages, are effectively denied opportunities for human capital formation.

Since the arrival of the new communication technologies to the continent (notably the Internet), greater emphasis has been placed on distance education in an effort to enhance the ability of many rural inhabitants to have access to opportunities for training and capital formation. In fact, in 1995, the African Virtual University was launched in Nairobi followed by efforts to identify and train staff in the use of electronic teaching media. The Internet is expected to help these virtual institutions of higher learning deliver more services to hitherto underserved regions and communities. Unfortunately, most rural areas in Africa do not now have access to electricity and telephones and hence, cannot avail themselves of the Internet and its services. In addition, these virtual universities, like traditional educational institutions in the continent, deliver their lectures in European languages, a process that limits significantly the number of people who can benefit from these services (World Bank, 1998c, p. 55).

Although enrollment in university education has improved in several countries during the last decade, deteriorating political and economic conditions have forced many of the graduates to migrate to more stable economies (mostly in the industrial West—Western Europe, North America, Japan, Australia and New Zealand) in search of opportunities for self-actualization.

The failure of African countries to invest in human capital development has resulted in a severe shortage of the skilled workers that these economies need for wealth creation and economic growth. In fact, very high rates of illiteracy, especially among women and girls, and those who reside in rural areas characterize the majority of countries in the continent. According to World Bank (1998b, 2005) data, illiteracy rates in the African countries are among the highest of any country in the world. Today, most governments in Africa are still unable to adequately and effectively provide the educational facilities that their economies need to maintain a well-trained and skilled labor force. As a result, the region continues to suffer from poor economic performance and subsequently extremely high rates of poverty and deprivation. Such poverty has contributed significantly to Africa's continued marginalization in international trade and global affairs.

Associated with capital formation is the issue of knowledge creation and its effects on economic growth and development. Exactly what does knowledge do? How does it affect development? According to the World Bank (1998c, p. 1), "[k]nowledge also illuminates every economic transaction, revealing preferences, giving clarity to exchanges, informing markets." Knowledge is essential for the effective functioning of markets. Unfortunately creating and disseminating knowledge is very costly and today most of it is created by the rich and industrial countries of the West. Poor countries, however, can acquire knowledge from the industrialized countries, as well as create certain kinds of it. To create knowledge, it is necessary that the appropriate political, social, and economic environment is provided.

Knowledge is very important for wealth creation and economic growth. For example, information about prenatal care can result in healthier babies, even for families with relatively low incomes. In fact, in Africa today, an important strategy to fight HIV/AIDS and prevent the pre-mature deaths of millions of people is to provide at-risk groups with accurate and relevant information about the ways in which the disease is transmitted. It has been suggested that Africans should not reinvent the wheel but should simply acquire the knowledge that they need from the industrialized countries. It is important to caution, however, that care must be taken in order not to displace local technologies that may actually be more effective than the imported ones. Making policy on the importation of knowledge, like other public policies, should be an inclusive and participatory process. World Bank (1998c, p. 5) experience in developing countries has determined that when consultants work closely with the local people, instead of just providing them with information, the technology transferred is more appropriate and relevant to solving the problem in question. The two-way communication significantly improves information dissemination and enhances the adoption by local users, of knowledge that complements local technologies.

Unfortunately the suggestions being made today to help African countries close the knowledge gap between themselves and the rest of the world and within each country (between relatively educated urbanites and the poorly educated or mostly illiterate rural inhabitants) are most likely to place the African countries at the mercy of international institutions. Multilateral agencies such as the IMF and the World Bank, as well as multinational companies, have been mentioned as important conduits through which African countries can avail themselves of information created in the developed countries (see, e.g., World Bank, 1998c, pp. 1–56). If the structural adjustment programs imposed on the African countries by the Bretton Woods institutions are any indication, it is not likely that these multilateral agencies would be able to successfully help Africans acquire and utilize knowledge effectively. In fact, the wide gap that currently exists between HIV/AIDS care in the industrialized countries and Africa is a clear indication that Africans cannot rely on the generosity or magnanimity of international organizations and the industrialized West for a solution to their development issues. African countries must therefore develop their own policies for creating, acquiring, and disseminating knowledge instead of waiting for the international organizations to take the initiative.

Where illiteracy rates are high, creation of knowledge is quite difficult and its dissemination is even more problematic. Low rates of literacy can also make it very difficult for a country to make effective and fuller uses of the global stock of knowledge. Hence, universal basic education must be the starting point for any public policy to secure viable and sustainable solutions to the problem of information generation and dissemination in Africa (World Bank, 1998c, pp. 1–14).

In addition to the fact that they suffer from a severe shortage of human capital, the African countries also lack well-developed physical infrastructures such as railroads, airports, sewage disposal systems, highways, communication structures, and other facilities that are critical for maintaining a productive and viable economic system. In many countries in the continent, these structures either do not exist or if they do, function extremely inefficiently and services are allocated capriciously (see, e.g., Ostrom, Schroeder and Wynne, 1993). Throughout the continent, most countries must depend on road (land) transportation since effective regional and air transport networks, which can exploit technological economies of scale, have not yet been developed.

Most Africans are employed in the rural agricultural sectors (see, e.g., World Bank, 1998a, p. 286; ADB, 1997, p. 210) and produce foodstuffs that are sold in the urban sectors. As a consequence, farm-to-market roads are very important determinants of economic performance in most of Africa. These roads provide farmers with effective access to urban markets, allowing these farmers to efficiently transport their products to where they can be sold. In addition, farm-to-market roads allow for the transportation of cash crops (e.g., cocoa, coffee, bananas, and palm kernel) from the rural areas to the national export zones, and for the transfer of essential farm inputs (e.g., fertilizers and insecticides) from the urban industrial centers to the farms. Unfortunately, since independence, public policy in many of these countries has not emphasized the construction and maintenance of these important wealth-creating structures. Instead, public policy has favored the provision of roads and other transportation systems in politically sensitive areas such as urban centers and politically dominant communities. As with health and education systems, most spending on roads and other forms of communication infrastructures favors urban areas with a total neglect of the economically important rural agricultural sectors. The result has been the continued deterioration in agricultural performance and the inability of many of these countries to achieve self-sufficiency in foodstuff production.

Other critical infrastructures for development include dams, bridges, irrigation systems for farming, rural dispensaries, clinics, and hospitals for primary health care (including preventive care), postal and mail delivery systems, financial institutions, and adult education centers. Although African countries continue to suffer from a shortage of physical infrastructure, many researchers believe that inefficient and inadequate maintenance of existing structures is a much more serious problem (see, e.g., Ostrom, Schroeder and Wynne, 1993). In many African countries, postal and telephone systems owned and operated by the government are so inefficient that many multinational companies have opted to operate their own systems. Many public utilities are in a state of serious disrepair and lack the spare parts to function effectively. In some countries, corruption has exacerbated the problem of inefficient and capricious delivery of infrastructural services. Unreliability and unpredictability in the allocation of public goods and services continue to negatively impact wealth creation and economic growth in Africa (Stepanek, 1999, pp. 41–60). During a recent research trip to various urban centers in Nigeria, I discovered that many small business owners have resorted to owning gasoline-powered portable electric generators as insurance against frequent power outages. Unfortunately, I could not secure any data on the number of such generators, nor was I able to get any information on the environmental consequences of these alternative energy sources.

In order to improve their ability to use their resources effectively and efficiently to create the wealth that they need, Africans must provide themselves with adequate, viable, and sustainable economic infrastructures.

Excessive External Debt

Another important characteristic of African economies is that most countries have extremely high levels of external debt. In 1980, total external debt of the African countries was U.S. $111,893 million. By 2000, the continent's total external debt had risen to $298,386 million (World Bank, 2002b, p. 174). The 2000 figure was a decline from a high of $335,046 million in 1995; however, the decrease was not significant. Since the nominal GDP for the continent in 2000 was $553,159 million (World Bank, 2002b, p. 19), Africa's foreign debt was over 50 percent of its current output.

External debt for sub-Saharan Africa grew faster than that for the continent as a whole during the period 1980 to 2000, reaching a high of $229,983 million in 1999 and falling to $213,914 million in 2000. Thus, in 2000, sub-Saharan Africa's total external debt was 3.5 times higher than it was in 1980. Examining the growth of debt in individual African countries may be more instructive. For example, in Lesotho, external debt grew from $72 million in 1980 to $721 million in 2000 or a little over ten times as much as it was in 1980. Growth in external debt in Mozambique was equally phenomenal, rising from $49 million in 1980 to $6,185 million in 2000 or 126 times (World Bank, 2002b, p. 174). Except for a few countries, rapid growth in external debt in Africa appears to have been universal. In real terms, the growth in the continent's external debt was just as phenomenal. For example, in 1980, total external debt in Africa was $104,087 million (1995 U.S. dollars), but by 2000, it had risen to $317,433 million. In 2000, the continent's real GDP (1995 U.S. dollars) was $588,385 million, and as a consequence, its external debt was 53.9 percent of the real GDP, an increase from 28.89 percent in 1980 (World Bank, 2002b, pp. 15, 43, 174).

The latest data on external debt in Africa (World Bank, 2005, p. 172) show that the debt situation in the continent has not improved despite the efforts of many external actors such as the IMF, the World Bank, and the G8 countries to supposedly help the highly indebted African countries deal more effectively with their debt.

Economists use several measures to determine the debt burden on national economies. These include total long-term debt, debt service, and debt service as a percentage of the export of goods and services. Of all these measures, the latter is considered a more effective indicator of the debt burden because it represents actual resources that are remitted to foreign creditors by the domestic economy. In Africa, the resources used to service the debt are usually hard currency derived from the export of goods and services. These are scarce resources that could be used to import essential inputs for domestic industries and to increase spending on welfare enhancing areas such as education, sanitation and health care, HIV/AIDS prevention education, nutrition (especially for the young), prenatal care, and job training for urban youth. Unfortunately, these resources must be remitted abroad to meet debt service obligations. Debt service ratios (ex post, depicting the amount actually paid after debt relief and/or arrears, see World Bank, 1998a, pp. 184–185; World Bank, 2002b, pp. 178–179) for the African economies in 1999 ranged from a low of zero percent for Togo and Botswana to a high of 89 percent for Burundi. The average for sub-Saharan Africa was 19 percent. Africans must devote as much as 15 percent or more of their export earnings to debt service (World Bank, 2002b, pp. 178–179; World Bank, 2005, pp. 176-177). The transfer of such significant amounts

Table 4.1: Gross National Income Per Capita (GNI) and Growth Rates for Low-income African Countries

Country	*Real GNI per capita, 2000 (U.S. $)*	*Average annual growth rate (%), 1988–2000*
Ethiopia	100	1.4
Burundi	110	-4.1
Sierra Leone	130	-6.1
Guinea-Bissau	180	-1.3
Niger	180	-1.5
Mozambique	210	3.4
Burkina Faso	230	2.0
Rwanda	230	-3.0
Mali	240	0.9
Angola	240	-8.7
Nigeria	260	0.6
Madagascar	260	-0.7
Tanzania	280	0.5
São Tomé & Principe	290	-0.8
Central African Rep.	290	-0.7
Togo	300	-1.2
Zambia	300	-2.2
Uganda	310	3.7
Sudan	320	0.0
Ghana	350	1.6
Kenya	360	0.0
Mauritania	370	1.2
Benin	380	1.5
Comoros	380	-2.8
Guinea	450	1.8
Zimbabwe	480	-0.4
Senegal	500	0.6
Lesotho	540	-0.4
Cameroon	570	-2.5
Congo-Brazzaville	630	-5.5
Côte d'Ivoire	660	0.1

Source: World Bank, *African Development Indicators, 2002*, (World Bank: Washington, D.C., 2002b), p. 5.

of resources abroad in the form of debt service significantly constrains the ability of the state to devote enough resources to those areas that are critical for wealth creation and economic growth (see, e.g., UNDP, 1990). In fact, throughout the continent, it is becoming apparent that many countries cannot continue to remit scarce foreign exchange abroad to service the debt while millions of local people die from AIDS. Citizens of several African countries have suggested that spending on education to prevent HIV infection be given top priority over remittances for debt service.

POOR ECONOMIC PERFORMANCE

During most of the post-independence period, most economies in Africa, especially those in sub-Saharan Africa, have encountered primarily poor economic performance. According to the World Bank (2002b; also see Tables 4.1 and 4.2), only a small number of African countries experienced reasonable rates of economic growth during the period 1988–2000. Angola registered the worst performance of all the countries in Africa during this period, achieving a growth rate in gross national income (GNI) per capita of –8.7 percent. The majority of the low-income countries either regressed significantly during this period or registered only modest rates of growth (see Table 4.2).

In 2000, Ethiopia, with a GNI per capita of only U.S. $100, was the poorest country in Africa. By 2002 (World Bank, 2003, pp. 253–255), Ethiopia had been joined by other African countries, including Burundi ($100), and Democratic Republic of Congo ($90). Of the world's poorest countries, a large number of them can be found in Africa (see, e.g., UNDP, 2003, 2005). Today in Africa, only South Africa and Algeria, and to a certain extent, Mauritius, have viable manufacturing sectors that can compete (in both price and quality of output) with those of the newly industrializing countries such as Brazil, Mexico, Malaysia, and Thailand. Although

Libya and Gabon have relatively high per capita incomes, most of their wealth is derived primarily from the exploitation of raw materials, notably petroleum. These countries still have not yet developed well-integrated manufacturing and industrial sectors. Countries such as Cameroon and Nigeria have the potential to develop globally competitive manufacturing sectors. However, corruption and non-democratic institutional environments continue to constrain the development and sustaining of strong and competitive industrial sectors (see World Bank, 2005).

Table 4.2: Gross National Income (GNI) Per Capita and Growth Rates for Middle-income African Countries

Country	*Real GNI per capita, 2000 (U.S. $)*	*Average annual growth rate (%), 1988–2000*
Morocco	1,180	0.7
Swaziland	1,290	0.7
Cape Verde	1,330	2.6
Egypt	1,490	2.6
Algeria	1,590	-0.6
Namibia	2,050	2.2
Tunisia	2,090	3.0
South Africa	3,020	-0.3
Gabon	3,180	0.0
Botswana	3,300	2.2
Mauritius	3,800	4.2
Seychelles	7,310	1.9

Source: World Bank, *African Development Indicators, 2002*, (World Bank: Washington, D.C., 2002b), p. 5.

One must note that data on South Africa should be interpreted with caution. While the country is considered middle-income, it must be understood that apartheid development policies (1948–1994) significantly skewed the distribution of income and wealth (i.e., the overall allocation of resources) in favor of the white minority and forced the country's black population to live in poverty and deprivation. Apartheid was abolished in 1994 and a new non-racial democratic dispensation established. However, it will take some time before resource allocation is made equitable and socially optimal.

South Africa's post-apartheid government is making concerted efforts to enhance entrepreneurship among the country's various historically marginalized and deprived groups, increase employment opportunities for all its citizens, improve wealth creation and economic growth, and significantly reduce historical inequities. Unfortunately, the gap in living standards between the historically privileged white minority and the rest of the country's citizens created by many years of apartheid (mis)rule is so large that many people doubt that current public policies are aggressive enough to eliminate them in the next fifty years.

Table 4.3: Gross National Income (GNI) Per Capita and Gross Domestic Product (GDP) Per Capita Growth Rates for Selected Regions of the World

Region	*Real GNI per capita (U.S. $, weighted average)*		*Average annual growth rate of GDP per capita (%)*	
	2000	2002	1999–2000	2001–2002
Sub-Saharan Africa	480	450	0.5	0.9
East Asia and Pacific	1,060	950	6.5	5.8
South Asia	460	460	3.8	2.6
Europe and Central Asia	2,010	2,160	6.3	4.6
Middle East and North Africa	2,040	2,230	..	..
Latin America and Caribbean	3,680	3,280	2.3	-1.9
Low and Middle income countries	1,230	1,170	4.2	2.0

Sources: World Bank, *World Development Report, 2002*, (Oxford University Press: New York, 2002c), pp. 232–233; World Bank, *World Development Report, 2003*, (Oxford University Press: New York, 2003), p. 253.

Table 4.3 provides data on economic performance in selected regions of the world. During the period 1999–2000, sub-Saharan Africa registered a growth rate in per capita GNI of 0.5 percent. On the other hand, East Asia and the Pacific performed impressively, registering a growth rate for the period of 6.5 percent. South Asia, a region that is comparable to sub-Saharan Africa because of its high population growth rates and relatively high poverty levels, encountered reasonably healthy growth in per capita income during the period 1999–2000. In fact, despite recent financial problems in East Asia and the Pacific, the region has had relatively healthy economic performance during the last several decades. For example, it registered growth rates in per capita income of 7.2 percent, 7.4 percent, and 5.6 percent during the periods, 1985–1995, 1995–1996, and 1996–1997 respectively. On the other hand, sub-Saharan Africa regressed economically during the period, 1985–1995 (-1.1 percent), and grew modestly (1.9 percent; 1.2 percent) during the periods 1995–1996 and 1996–1997 respectively (World Bank, 1997, 1998b).

In 2000, the weighted average per capita income for sub-Saharan Africa was only $480 or 13 percent of that of Latin America and Caribbean and 45 percent that of East Asia and the Pacific (Table 4.4). Since then, there has been deterioration resulting in a fall in per capita income for the region to $450 in 2002. Although other regions of the world have suffered similar declines, they are still generally better off than sub-Saharan Africa (see Table 4.3).

Africa, especially the sub-region called sub-Saharan Africa, is in crisis. During the last forty years, most policy makers in the region have either been unwilling or unable to devote the appropriate level of effort to economic, social, and political transformation of their societies. Instead, many state structures and human capital in the public sectors of the countries of this part of the world have been devoted to crisis management in order to create an environment for (1) incumbent leaders to continue to monopolize political power and the allocation of resources; (2) the effective plundering of the national economy to generate benefits for the ruling elites and their domestic and foreign benefactors; and (3) generally maintaining a semblance of peaceful coexistence of population groups in order to attract foreign resources. Preoccupation with crisis management and political survival at all cost has made it very difficult for many post-independence governments in Africa to place appropriate emphasis on wealth creation and the effective alleviation of poverty and the general improvement of the quality of life for historically marginalized groups and communities, especially women and children, as well as rural peasants.

It has been argued that many countries in Africa, which today are among the poorest in the world, had per capita incomes that were either higher than or at least equal to those in many countries in East Asia and the Pacific in the late 1950s and early 1960s. Given the fact that the African countries also had significant endowments of natural resources, they were expected to outperform their less endowed Asian counterparts and achieve rapid economic development in the post-independence period. For example, in 1967, Ghana's per capita income of $240 was higher than that in South Korea ($140), Papua New Guinea ($190), Indonesia ($50), and Thailand ($170) (World Bank, 1991, pp. 14–15). In less than thirty years, the Asian countries, as a result of higher levels of economic freedom (e.g., bureaucracies that have been quite friendly to entrepreneurship and wealth creation) and significant emphasis on investments in basic education and human capital formation (see, e.g., Stapanek, 1999, pp. 37–61), have outperformed Ghana and other African economies. Today, several of these Asian countries are considered newly industrialized, while Ghana and its neighbors continue to suffer from high rates of poverty and deprivation. In 1997, per capita income in Ghana was $370 and that in South Korea was $10,550. Thus, South Korea, whose per capita income in 1967 was lower than that in Ghana, had per capita income in 1997 that was 28.5 times as much as that in Ghana. In terms of purchasing power parity estimates of GNP per capita for 1997, the figures for Ghana and South Korea were $1,790 and $23,500 respectively (World Bank, 1998b, p. 190). Like Ghana, African countries (except for a few like Botswana and Mauritius) have failed to achieve the type of economic performance that was expected of them at independence.

It is important to note that the politics of the Cold War significantly impacted the success of the East Asian countries. U.S. military aid, preferential trade arrangements with the United States, geo-strategic positioning (especially of Taiwan, South Korea, and Thailand), all had significant impact on economic performance in the region. It has been argued that economic take-off in this region was a function of a partnership between state bureaucrats and non-competitive conglomerates in generating industrial policy. Some scholars have even argued that strategic state intervention in the private sector, which in many ways limited economic freedom (e.g., land reform, massive tax-fueled public investments in education, and severe labor repression) was important in these East Asian economic growth models (e.g., Johnson, 1982; Deyo, 1981, 1989). However, based on research conducted by Gwartney and Lawson (2000, pp. 11–14) on economic freedom, entrepreneurs in the East Asian countries (from 1970–1997) were still more likely to have greater levels of economic freedom than those in the African economies (see Table 4.4).

As argued by Stepanek (1999, p. 52), many "Asian countries maintained strong markets and trade regimes throughout the era of public planning." Thus, while African governments were stunting entrepreneurship and consequently, wealth creation, with excessive planning and capricious regulation,

Table 4.4: Economic Freedom Ratings for Several African and Asian Countries

	Economic freedom rating						
Country	1970	1975	1980	1985	1990	1995	1997
Algeria	..	..	..	..	2.9	5.0	4.3
Benin	..	5.1	4.9	4.8	5.7	4.7	4.9
Botswana	..	3.9	4.7	5.6	6.0	6.8	6.6
Burundi	..	3.2	3.2	4.1	3.9	3.5	4.2
Cameroon	..	..	5.1	5.2	5.5	5.2	5.1
CAR	..	..	5.2	4.6	4.4	4.4	4.3
Chad	..	..	..	5.2	5.2	5.1	4.5
Congo, DR	4.6	3.2	2.7	3.7	3.2	3.2	3.1
Congo, R.1	..	..	5.1	4.4	4.4	4.8	4.2
Côte d'Ivoire	..	..	4.9	5.4	4.9	5.2	5.7
Egypt	..	4.2	4.1	4.6	4.3	6.0	6.6
Gabon	..	..	3.8	5.2	5.2	5.7	5.1
Ghana	3.3	2.5	2.1	2.6	4.8	6.1	6.4
Guinea-Bissau	..	..	..	..	3.8	4.1	4.0
Hong Kong*	9.4	9.3	9.6	9.3	9.3	9.8	9.4
Indonesia*	4.8	5.0	5.2	5.9	6.8	7.3	7.2
Kenya	5.0	4.8	4.8	5.1	5.1	6.2	6.8
Madagascar	5.6	4.1	4.1	4.4	3.8	3.9	3.9
Malawi	..	5.0	3.9	4.4	4.7	4.1	4.6
Malaysia*	6.5	6.4	7.1	7.3	7.7	7.6	7.5
Mali	..	4.8	5.3	5.3	5.0	5.1	4.7
Mauritius	..	4.6	4.7	6.4	6.0	7.9	7.6
Morocco	5.5	4.9	4.0	4.8	4.6	5.6	6.0
Namibia	..	..	..	..	5.2	5.3	6.4
Niger	..	5.5	5.1	5.0	4.4	4.6	4.8
Nigeria	4.0	3.8	3.1	3.6	3.6	3.4	4.7
Rwanda	..	2.1	3.7	..	3.9	3.9	3.7
Senegal	..	..	5.0	4.9	5.0	4.2	4.7
Sierra Leone	..	3.9	4.1	3.0	2.9	3.7	3.2
Singapore*	7.7	7.6	8.0	8.4	9.1	9.4	9.4
Somalia	..	..	..	..	3.3	..	..
South Africa	7.6	6.2	6.0	5.6	5.9	6.6	7.3
South Korea*	6.3	5.6	5.7	6.0	6.6	7.7	7.3
Taiwan*	6.6	6.1	6.8	7.1	7.6	7.8	7.1
Tanzania	4.3	3.2	4.1	3.0	3.5	5.0	5.6
Thailand*	6.4	5.6	5.8	6.1	6.8	7.6	8.2
Togo	..	..	4.4	5.9	4.9	4.7	4.6
Tunisia	4.3	4.5	4.4	4.1	5.0	6.1	6.3
Uganda	..	..	2.8	2.7	2.7	4.6	6.1
Zambia	..	4.3	4.7	3.1	2.5	4.5	5.5
Zimbabwe	..	..	4.1	4.0	4.5	5.4	5.0

Note: The ratings range from zero to 10. Higher ratings indicate the existence of institutions and policies more consistent with economic freedom. Asterisk indicates an Asian country. The data on South Africa must be interpreted with caution. Although the country has enjoyed significant levels of economic freedom, especially when compared with other African countries, such freedom was only guaranteed the country's white population. The ability of the majority black population (Africans, Indians, and coloreds) to freely engage in trade was strictly regulated by the apartheid system implemented in the country in 1948. Apartheid was abolished in 1994 following the coming to power of Nelson Mandela and the African National Congress.

Source: J. D. Gwartney and R. Lawson, *Economic Freedom of the World: 2000 Annual Report*, The Fraser Institute: (Vancouver, BC, 2000). Also J. D. Gwartney and R. Lawson, *Economic Freedom of the World: 2002 Annual Report*, (The Fraser Institute: Vancouver, BC, 2002) for an update of the ratings.

the East Asian governments were enhancing the ability of domestic markets to operate effectively, resulting in more improved economic performance. Stepanek (1999, p. 52) cautions, however, that 'there was close cooperation between government and industry. . . . Large firms and selected industries did not act alone but were part of a purposeful and less-than-transparent public structure.'

It was also determined that the Asian countries emphasized education during their take-off stage. According to Stepanek (1999, p. 53), primary education in Asian countries "had been a priority as long as the 1950s. General education created a skilled labor force. The pattern of income and asset distribution was more egalitarian than in other countries at a similar level of development, which probably contributed to greater domestic savings and investment." As economist Dani Rodrik (1994, p. 9) has noted, "[h]uman capital makes investment more productive, facilitates the transfer and adoption of advanced technology from abroad, and enables the establishment of meritocractic, efficient, and capable administration."

Training and education provided by several universities and colleges in the United States helped South Korea, Taiwan, and several other Asian countries build and sustain critical institutions for wealth creation and economic growth. One of the most important development lessons that Africa can learn from the East Asian countries is to place emphasis on education and human capital formation, and provide domestic economies with institutional arrangements that guarantee economic freedom.

During the last five decades, as a result of rapid economic growth, many regions of the world have significantly improved the quality of life of their citizens. Unfortunately, the kind of economic growth that has enhanced the ability of many of these countries to achieve food security and significantly raise domestic standards of living has not been universal. Although Africa has seen a few successes, the last fifty years has been characterized primarily by extremely poor economic performance. In addition to the fact that few countries in the continent have achieved food security, most Africans are severely impoverished and suffer from high levels of poverty and material deprivation. Based on various measures of development, including the United Nations Development Program's human development index (HDI), of the thirty poorest countries in the world in 2003, most of them were in Africa. In addition, Africa is not only the poorest region of the world, but it is the only one with relatively bleak prospects for the new millennium. Unless each African country provides itself with institutional arrangements that can enhance indigenous entrepreneurship and maximize the creation of wealth, while at the same time adequately constraining state custodians (i.e., civil servants and politicians) and preventing them from plundering their economies, the continent will continue to suffer from high rates of poverty, as well as remain indefinitely on the periphery of global affairs. Perhaps more important is the fact that most of the countries in the continent will continue to depend on the industrialized countries of the West for budget subventions (UNDP, 2003, 2005). Hence, without the introduction of political dispensations that promote indigenous entrepreneurship, guarantee economic freedom, and enhance the peaceful coexistence of each country's various population groups, economic growth and development will remain elusive.

In the above section, we have presented a relatively bleak and depressing picture of both policy failure and a widening gap between previously poor and deprived developing societies (e.g., several countries in Asia) that have managed, through rapid economic growth, to pull themselves out of economic decay, and poorly managed African economies, which remain essentially in a state of continuing deterioration. Poverty in Africa is a very complex problem. Dealing effectively with it requires significant transformations in the critical domains to make them more supportive of entrepreneurship and wealth creation (especially among indigenous peoples). It also requires public policies that enhance the ability of all relevant stakeholders to devise and implement their own programs to deal with poverty and other social issues unique to their localities (Stepanek, 1999, pp. 37–61). Imposing solutions or priorities determined by center elites and their international (i.e., foreign) benefactors (e.g., IMF and World Bank) is not likely to have much positive effect on poverty alleviation in the continent.

Population

During the last few decades, population-related crises in Ethiopia, the Sudan, Somalia, Chad, Rwanda, and the Great Lakes region have reminded the world of the effects of excessive population growth on Africa and its relatively fragile ecosystem. Newspapers, television, and other media in the West have publicized population problems (especially famine and malnutrition) in Somalia, Ethiopia, the Sudan, and other parts of the Sahel. Unfortunately, these are not the only African countries that have suffered or continue to suffer from population-related problems such as food insecurity, malnutrition, overburdened health care systems, and ecosystem degradation. The failure or inability to achieve food security is a problem that is pervasive throughout most of the continent. Rapid population growth intensifies the competition for scarce resources and puts pressure on an already fragile ecological system. As argued by several researchers (e.g., Schnitzer, 1994, p. 328), the number of poorly fed and malnourished Africans has risen in recent years to about 20 percent of the continent's population. Perhaps more important is the fact that prospects for the future look relatively bleak—many countries in the continent continue to register very healthy growth rates in their populations but their economies are not performing well enough to fully and effectively meet the needs of the ever-expanding population.

Starvation has already taken the lives of many Africans, most of them young people in their most productive years. In addition, many of the people who have survived have been permanently damaged and are not likely to recover well enough to become fully productive and function at their full capacity. Many people whose growth has been severely stunted by poor nutrition and malnourishment are likely to remain wards of their societies for the rest of their lives. Hence, in addition to lost production, society must feed, clothe and care for these people for many years to come. Many of Africa's malnourished people are also the most susceptible to infections and are likely to get sick and increase the demand for health care services, further putting a lot of stress on already over-burden health care systems.

One, however, must recognize the horrible impact of AIDS on Africa's population. International organizations and other agencies fighting HIV/AIDS in the continent, state that unless African countries develop and implement more effective prevention programs (or a cure is found for the disease), the pandemic is likely to decimate as much as 20 percent of Africa's productive population. Unfortunately, HIV/AIDS cannot be considered an effective, sustainable, or morally acceptable way to deal with excessive population growth.

Urbanization has emerged as another population-related problem for most of Africa. Since the mid-1950s, many African countries have been abandoning the rural agricultural sectors in favor of urban centers. Although many reasons have been advanced to explain this explosion in rural-to-urban migration, the most important of them is decreasing returns to agriculture (due primarily to poor farming techniques, lack of appropriate technology, and excessive taxation of agriculture by the state to generate benefits for the urban sectors) and the absence of opportunities for social and economic advancement. In some regions of Africa, migration has been due to excessive population growth and overcrowding on the farms. Increases in the rural population, coupled with inefficient and antiquated farming practices, have significantly reduced the amount of land available for agriculture, the occupation of the majority of the people who reside in the rural areas. As a consequence, many displaced farmers have been forced to exit the rural sector in search of more favorable opportunities for advancement—usually in the urban industrial centers.

Today in Africa, most urban centers are severely overcrowded. Many cities are not able to properly house their inhabitants, existing health care systems cannot keep up with the demand for services, sewage disposal systems cannot handle all the waste generated by citizens, and shortages of essential services have become endemic. During the first decade of the new century, several African cities are expected to have populations of more than a million people, and unless the productive capacities of these urban centers are increased significantly, living standards of these Africans will continue to deteriorate. Dealing with the problem of excessive population growth should be part of a comprehensive reform process that allows Africans to reconstruct and reconstitute the postcolonial state and compact, for themselves, institutional arrangements that effectively constrain state custodians, enhance wealth creation, and significantly improve the peaceful coexistence of each country's diverse population groups. These institutional arrangements should eliminate (or at the least, minimize) the types of perverse economic policies that have contributed significantly to rural poverty and marginalization, and subsequently to rural-to-urban migration.

Economic Dependence

The European countries that colonized Africa structured the colonial economies to serve as suppliers of raw materials to the metropolitan economies and markets for the sale of excess output from Europe's industries. Each European colonial power made an effort to "integrate" the economies of its African colonies into the metropolitan economy and in the process, created a one-sided dependency that has lasted to this day (see, e.g., Stepanek, 1999, pp. 17–61). Today, many African countries are as dependent on the West European economies as they were during the colonial period. The African countries depend on their former colonizers for trade, development and military assistance, food aid, foreign direct investment, just to name a few. The francophone African countries, whose economies are further "integrated" into the French economy through the currency union called the CFA Franc Zone, exhibit an even greater level of dependence on their former colonizer. Unfortunately, as has been demonstrated by other researchers (e.g., Davenport, 1992), this is a one-sided dependency that produces net benefits primarily for France and marginalizes the African countries.

Africa's most important trade partner since the 1960s is the European Economic Community (now the European Union). Over the decades, while other developing regions of the world have been able to lessen their trade dependency on the EU, African countries have actually become more dependent on their former colonizers for trade (see, e.g., IMF, 2003; Davenport, 1992). Although the EU is an important market for African economies, the latter have been losing their strategic significance to the Europeans. Continued European integration, with the formation of the EU, is expected to further marginalize the African economies and push them to the periphery of the global system.

In the 1950s, as African colonies prepared for independence, it was suggested that foreign financial flows, especially official development assistance (ODA), could be used to augment domestic savings and significantly raise the level of capital formation in the new countries (Millikan and Rostow,

1957). Many development economists of the time believed that each African country would eventually be able to undertake its own capital formation programs without further assistance from abroad. What was needed at the time of independence and shortly afterwards was "seed" money from former colonizers to get the process going. Since independence in the 1950s and 1960s, African countries have received a significant amount of development aid from the industrialized countries, especially those of the EU (World Bank, 1998b, 1998c, 2002a, 2002b). Despite the fact that Africa has done very well attracting development aid during the last fifty years, the region has remained very poor and deprived. Many reasons have been given to explain why this massive flow of aid has failed to improve wealth creation and economic growth on the continent. First, during the Cold War, Western aid donors favored African countries with relatively high military expenditures (see, e.g., UNDP, 1992, pp. 42–45).

Second, the African countries have usually allocated very little aid to areas such as basic education, primary health care, nutrition, safe drinking water, and family planning—social and economic sectors that are critical to economic growth and development. According to UNDP (1992, p. 45) data, less than 6.5 percent of bilateral ODA to poor countries, including those in Africa, is allocated to those important development areas.

Third, the granting of ODA greatly favors those countries whose leaders are friendly with the donor countries, and as a consequence, national leaders are forced to accept, for example, Western ideology (at least publicly) and approach to the allocation of resources in order for the country to retain its friendly relations with the West and continue to receive aid. Of course, during the Cold War, African countries that supported the Soviet Union at international forums (e.g., the United Nations) were favored with military and "development" aid from the Warsaw Pact countries and those that supported the United States and its allies were generously rewarded by the United States and other Western countries. At these international forums, African countries found it very difficult to pursue an independent or so-called "non-aligned" path for fear of losing critical food, military, and development aid. In addition, most development aid is conditional, usually requiring that the recipient country either agree to undertake certain domestic policy reforms or perform certain designated services for the donor. Lack of control over ODA may constrain the ability of African policy makers to use the resources effectively to enhance domestic wealth creation efforts.

Fourth, quite often, policy regarding aid in the developed countries is driven by the objectives of special interest groups instead of a genuine desire to improve the wealth-creating capacities of the poor countries. For example, private companies in the donor countries may see ODA as a vehicle for helping them get rid of excess or technologically obsolete output. Unfortunately, the technology transferred through this process is rarely appropriate for African economies and ends up being abandoned after arrival in the continent.

Fifth, in the case of food aid, the dumping of foreign goods in the African country may destroy the markets for domestic production, discourage investment in agriculture, and prevent the local economy from achieving self-sufficiency in foodstuff production.

Finally, the failure of African policy makers to utilize ODA effectively and efficiently is due primarily to a lack of appropriate incentive structures. Existing laws and institutions have allowed ruling elites to redistribute income and wealth, including foreign flows, in their favor and at the expense of the general population. The absence of accountable and transparent governance structures implies that aid resources can be distributed capriciously, usually favoring politically dominant groups in order to generate support for the regime and help it remain in power. Rarely are these resources used to enhance wealth creation and economic growth. In fact, many regimes continue to rely on foreign aid as a source of funds to be used to bribe competitive elites and purchase security for the government. Loss of 'development aid' is said to have contributed significantly to the collapse of many authoritarian regimes in Africa. For example, the loss of Soviet military and development aid played an important role in the demise of several Afro-Marxist governments in Africa, including those in Somalia and Ethiopia (Decalo, 1992; Stepanek, 1999).

In the 1960s, it was suggested that Western-based multinational companies could serve as a conduit to bring needed investment resources to the African countries to help the latter jump-start industrial development. This approach to development in Africa and other developing regions of the world was not without its critics. The involvement of multinational companies in developing countries, including those in Africa, is viewed from three main perspectives: deprivation, group mobilization, and the liberal perspective (Rothgeb, 1991).

According to the deprivation view, the penetration of African economies by foreign capital undermines the "legitimacy of the ruling elite and accentuate[s] class differences so that the masses become enraged and resort to violence" (Rothgeb, 1991, p. 11). Foreign capital flows are said to increase inequality in the distribution of income and wealth, resulting in the creation of a favored class. Rothgeb (1991, p. 12) argues that "[t]his happens because of the asymmetrical nature of the relationship between rich and poor actors, which favors wealthier actors to such an extent that they are able to dominate the poor partners." It is also argued that the presence of foreign capital in the poor country creates a domestic ruling elite that is dominated by foreign interests. As the argument goes, the domination of the national elites by the executives of multinational companies is due partly to the fact that manufacturing and mining investment, which the African ruling elites consider to be very critical to their development, places the owners of foreign capital in a position to have enormous control over public policy in the country in question (Mahler, 1981; Sunkel, 1979). In addition, foreign investors provide domestic policy makers with the resources that the latter need to purchase regime security and continue to monopolize governance and the allocation of resources. In exchange, the ruling coalition can restructure property rights and develop investment schemes to favor foreign investors in their efforts to exploit domestic resources, including labor (Galtung, 1971, p. 84). The mass of the people see that the bulk of the benefits generated by foreign investment accrue primarily to the national elites and their foreign benefactors. They see foreign capital penetration of the domestic economy as exacerbating existing inequalities and inequities in the distribution of resources, and as a result, levels of domestic political conflict rise (Rothgeb, 1991; Mahler, 1981; Gurr and Duvall, 1973).

According to the group mobilization perspective, dependence on foreign capital flows produces shifts in the wealth position of the various groups in society. The presence of foreign investment in the domestic economy produces an equilibrium in which some groups win at the expense of others; in other words, the welfare of some groups is enhanced and that of other groups deteriorates. Winners usually secure additional resources and hence increase their overall endowments. Losers suffer a decrease in their stock of wealth (Rothgeb, 1991; Olson, 1963). As argued by Tilly (1978), after the social change produces winners and losers, the former attempt to use their increased wealth to improve their participation in governance—the winners mobilize, capture, and retain additional leadership positions in the national political system. Losers, on the other hand, engage in defensive mobilization, in an effort to, at the minimum, retain their existing political positions. This process can lead to conflict, which should not necessarily be of the destructive type if the country has institutional arrangements that provide viable structures for peaceful resolution of conflict. Hence, whether such conflict leads to political violence or not is determined by the country's existing laws and institutions (Mason, 1984).

Liberals argue that a significant part of the conflict that exists in developing countries arises from resource scarcity. Unlike proponents of the deprivation view, however, liberals believe that foreign capital is critical for economic development in poor countries, and that it can provide enormous benefits to the peoples of these societies. In fact, they argue that foreign capital can reduce domestic conflict through the creation of jobs for the people, and enhance the ability of domestic businesses to grow and eventually become globally competitive. Liberals also argue that foreign investment can significantly increase what are usually very meager tax bases and provide the government with the resources that it needs to deal with poverty and other pressing societal problems. Foreign capital, of course, is also expected to bring to the poor country valuable knowledge (i.e., technology) that can improve the utilization of resources, including labor (Rothgeb, 1991).

We must note, as has been argued by several scholars (see, e.g., Ayoob, 1995), that elite dependence on foreign capital and other foreign benefactors derives partly from the failure or unwillingness of their law makers to develop legitimacy, or secure compliance from the governed. As a consequence, many of the elites who are part of what are essentially illegitimate regimes, must look elsewhere (usually abroad) for resources, which they can use to bribe those who have developed enough violence potential (e.g., military officers) to be able to destabilize the government. Obsession of Africa's ruling elites with the maintenance of regimes that have not been legitimized by the people has often resulted in the neglect of the traditional duties of government, such as the provision of public goods and the maintenance of law and order, including the protection of the individual and his property.

The three views elaborated above can be reconciled by viewing foreign capital penetration of African economies through the lenses of public choice theory. According to the latter, how well foreign investment performs in a country is determined by the nature of the incentives faced by traders in national markets. Foreign capital penetration of an African country is less likely to create destructive conflict between local groups or social cleavages if domestic institutional arrangements can effectively and adequately handle the increased demand for greater economic and political participation that may accompany the inflow of capital. However, if local institutions are either incapable of effectively handling such increased demand for participation, or favor some groups and thus artificially place others at a competitive disadvantage, then conflict will arise (Mbaku, 1993, 1997; Doxey, 1961).

When foreign capital penetrates a poor country, it is likely to create jobs and other opportunities for economic and social advancement that will be competed for by the various groups that exist in the country. If the latter's institutional arrangements provide dependable, fair, effective, and predictable avenues for groups and individuals to compete for the new economic opportunities, then conflict, especially of the destructive nature, many not arise. If conflict does arise, it would not lead to political violence or instability. With appropriate laws and institutions, foreign capital should provide essential resources for wealth creation and economic growth. In addition, the appropriate institutional arrangements should constrain state custodians and prevent them from colluding with foreign entrepreneurs to pursue perverse economic policies that may generate benefits for them and their foreign benefactors but impose severe costs on the rest of society. Thus, effective and relevant institutional arrangements should serve to:

- improve the functioning of foreign capital as an instrument of domestic development;
- prevent political opportunism (e.g., corruption and rent seeking) on the part of both domestic elites and foreign capitalists;
- provide fair, effective, and predictable structures for individuals and groups to compete for the benefits of foreign investment, in particular, and economic growth, in general;
- provide a system of well-defined and enforced property rights, especially in natural resources;
- prevent foreign entrepreneurs from exploiting the country and its resources, while providing these investors with the opportunity to earn a fair return for the resources that they have committed to the domestic economy; and
- improve the ability of both domestic and foreign entrepreneurs to undertake wealth-creating activities.

Whether investments (domestic or foreign) contribute positively to economic growth and development in Africa is determined by the nature of incentives faced by participants in the continent's economies. Of course, the incentive structures in a country are determined by that country's institutional arrangements. Thus, as Africans prepare themselves for development in the new century, they must engage in democratic constitutional reforms to provide themselves with laws and institutions that adequately constrain the state (and thus minimize political opportunism by state custodians), enhance wealth creation, and promote the peaceful coexistence of each country's various population groups. Unless such reforms are undertaken, the continent's legacy of perverse economic policies will continue and the African people will remain poor and deprived.

BEYOND AFRICA'S ECONOMIC CRISIS: SOME PROPOSALS

In order to address Africa's economic crisis, several steps need to be taken. A critical measure would be for Africans to engage in institutional reforms to develop laws that provide the appropriate foundation for establishing viable and efficient institutions to uphold the constitution and the rule of law. These include (1) a professional and neutral military; (2) a properly constrained police force; (3) an independent judiciary; (4) an independent media; (5) an independent central bank; (6) a professional civil service; and (7) an efficient and representative parliament. How well these institutions maintain the rule of law in the country (including the enforcement of property rights) will determine the extent to which groups coexist peacefully and the ability of entrepreneurs to create the wealth that each country needs to confront poverty and deprivation and deal with other societal problems.

CONCLUSION

In this chapter we have provided a brief review of the African economies. Despite more than fifty years of independence, Africans remain poor and highly deprived. In fact, available evidence points to the fact that Africa is the poorest region of the world and the one with bleak prospects for the future. Weak, inefficient, and nonviable institutional arrangements in the African countries are partly responsible for continued underdevelopment in the continent. Institutions are very important for wealth creation and economic growth.

References

African Development Bank (1997). *African Development Report, 1997*. New York: Oxford University Press.

Agbese, P. O. (1998). "Foreword: Africa and the Dilemmas of Corruption", in J. M. Mbaku (ed.). *Corruption and the Crisis of Institutional Reforms in Africa*. Lewiston, NY: Edwin Mellen Press.

Ayoob, M. (1995). *The Third World Security Predicament: State Making, Regional Conflict, and the International System*. Boulder, CO: Lynne Rienner.

Commonwealth (1999). *Commonwealth Universities Handbook, 1999: A Directory of the Universities of the Commonwealth and the Handbook of their Association*. 2 Volumes. London: Association of Commonwealth Universities.

Davenport, M. (1992). "Africa and the Unimportance of Being Preferred". *Journal of Common Market Studies*. Vol. 30. No. 2, pp. 233–251.

Decalo, S. (1992). "The Process, Prospects and Constraints of Democratization in Africa". *African Affairs*. Vol. 9. No. 362, pp. 7–35.

Deyo, F. C. (1981). *Dependent Development and Industrial Order: An Asian Case Study*. New York: Praeger.

Deyo, F. C. (1989). *Beneath the Miracle: Labor Subordination in the New Asian Industrialization*. Berkeley, CA: University of California Press.

Doxey, G. V. (1961). *The Industrial Color Bar in South Africa*. Cape Town: Oxford University Press.

Europa (1998). *The World of Learning, 1999*. 49th ed., London: Europa Publications.

Galtung, J. (1971). "A Structural Theory of Imperialism," *Journal of Peace Research*. Vol. 8. No. 2, pp. 81–117.

Gurr, T. and Duvall, R. (1973). "Civil Conflict in the 1960s: A Reciprocal Theoretical System with Parameter Estimates", *Comparative Political Studies*. Vol. 6. No. 2, pp. 135–169.

Gwartney, J. D. and Lawson, R. A. (2000). *Economic Freedom of the World: 2000 Annual Report*. Vancouver, BC: The Fraser Institute.

Gwartney, J. D. and Lawson, R. A. (2002). *Economic Freedom of the World: 2002 Annual Report*. Vancouver, BC: The Fraser Institute.

Ihonvbere, J. O. (1994). *Nigeria: The Politics of Adjustment & Democracy*. New Brunswick, NJ: Transaction.

IMF (2003). *Direction of Trade Statistics, 2003*. Washington, D.C.: IMF.

Johnson, C. A. (1982). *MITI and the Japanese Miracle: The Growth of Industrial Policy, 1925–1975*. Stanford, CA: Stanford University Press.

Jua, N. (1998). "Cameroon: Jumpstarting an Economic Crisis", in Mbaku, J. M. (ed.). *Corruption and the Crisis of Institutional Reforms in Africa*. Lewiston, NY: Edwin Mellen Press.

LeVine, V. T. (1975). *Political Corruption: The Ghanaian Case*. Stanford, CA: Hoover Institution.

MacGaffey, J. (1983). "How to Survive and Become Rich Amidst Devastation: The Second Economy of Zaire". *African Affairs*, Vol. 82. No. 328, pp. 351–366.

Mahler, V. (1981). "Mining, Agriculture, and Manufacturing: The Impact of Foreign Investment on Social Distribution in Third World Countries". *Comparative Political Studies*. Vol. 14. No. 3, pp. 267–297.

Mason, D. (1984). "Individual Participation in Collective Racial Violence: A Rational Choice Perspective". *American Political Science Review*. Vol. 78. No. 4, pp. 1040–1056.

Mbaku, J. M. (1993). "Markets and the Economic Origins of Apartheid in South Africa". *The Indian Journal of Social Science*. Vol. 6. No. 2, pp. 139–158.

Mbaku, J. M. (1997). *Institutions and Reform in Africa: The Public Choice Perspective*. Westport, CT: Praeger.

Mbaku, J. M. (2007). *Corruption in Africa: Causes, Consequences and Cleanups*. Lanham, MD: Lexington Books.

Millikan, M. F. and Rostow, W. W. (1957). *A Proposal: Key to an Effective Foreign Policy*. New York: Harper & Brothers.

Olson, M. (1963). "Rapid Growth as a Destabilizing Force". *Journal of Economic History*. Vol. 23. No. 4, pp. 529–552.

Ostrom, E., Schroeder, L. and Wynne, S. (1993). *Institutional Incentives and Sustainable Development: Infrastructure Policies in Perspective*. Boulder, CO: Westview Press.

Rodrik, Dani (1994). "King Kong Meets Godzilla: The World Bank and the 'East Asian Miracle'". In Albert Fishlow et al (ed.). *Miracle or Design? Lessons from the East Asian Experience*. Washington DC: Overseas Development Council.

Rothgeb, J. M. Jr. (1991). "The Effects of Foreign Investment Upon Political Protest and Violence in Underdeveloped Societies". *The Western Political Quarterly*. Vol. 44. No. 1, pp. 9–38.

Schnitzer, M. C. (1994). *Comparative Economic Systems*. Cincinnati, OH: South-Western.

Stepanek, J. E. (1999). *Wringing Success from Failure in Late-Developing Countries: Lessons from the Field*. Westport, CT: Praeger.

Sunkel, O. (1979). "Big Business and 'Dependencia'", in G. Modelski (ed.). *Transnational Corporations and World Order*. San Francisco: Freeman.

Tilly, C. (1978). *From Mobilization to Revolution*. Reading, MA: Addison-Wesley.

UNAIDS (1998). *AIDS Epidemic Update: December 1998*. New York: UNAIDS. Retrieved from http://www.who.org, December 20, 1998.

UNAIDS (2003). *AIDS Epidemic Update: December 2003*. New York: UNAIDS. Retrieved from http://www.thebody.com/unaids/aids2003.html, December 19, 2003.

UNAIDS (2005). 2006 Report on the Global AIDS Epidemic, New York: UNAIDS. Retrieved from http://www.unaids.org/en/HIV_data/2006GlobalReport/default.asp, September 14, 2006.

UNAIDS/UNICEF/WHO (2003). Joint Press Release: 60 Million Africans have been Touched by AIDS, Says UNIADS Executive Director, New York: UNAIDS. Retrieved from http://www.thebody.com/unaids/africa_aids.html, December 19, 2003.

UNDP (1990). *Human Development Report, 1990*. New York: Oxford University Press.

UNDP (1992). *Human Development Report, 1992*. New York: Oxford University Press.

UNDP (1997). *Human Development Report, 1997*. New York: Oxford University Press.

UNDP (2002). *Human Development Report, 2002*. New York: Oxford University Press.

UNDP (2003). *Human Development Report, 2003*. New York: Oxford University Press.

UNDP (2005). *Human Development Report, 2005*. New York: Oxford University Press.

WHO (1998). AIDS Epidemic Update: December 1998. Retrieved from http://www.who.org, December 19, 1998.

World Bank (1997). *World Development Report, 1997*. New York: Oxford University Press.

World Bank (1998a). *African Development Indictors, 1998/99*. Washington, D.C.: World Bank.

World Bank (1998b). *World Development Indicators, 1998*. Washington, D.C.: World Bank.

World Bank (1998c). *World Development Report, 1998/99*. New York: Oxford University Press.

World Bank (2002a). *World Development Indicators, 2002*. New York: Oxford University Press.

World Bank (2002b). *African Development Indicators, 2002*. Washington, D.C.: World Bank.

World Bank (2002c). *World Development Report, 2002*. New York: Oxford University Press.

World Bank (2003). *World Development Report, 2003*. New York: Oxford University Press.

World Bank (2005). *African Development Indicators, 2005*. Washington, D.C.: World Bank.

World Bank (2006). *World Development Report, 2006*. New York: Oxford University Press.

Chapter 5

The Travails of Democratization in Africa

George Klay Kieh, Jr.

INTRODUCTION

Since the end of the "Cold War" in 1990, "democratization" has become one of the major buzzwords in the academic literature, policy circles and in the corridors of "daily talk and chat." The end of Stalinist socialism in Central and Eastern Europe and the subsequent efforts to establish a new "liberal democratic order," as well the cracking of the authoritarian armor in Africa, Asia, Central and South America precipitated the emergence of a wave of optimism regarding the "democratization contagion." As Diamond (2003, p.1) notes, "...democracy—a system of government in which the people choose their leaders at regular intervals through free, fair and competitive elections—has expanded in the world."

In Africa, democratization is being reified as continent's "savior," especially since the region has been strangulated by the authoritarian albatross since the post-independence era. Moreover, the United States, the other Western powers and Japan and the Bretton Woods Institutions—International Monetary Fund and the World Bank—have rhetorically made democratization the *terra firma* of their policies toward Africa. For example, the progress toward democratization is a premier prerequisite for heavily indebted African states to qualify for debt relief (Mbaku, 2007).

So, amidst all of the hoopla, what is the state of democratization in Africa? What are the obstacles to the successful prosecution of the democratization project on the continent? What steps need to be taken to address the obstacles? These questions will constitute the kernels of the chapter.

CONCEPTUALIZATION

In this study, I define democratization as a process through which individuals and groups are empowered, become major stakeholders in the affairs of their polity and enjoy and exercise cultural, economic, environmental, political, religious, security and social rights and freedoms.

THE ELUSIVE QUEST FOR DEMOCRATIZATION IN AFRICA: A BACKGROUND

The struggle for democratization in Africa has been waged in three phases: The first, second and the third waves. In this part of the chapter, the focus will be on the first and second waves. The purpose is to establish a historical context for examining the state of the third wave.

The "First Wave of Democratization:" 1884-1960s

The "first wave of democratization" in Africa was focused on resisting colonialism and its attendant repressive and exploitative systems. As I have argued in chapter 1, colonialism adversely affected Africa in various ways—ranging from cultural to social. Every African group—ethnic, regional, etc. —was impacted by the myriad deleterious effects of colonialism. Against this background, Africans were able to organize broad-based anti-colonial coalitions that cut across the various divides. Unity and collective resolve were brought to bear on the prosecution of the various anti-colonial struggles throughout the continent whether through armed struggles or non-violent means. The various anti-colonial struggles had a shared agenda that revolved around the importance of the colonial state respecting the cultural, economic, environmental, political, religious, security and social rights and freedoms of all Africans; and the ultimate abolition of colonial rule

By the mid 1940s, the "first wave" began to bear dividends as the various European colonial empires throughout Africa began to show signs of stress. The development was caused by a confluence of factors. The most important one was the toll of the various anti-colonial struggles on the various colonial empires. The cumulative effects of the various struggles exacted tremendous pressures on the political and economic base of the colonial order.

Exhausted by the impact of the anti-colonial struggles and the other ancillary factors, all of the European colonial powers except Portugal (it held onto its colonial empire consisting of Angola, Cape Verde, Guinea Bissau and Mozambique until 1975) were forced to dismantle their respective colonial empires. So, by the early 1950s, the "wave of independence" began to sweep across the African continent beginning in North Africa then to the rest of the continent. By the 1960s, the continent was gripped in a state of ecstasy as one country after another broke the yoke of colonialism. Ramsay (1993, p.3) captures the essence of the celebration that was going on in the various sub-regions and newly independent states of the continent:

> The times were electric. In country after country, the flags of Great Britain, Belgium and France were replaced by the banners of new states, whose leaders offered idealistic promises to remake the continent and thus the world. Hopes were high, and the most ambitious of goals seemed obtainable. Even non-Africans spoke of the resource rich continent as being on the verge of a developmental take off.

Having grudgingly accepted the reality that their colonial empires had collapsed, the various imperialist powers sought to devise ways in which they could still maintain control over the newly independent states. The most effective instrument of control created by the imperialist powers was neo-colonialism. According to Nkrumah (1965, p.1), "The essence of neo-colonialism is that the State which is subject to it is, in theory, independent and has all the outward trappings of international sovereignty. In reality its economic system and thus its political policy is directed from outside."

Very few African states such as Ghana rejected the imposition of this new form of metropolitan-based control. However, in countries such as Cote d'Ivoire, France maintained its control through the compradorial regime of Houphet Boigny, who was tutored in neo-colonial peonage during the colonial period.

The "Second Wave of Democratization:" 1961-1990

Barely a year after the climax of the celebration of the demise of colonialism, the peoples of Africa, with few exceptions, realized that they were the victims of a monumental hoax. This was because they came to the realization that no fundamental change was going to occur, despite the end of colonialism (Kieh and Agbese, 2004). The crux of the evidence was that the portrait of the state that was inherited from colonialism was maintained. The only superficial change was the replacement of the European colonial state managers by indigenous African ones—a phenomenon akin to the one that Fanon (1967) refers to as "black skin white masks."

The failure of the African ruling classes to exorcise the colonial demon set the constituent states on the path to underdevelopment. At the political level, the ruling classes, among other things, established a culture of the one-party state. In order to maintain the emergent political order, authoritarianism became the pervasive model of governance. The resultant was that the ruling classes lost legitimacy and increasing relied on the use of repression as the mainstay of state-society relations. According to Freedom House (2002), by 1989, only three African states—Botswana, Gambia and Mauritius—were classified as "free;" 16 were designated as "partially free;" and the majority—32 states—were classified as "not free." Put into a larger context, 48 African states were authoritarian, while only three were democratizing.

Economically, the peripheral capitalist mode of production failed to create jobs and improve the standard of living of the members of the subaltern classes. However, amidst growing mass impoverishment, the members of the ruling classes, their families and surrogates were engaged in the private accumulation of capital through the plundering and pillaging of the public treasury. With their ill gotten wealth, the members of the ruling classes and their relations enjoyed high standards of living replete with the necessities of life.

In the social domain, the ruling classes made perfunctory efforts to address the challenges of education, health care, access to clean drinking water, acceptable sanitation and housing. For instance, while public schools were experiencing neglect from the neo-colonial state, the members of the ruling class had no problem using state resources to send their children and other relatives to schools in the United States and Europe. Similarly, despite the pressing need for the development of a functional and effective public health system, the members of the African ruling classes were busy commandeering state funds to pay for their expensive "health trips" to Europe and the United States.

Culturally, amid the crisis of legitimacy, the ruling classes used ethnicity instrumentally as a vehicle for dividing the members of the subaltern classes. One of the major ways in which this was done was through the privileging of one ethnic group over the others. Specifically, this involved giving the members of the so-called privileged ethnic group unfettered access to state resources, while simultaneously depriving the members of the peripheral ethnic groups. Ultimately, this led to a series of conflicts between and among ethnic groups, and diverted attention from the class character of the problematic.

In a related way, the ruling classes fostered religious intolerance and polarization as part of their "grand strategy" of keeping the members of the subaltern classes divided. By so doing, the ruling classes were able to erode the basis of class solidarity, the critical imperative that was exigent for the subalterns to wage class struggles against the members of the ruling classes. In other words, just like ethnicity, religion was used as an instrument of division to help divert the attention of the members of the subaltern classes away from the ruling classes, the fundamental sources of their predicament.

Despite the deployment of the "divide and rule" strategy by the ruling classes, political conscious and progressive Africans were able to mobilize some members of the subaltern classes to wage the "second wave of democratization." The "second wave" was ostensibly designed to end authoritarian rule on the continent, and to replace it with a new pro-people, pro-democracy and pro-development order. Characteristically, the ruling classes and their regimes responded to the "second wave" with unadulterated violence, including the murder of scores of pro-democracy activists. The United States and the Soviet Union and their respective allies played pivotal roles in providing the oxygen that kept authoritarianism well and alive on the continent. However, the violent responses from the continent's repressive regimes did not end the "second wave." Instead, it emboldened the pro-democracy activists on the continent.

The resultant "tugs and pulls" between the continent's authoritarian regimes on the one hand, and the various pro-democracy groups, on the other, provided the opportunity for the military to hijack the democratic struggle. Beginning with the "Free Officers" led coup in Egypt in 1952, military intervention in African politics became the mainstay of the continent's political landscape. In the 1960s, there were 23 successful military coups on the continent (Kieh, 2004, p. 44). During the decades of the 1970s and the 1980s, there were a total of 42 coups (Kieh, 2004, p.44).

Additionally, several African states degenerated into civil wars. Sudan and Senegal were the forerunners, followed by several other states—Nigeria, Angola, Mozambique, Chad, Ethiopia, Mali, Niger, Somalia and Liberia, among others. By the end of the decade of the 1980s, there were ten civil wars raging in Africa (Kieh, 2002, p.46). Some of these wars were resolved, while others continued. However, in the case of the former, the post-conflict peace-building projects failed to address and seriously tackle the roots causes of the conflicts that generated the wars.

Overall, the "second wave" produced a combination of successes and failures for the various pro-democracy movements. But, on balance, the "second wave" failed to achieve its primary objective of caging the authoritarian genie. This provided the coupists, militarists and warlords with increased opportunities to use mass grievances as pretexts in waging their various wars designed to enable them to accumulate capital.

FAREWELL TO AUTHORITARIANISM AND SOCIO-ECONOMIC MALAISE? THE JOURNEY OF THE "THIRD WAVE OF DEMOCRATIZATION"

Background

The end of the Cold War profoundly affected the struggle for democratization in Africa in three major ways. First, the collapse and subsequent disintegration of the Soviet Union deprived the Kremlin's client states of the political, economic and military support that was indispensable to the maintenance of authoritarianism. Second and related, the United States and its allies were deprived of the major alibi they had used to justify support for their authoritarian client states. So, the United States, Britain and France reluctantly abandoned their various client regimes. Third, pro-democracy groups ceased the opportunity to press for the liberalization of the political space and for other fundamental changes. Thus, the "third wave of democratization" was set into motion. Nzongola-Ntalaja (1998, p. 9) provides the following summation of the origins of the phenomenon:

> Since 1988, the people of Africa have risen to replace one party and military dictatorships with multiparty democracy. From its violent outbreak in October 1988, in the streets of Algiers, this new social movement for democracy has manifested itself all over the continent...

Subsequently, the first half of the 1990s saw widespread political turbulence across the African continent (Bratton and van de Walle, 1997, p.3). Commenting on the emergence of the "third wave," Africa News (1992, p.1) exclaimed, "Africa is experiencing a revolution as profound as the wave of independence that began to sweep the continent three decades ago."

Almost two decades have elapsed, since the inception of the "third wave of democratization." This provides an appropriate time span for evaluating the impact of the phenomenon on the continent. In this regard, the political and socioeconomic outcomes of the phenomenon will be evaluated.

Political Democratization

A Political Democratization Index (PDI) is used to measure the state of political democratization in Africa. The index consists of two clusters of variables: political rights and civil liberties (see Table 5.1). The former embodies measures of the electoral process, political pluralism and participation and the functioning of the government. The latter cluster comprises measures of the freedom of expression and belief, the freedom of association and organization, the rule of law and personal autonomy.

According to the results, in the area of political rights, eleven African states made substantial progress in 2006. Twenty-three states made some progress. Specifically, this group is characterized by some progress in the area of political liberalization amid the lacunas of authoritarianism. Another eleven states made very little progress in the areas of political democratization. This category, including countries such as Gabon, took symbolic steps in liberalizing the polity. In other words, authoritarianism remained at the core of the political system; however, a modicum of political liberalization such as the establishment of a nominal multiparty system occurred. Eight countries remained resistant to political democratization; hence, they made virtually no progress in any of the categories of political democratization; this group is anchored by Libya.

In terms of the respect for civil liberties, eight countries made substantial progress. Thirty-one countries made some progress in the promotion of these rights; these are the states that made some progress in some of the areas of civil liberties, while retaining the authoritarian stranglehold over the other areas. Cameroon and six other states made very little progress. That is, they implemented some token measures ostensibly to placate domestic and international critics. Seven states, with the Sudan as the anchor, made absolutely no progress in the promotion and protection of civil liberties.

Overall, based on the PDI, eleven countries in Africa were considered free; these are the states, such as Cape Verde, that made substantial progress in the combined areas of political rights and civil liberties Twenty-three countries made some progress toward political democratization. Another group of sixteen states made very little progress; these are the states that have taken some symbolic steps in an effort to provide the façade of political democratization. The final category consists of three states— Libya, Somalia and Sudan—that have refused to take any step toward political democratization.

In addition, there are several other general trends. First, there is the problem of the holding fraudulent elections even within a multi-party context. For example, during the 2007 state and national elections, the Obasanjo regime put into place a fraudulent process that was highlighted by rigging and sundry other irregularities (The Epoch Times, 2007). The ultimate goal was to secure victory for the ruling People's Democratic Party (PDP) and President Obasanjo's handpicked successor, Musa Yar' Ardua. In essence, the fact that several political parties contested the elections did not mean that they were competitive, free and fair. That is, the multiplicity of the political parties that participated in the elections simply served as a veneer for legitimation. This is because there were visible signs that President Obasanjo, having failed in his effort to stage a "constitutional coup" in order to perpetuate his rule, was determined to ensure that "Obasanjoism" would continue even without Obasanjo. Basically, "Obasanjoism" is an autocratic governance architecture decorated with the trappings of political democratization. In fact, during the electoral campaign, President Obasanjo clearly gave an indication that the elections would be plagued with fraud, when he stated, "April polls are a matter of life and death for the ruling People's Democratic Party (PDP)" (Benson et al, 2007, p.1).

Second, the dominant political parties and politicians represent various factions and fractions of the ruling classes. They are able to exert great influence over the electoral process and outcome because they control state power; they have financial and logistical resources; and they enjoy the support of the United States, Britain, France, the International Monetary Fund and the World Bank. In other words, the elections are usually contests among recycled politicians, repackaged "born again democrats" and the emerging corps of opportunists. Those political parties and candidates that are outside of the orbit of power and wealth are usually banished to the periphery of the process.

Third and related, the various ruling class-based political parties do not provide any vision about the democratic reconstitution of the state. Instead, they focus on superficialities that have no bearing on improving the lives of the members of the subaltern classes. Those parties that advocate systemic transformation are often hamstrung in waging their campaigns by the inadequacy of financial and logistical resources.

Fourth, given the prevalence of abject poverty, elections are not usually about competing national visions embodied in political platforms. Instead, the ruling class-based political parties use their great advantage in resources to "buy votes" through the provision of food and other short-term benefits to the electorate. Thus, the elections provide voters the opportunity to engage in "rent-seeking behavior" (Kieh, 2006).

Fifth, in several African states, there is the oscillation between political liberalization and authoritarianism between elections. That is, usually prior to the holding of elections, there is an improvement in the progress toward the respect for and the promotion of political rights and civil liberties. However, after the elections, there is the reversal to authoritarianism. Among other things, this process of "forward and backwards" makes it very difficult to consolidate political democratization (Osaghae, 2005).

Table 5.1: The State of Political Democratization in Africa in 2006

Country	Political Rights	Civil Liberties	PDI	Status
Algeria	6	5	5.5	Not Free
Angola	6	5	5.5	Not Free
Benin	2	2	2.0	Free
Botswana	2	2	2.0	Free
Burkina Faso	5	3	4.0	Partly Fr.
Burundi	4	5	4.5	Partly Fr.
Cameroon	6	6	6.0	Not Free
Cape Verde	1	1	1.0	Free
Central African Republic	5	4	4.5	Partly Fr.
Chad	6	6	6.0	Not Free
Comoros	3	4	3.5	Partly Fr.
Congo	6	5	5.5	Not Free
Cote d'Ivoire	7	6	6.5	Not Free
Democratic Republic of the Congo	5	6	5.5	Not Free
Djibouti	5	5	5.0	Partly Fr.
Egypt	6	5	5.5	Not Free
Equatorial Guinea	7	6	6.5	Not Free
Eritrea	7	6	6.5	Not Free
Ethiopia	5	5	5.0	Partly Fr.
Gabon	6	4	5.0	Partly Fr.
Gambia	5	4	4.5	Partly Fr.
Ghana	1	2	2.5	Free
Guinea	6	5	5.5	Not Free
Guinea-Bissau	4	4	4.0	Partly Fr.
Kenya	3	3	3.0	Partly Fr.
Lesotho	2	3	2.5	Free
Liberia	3	4	3.5	Partly Fr.
Libya	7	7	7.0	Not Free

Madagascar	4	3	3.5	Partly Fr.
Malawi	4	3	3.5	Partly Fr.
Mauritania	5	4	4.5	Partly Fr.
Mauritius	1	2	1.5	Free
Morocco	5	4	4.5	Partly Fr.
Mozambique	3	4	3.5	Partly Fr.
Namibia	2	2	2.0	Free
Niger	3	3	3.0	Partly Fr.
Nigeria	4	4	4.0	Partly Fr.
Rwanda	6	5	5.5	Not Free
Sao Tome and Principe	2	2	2.0	Free
Senegal	2	3	2.5	Free
Seychelles	3	3	3.0	Partly Fr.
Sierra Leone	4	3	3.5	Partly Fr.
Somalia	7	7	7.0	Not Free
South Africa	2	2	2.0	Free
Sudan	7	7	7.0	Not Free
Swaziland	7	5	6.0	Not Free
Tanzania	4	3	3.5	Partly Fr.
Togo	6	5	5.5	Not Free
Tunisia	6	5	5.5	Not Free
Uganda	5	4	4.5	Partly Fr.
Zambia	3	4	3.5	Partly Fr.
Zimbabwe	7	6	6.5	Not Free

Source: Freedom House, *Freedom in the World, 2007*, (New York: Freedom House, 2007), pp. 1-12.

Note: The ratings are distributed thus: 1.0-2.5 (Free); 3.0-5.0 (Partly Free); and 5.5-7.0 (Not Free).

Socio-Economic Democratization

What has been the impact of the "third wave of democratization" on the material conditions of the African peoples? A Socio-economic Democratization Index (SEDI) was constructed to address the question. As Table 5.2 shows, in 2004, only two African states—Mauritius and Seychelles made high level of progress in the efforts to address the basic human needs of their citizens. In the case of Mauritius, this means that it made substantial progress in the areas of political and socio-economic democratization. As for the Seychelles, the results are interesting because as Table 5.1

indicates, the country only made some progress in the area of political democratization—with a "partly free status."

In terms of medium level of progress, there were 20 countries in this category. Specifically, the states in this cluster made appreciable amount of progress in attempting to provide for the needs—education, health care, etc. —of their respective citizens. However, Libya, the top ranked state in this category, was one of the most repressive countries—it made no effort toward political democratization.

Unfortunately, the majority of the African states made low level of progress in the area of socio-economic democratization during the period. 29 of the 53 states (54.7%) on the continent did a poor job in addressing the basic human needs of their citizens. Interestingly, this includes countries such as Benin and Mali that made substantial progress in the area of political democratization. In other words, in these cases, increased political democratization did not correspondingly lead to increased socio-economic democratization.

Table 5.2: The Human Development Index of African States for 2004

Country	Human Development Index
Algeria	0.728
Angola	0.439
Benin	0.428
Botswana	0.570
Burkina Faso	0.342
Burundi	0.348
Cameroon	0.506
Cape Verde	0.722
Central African Republic	0.353
Chad	0.368
Comoros	0.556
Congo	0.520
Cote d'Ivoire	0.421
Democratic Republic of the Congo	0.391
Djibouti	0.494
Egypt	0.702

Equatorial Guinea	0.653
Eritrea	0.454
Ethiopia	0.371
Gabon	0.633
Gambia	0.479
Ghana	0.532
Guinea	0.445
Guinea-Bissau	0.349
Kenya	0.491
Lesotho	0.494
Liberia	-
Libya	0.798
Madagascar	0.509
Malawi	0.400
Mali	0.338
Mauritania	0.486
Mauritius	0.800
Morocco	0.633
Mozambique	0.390
Namibia	0.626
Niger	0.311
Nigeria	0.448
Rwanda	0.450
Sao Tome and Principe	0.607
Senegal	0.460
Seychelles	0.842
Sierra Leone	0.335
Somalia	-
South Africa	0.653
Sudan	0.516
Swaziland	0.500
Tanzania	0.430
Togo	0.495
Tunisia	0.760
Uganda	0.502
Zambia	0.407
Zimbabwe	0.491

Source: United Nations Development Program, *Human Development Report, 2006*, (New York: Oxford University Press), pp. 283-286.

Score: The score is distributed thus: High (0.800 and above); medium (0.500-0.799); and low (below 0.500).

THE OBSTACLES TO DEMOCRATIZATION

The "third wave of democratization" in Africa has been hamstrung by several factors. The core obstacle is the failure to deconstruct, rethink and democratically reconstitute the neo-colonial state. Even in those African states that are making progress in the area of political democratization, the neo-colonial state has been left in tact. Thus, the neo-colonial that has visited repression and socio-economic malaise on the subaltern classes in Africa since the post-colonial era is shepherding the critical process of democratization. There is no wonder then why it is difficult to consolidate democratization in the political, socio-economic and the other sectors.

Another major obstacle is the lack of visionary leadership. With few exceptions, the states on the continent are ruled by leaders who lack a sense of genuine commitment to the improvement of the lives of the members of the subaltern classes. In many cases, recycled and repackaged politicians and the emergent new genre of opportunists—erstwhile so-called "political activists" who have joined the ruling classes they used to lambast—are the ones ruling as presidents, prime ministers, cabinet ministers, legislators and judges. The ideational bankruptcy of the ruling classes is vividly reflected, among other things, in their lack of a transformative vision that would provide the leadership in democratizing the various sectors of society (Adejumobi, 2000).

Yet, there is the related conundrum of the acquisitive impulse. The ruling classes use the state as an instrument for facilitating their private accumulation of capital. And this is done in various ways—from the embezzlement of public resources to the use of government positions and connections to extract bribes from those who seek state services. This is why the control of state power is indeed a "life and death matter" for the various factions and fractions of the ruling classes. In short, the faction or fraction that controls state power has concomitant control over the sources for the illicit accumulation of wealth.

The "hegemonic presidency" is another major obstacle to the advancement of democratization on the continent. In this context, the immense and unchecked powers of the presidency enable the institution to subordinate the legislature and the judiciary to its dictates. Moreover, the presidency tends to violate the constitution and statues with impunity. The emergent "third term phenomenon" is an excellent example of the way in which the excessive presidential powers have been able to strangulate and undermine democratic progress on the continent.

Also, most of the political parties on the continent are plagued with critical pathologies. A major problem is the tendency for these political parties to revolve around a personality. Either the political party was specifically organized to promote the presidential ambition of an individual and/or the party is dominated by a single individual—an incumbent president or the leader of the party. Within the context of such patron political parties, the dominant figure has the definitive word on virtually every issue—from the selection of candidates to the crafting and implementation of policies. Another pathology is that the political parties lack clearly articulated ideological compass. Hence, their "platforms" tend to be guided by conflicting ideological postulates; and this underscores the opportunistic foundation of their visions. Also, the parties tend to have narrow membership base. That is, rather than recruiting members from across the broad spectrum of socio-economic identities, these parties tend to focus on narrow segments of the society.

The dominant forces in the international system obstruct the promotion of democratization on the continent, their pro-democracy rhetoric notwithstanding. One way is the insistence that "liberal democracy "based on a peripheral capitalist political economy is the only acceptable model of democratization on the continent. Hence, the African states that are democratizing have "forsaken all other" models (Kieh, 1999) and tried to follow the liberal democratization path. There are two major problems with this attitude. The totalitarian orientation of the edict makes a mockery of democratization and democracy. If one of the major tenets of democracy is the respect for competing views and visions, then the insistence on liberal democracy and peripheral capitalism as "one size fits all models" undermines this principle. The related problem is that the liberal democratic model is imposed by these dominant forces rather than evolving from the process of national dialogue within each African state.

TOWARD THE RETHINKING OF THE DEMOCRATIZATION PROJECT: SOME SUGGESTIONS

The democratization project currently underway in Africa needs rethinking, if it is to succeed in rescuing the continent from the throes of authoritarianism, socio-economic malaise and the other tentacles of the crippling crises of underdevelopment. Against this background, I suggest several ideas. First and foremost, the neo-colonial state in Africa needs to be deconstructed, rethought and democratically reconstituted in terms of its nature, mission, character, values, institutions, rules, processes and policies. The ultimate goal must be to make the interests and welfare of the people the centerpiece of the state-building project. Such a pro-people, pro-democracy and pro-development new state will be well positioned to promote and consolidate democratization and to ultimately lead to the establishment of a full-fledged democracy.

The related issue is that the exclusive focus of the current democratization project on individual political rights and freedoms will not lead to the consolidation of genuine democratization and democracy on the continent. This is because although political freedoms are important, they are not sufficient to usher in a democratic order. Alternatively, democratization needs to be conceived of, and pursued as a multidimensional phenomenon—cultural, economic, environmental, political, religious, security and social. Hence, it must revolve around efforts to promote individual and group rights in these areas.

Another major requirement is the need for a new crop of African leaders, who are committed to pan-Africanism and the welfare of the African peoples. These "servant-leaders" will not, among other things, mortgage the continent's interests to the barons of neo-liberalism. Also, they will not privatize and criminalize the state for the purposes of engaging in the private accumulation of capital and wealth. Instead, they will make holistic democracy with its associated development their goal.

CONCLUSION

The chapter has attempted to examine three related issues: the state of democratization on the continent; the obstacles; and some suggestions for the way forward. The chapter began with a discussion of the struggle against colonialism ("the first wave of democratization"). One of the major reasons for the success of the struggle was that various broad nationalist movements were organized across the continent. And these organizations work together in waging the anti-colonial struggles.

But, the gains of the "first wave" were squandered by the emergent neo-colonial state and its ruling class. That is, the first generation of African leaders and the subsequent ones failed to democratically reconstitute the neo-colonial state that thcy inherited. Instead, the kept the state intact, and pursued policies that were similar to the colonial ones. This necessitated the waging of the "second wave" by various pro-democracy forces on the continent. The success of the "second wave" was undermined by vitriolic state repression and the support of the United States and the Soviet Union for their various authoritarian client regimes.

By the early 1990s, changes in the international system helped to create the requisite space for the waging of the "third wave of democratization." Although the "third wave" has had some successes in terms of liberalizing the political space, the majority of the states on the continent are either still sandwiched between authoritarianism and political liberalization or totally resistant to political democratization. On the other hand, the "third wave's" record in the area of socio-economic democratization has been dismal: The overwhelming majority of the states on the continent are doing a poor job in addressing the human needs of their respective citizens. Even some of the states that have made great strides in the area of political democratization are doing quite poorly in terms of socio-economic democratization.

Various obstacles were identified as the stumbling blocks to the successful prosecution of the democratization project on the continent. The core lacuna is the neo-colonial state. Since it is intrinsically anti-people, anti-democracy and anti-development, the neo-colonial state has made it difficult for democratization to take hold. Even when some progress has been made, the neo-colonial state, as the overarching architecture, reverses the gains.

Finally, several suggestions were proffered as prescriptions for addressing the obstacles to democracy. The key suggestion is the exigency of deconstructing, rethinking and democratically reconstituting the state, so that it can be made relevant to the lives of the majority of the peoples of Africa. A major derivative is the urgent need for a new generation of African leaders, who are committed to the welfare of the continent's subaltern classes.

References

Adejumobi, Said (2000). *Africa and the Challenges of Democracy and Good Governance in the 21st Century*. Paper presented at the Conference of the Network of Inter-Governmental Organizations in Africa. Addis Ababa, Ethiopia.

Africa News (1992). "News Analysis: People Power 'Unstoppable.' December 23-January 6, p. 1.

Benson, Dayo et al (2007). "April Polls are a Matter of Life and Death, Obasanjo Insists." *Vanguard.* February 25, pp. 1-2.

Bratton, Michael and Nicholas van de Walle (1997). *Democratic Experiment in Africa*. New York: Cambridge University Press.

Fanon, Frantz (1967). *Black Skin White Masks*. New York: Grove Press.

Freedom House (2002). *Freedom in the World, 2002*. New York: Freedom House.

Freedom House (2007). *Freedom in the World, 2007*. New York: Freedom House.

Diamond, Larry (2003). "Universal Democracy?" *Policy Review*. No. 119, pp. 1-10.

Kieh, George Klay (2006). "Elections and Voting Behavior: The Case of the 2005 Liberian Elections." *UMOJA: Bulletin of African and African-American Studies*. Vol.1. No. 2, pp. 1-17.

Kieh, George Klay and Pita Ogaba Agbese (2004). "Introduction: The Military Albatross and Politics in Africa." In George Klay Kieh, Jr. and Pita Ogaba Agbese. *The Military and Politics in Africa: From Engagement to Democratic and Constitutional Control*. Aldershot, United Kingdom: Ashgate Publishing.

Kieh, George Klay (2004). "Military Engagement in African Politics." In George Klay Kieh, Jr, and Pita Ogaba Agbese (eds). *The Military and Politics in Africa: From Engagement to Constitutional and Democratic Control*. Aldershot, United Kingdom: Ashgate Publishing.

Kieh, George Klay (2002). "Civil Conflicts in Africa: Patterns and Trends." In George Klay Kieh, Jr. and Ida Rousseau Mukenge (eds). *Zones of Conflict in Africa: Theories and Cases*. Westport, CT: Praeger.

Kieh, George Klay (1999). "Democratization in Africa: A Balance Sheet." In John Mukum Mbaku (ed). *Preparing Africa for the Twenty-First Century*. Aldershot, United Kingdom: Ashgate Publishing.

Mbaku, John Mukum (2008). "The New Globalization and the Debt Crisis in Africa." In George Klay Kieh, Jr. (ed). *Africa and the New Globalization*. Aldershot, United Kingdom: Ashgate Publishing.

Nkrumah, Kwame (1965). *Neo-Colonialism: The Last Stage of Imperialism*. London: Thomas Nelson and Sons.

Nzongola-Ntalaja, Georges (1998). "The State and Democracy in Africa." In Georges Nzongola-Ntalaja and Margaret Lee. *The State and Democracy in Africa*. Trenton, NJ: Africa World Press.

Osaghae, Eghosa (2005). "The State of Africa's Second Liberation." *Interventions: International Journal of Post-Colonial Studies*. Vol. 7. No. 1, pp. 1-20.

Ramsey, Jeffress (1993). "Introduction." *Africa*. Guilford, CT: Dushkin/McGraw-Hill.

The Epoch Times (2007). "Nigerian Elections Not Credible, EU Observers Report." April 23, p.1.

United Nations Development Program (2006). *Human Development Report, 2006*. New York: Oxford University Press.

Chapter 6

Urbanization and Social Development in Africa

Ebenezer O. Aka, Jr.

INTRODUCTION

There have been major regional shifts in world population in recent years. The African continent, which is about four times the size of continental United States, has the fastest growing population that surpassed Europe since the 1980s, to become second to Asia. Table 6.1 indicates that in 1995, 12.9 percent of the world's people lived in Africa, while 9.0 percent lived in Europe, 59.2 percent in Asia, 8.4 percent in Latin America, and 5.1 percent in North America. According to the *World Population Prospects: The 2004 Revision and World Urbanization Prospect*, in 2000 and 2005 in Africa, it was 13.4 percent and 14.0 percent respectively, while 12.0 percent and 11.3 percent in Europe, 60.4 percent and 60.4 percent in Asia, 8.6 percent and 8.7 percent in Latin America, and 5.2 percent and 5.1 percent in North America respectively (http://esa.un.org/unpp. Accessed Online on 10/02/06). Africa had the highest number of people per square area in 1995, i.e., an arithmetic density of 24.6 per sq km, followed by both Asia and Latin America with population density of 23.5 respectively. In 2000 and 2005, in Africa it was 27 and 30 respectively, 32 and 32 in Europe, 115 and 123 in Asia, 25 and 27 in Latin America, and 14 and 15 in North America respectively (http://esa.un.org/unpp. Accessed Online on 10/02/06).

Africa is the least urbanized region of the world though its rate of urbanization of between 5.0 and 6.0 percent is among the highest in the whole world. In fact, urbanization rate outpaces the continent's annual population growth rate of about 3.5 percent (Brunn and Williams, 1993, p. 267). The absorption potential of the principal urban centers, of the rural to urban migrants, is relatively low such that the socio-economic conditions of a majority of the inhabitants who managed to force themselves inside those centers tend to be relatively poor. Africa is a poor and underdeveloped continent. According to the United Nations Economic Commission for Africa, 262 million Africans live on less than one dollar ($1.00) a day, 200 million have no access to health services and 274 million do not have safe water to drink. One of the paradoxes is that a majority of the African people are desperately poor while its land is extraordinarily rich in minerals and natural resources (Kristof, 1998). Since the Second World War, especially between 1960 and 1992, the social indicators depict that Africa scored lowest in the human development index (HABITAT, 1996, p. 100). For example life expectancy at birth in Sub-Saharan Africa in 1960 was 40 years, 51 years in 1992, 49.9 in 2000, and 49.1 in 2005, while during the same period, it was 70 years in 1960, 75.8 years in 1992, 76.7 years in 2000, and 77.6 years in 2005 in North America. Infant mortality rate in 1960 and 1992 were 165 and 101 per thousand live births respectively, and in 2000 and 2005 they were 98.8 and 94.2 respectively. These figures are high when compared to those of the whole world during the same periods at 128 in 1960, 60 in 1992, 61.5 in 2000, and 57.0 in 2005 (http://esa.un.org/unpp. Accessed Online on 10/02/06).

Table 6.1: World Distribution of Population by Region, 1995

Region	Population[1] (thousands)	Percent of World Population	Density (Population per sq km)
World	5,759,276	100.0	43.3
Africa	**744,009**	**12.9**	**24.6**
Asia (excl. former USSR)	3,407,594	59.2	23.5
Europe (excl. former USSR)	516,043	9.0	06.0
Latin America[2]	482,476	8.4	23.5
North America[3]	291,802	5.1	15.1
Oceania	28,790	0.5	3.6
Former USSR	288,562	3.6	12.9

Source: Brian J.L Berry et al, *The Global Economy in Transition*, 2nd ed., (Upper Saddle River, New Jersey: Prentice Hall, 1997) p. 52.

1. Projected
2. Latin America includes all countries south of the U.S. border: Mexico, Central America, the Caribbean, and South America.
3. North America consists of Canada and the United States.

The proportion of malnourished children of 31 percent has not changed since 1975, while the percentage of population with access to safe water has changed from 25 in 1975/80 to 45 in 1988/91 periods, and adult literacy rate has changed from 28 to 51 percent from 1970 to 1992 respectively. Relatively, these numbers are low despite the modest increases.

This chapter explores the issue of urbanization in Africa with its attendant social conditions and problems. Factors of urban growth are addressed, as well as the prospects and implications of Africa's largest cities in the prevailing social, economic, political, and cultural globalization and integration. The future of African cities in the new millennium is also discussed, as well as the recommendations and conclusions based on the findings.

POPULATION AND URBAN CHANGE

Demographic Change

Among the world's regions, Africa has one of the most rapid population growth rates of about 3.5 percent per year, and also the most rapid urban change (United Nations, 1996). According to the data, about 627 million people lived in Africa in 1990, which represented about 13 percent of the world's population, while about 199 million people representing 31.7 percent of Africa's total population resided in urban areas. In 2000 and 2005, African population was 812 million and 906 million respectively, while the world population was 6.1 billion and 6.5 billion respectively. During the same periods, urban population in Africa was 302 million and 360 million respectively, representing 37.1 percent and 39.7 percent of Africa's population respectively (http://esa.un.org/unpp. Accessed Online on 10/02/06). The most populous African region in 1990 was East Africa with about 194 million people, followed by West Africa with about 179 million people, and North Africa with about 143 million people. The least populous region was Southern Africa with about 41 million people, followed by Middle Africa with about 70 million people.

Many countries' populations grew more than threefold between 1950 and 1990. For example, Kenya (3.8 times), Malawi (3.3), Rwanda (3.3), Uganda (3.8), United Republic of Tanzania (3.2), Zambia (3.3), and Zimbabwe (3.6) in East Africa; the Democratic Republic of the Congo (formerly Zaire) (3.1) in Middle Africa; Libyan Arab Jamahirya (4.4) in North Africa; Botswana in Southern Africa; and Cote d'Ivoire (4.3), Ghana (3.1), Liberia (3.1), and Niger (3.2) in West Africa. From Table 6.2, the most populous country in Africa was Nigeria with about 96 million people, followed by Egypt with about 56 million people, and Ethiopia with about 47 million people. The least populous was Mauritius with about one (1) million people, followed by Gabon (1.1 million) and Botswana (1.3 million).

Table 6.2: Population and Urban Change in African Countries between 1950 and 1990[1]

Country	Population 1990 (000s)	Pop 1990/ Pop 1950	Urban Pop 1990 (000s)	% of pop in Urban Areas (Level of Urbanization)	
				1950	1990
East Africa	**194,067**		**36,602**		**18.9**
Burundi	5,503	2.2	345	1.7	6.3
Eritrea	3,082	2.7	487	5.9	15.8
Ethiopia	47,423	2.6	5,815	4.6	12.3
Kenya	23,612	3.8	5,565	5.6	23.6
Madagascar	12,571	3.0	2,993	7.8	23.8
Malawi	9,367	3.3	1,106	3.5	11.8
Mauritius	1,057	2.1	428	28.8	40.5
Mozambique	14,187	2.3	3,795	2.4	26.8
Rwanda	6,986	3.3	391	1.8	5.6
Somalia	8,677	2.8	2,101	12.7	24.2
Uganda	17,949	3.8	2,003	3.1	11.2
UnitedRep. of Tanzania	25,600	3.2	5,325	3.8	20.8
Zambia	8,150	3.3	3,422	8.9	42.0
Zimbabwe	9,903	3.6	2,826	10.6	28.5
Middle Africa	**70,014**		**21,703**		**31.0**
Angola	9,194	2.2	2,602	7.6	28.3
Cameroon	11,526	2.6	4,643	9.8	40.3
Central African Rep.	2,927	2.2	1,097	16.0	37.5
Chad	5,553	2.1	1,138	3.9	20.5
Congo	2,232	2.8	1,194	30.9	53.5
Gabon	1,146	2.4	523	11.4	45.7
Zaire (DRC, since1997)	37,436	3.1	10,506	19.1	28.1
North Africa	**142,791**		**62,585**		**43.8**
Algeria	24,935	2.8	12,899	22.3	51.7
Egypt	56,312	2.6	24,743	31.9	43.9
Libyan Arab Jamahiriya	4,545	4.4	3,744	18.6	82.4
Morocco	24,334	2.7	11,217	26.2	46.1
Sudan	24,585	2.7	5,544	6.3	22.5
Tunisia	8,080	2.3	4,438	31.2	54.9
Southern Africa	**41,483**		**19,313**		**46.6**

Botswana	1,276	3.3	295	0.3	23.1
Lesotho	1,792	2.4	348	1.0	19.8
Namibia	1,349	2.6	430	9.4	31.9
South Africa	37,066	2.7	18,240	43.1	49.2
West Africa	**178,901**		**58,792**		**32.9**
Benin	4,633	2.3	1,345	5.3	29.0
Burkina Faso	8,987	2.5	1,605	3.8	17.9
Cote d'Ivoire	11,974	4.3	4,841	13.2	40.4
Ghana	15,020	3.1	5,107	14.5	34.0
Guinea	5,755	2.3	1,484	5.5	25.8
Liberia	2,575	3.1	1,084	13.0	42.1
Mali	9,212	2.6	2,193	8.5	23.8
Mauritania	2,003	2.4	937	2.3	46.8
Niger	7,731	3.2	1,177	4.9	15.2
Nigeria	96,158	2.9	33,808	10.1	35.2
Senegal	7,327	2.9	2,919	30.5	39.9
Sierra Leone	3,999	2.1	1,287	9.2	32.2
Togo	3,531	2.7	1,005	7.2	28.5
AFRICA	**627,256**		**198,995**		**31.7**

Source: United Nations Center for Human Settlements (HABITAT), *An Urbanizing World: Global Report on Human Settlements, 1996*, (Oxford, New York: Oxford University Press, 1996), p. 85.

1. African countries with 1 million or more inhabitants in 1990.

African Urbanization or Urban Change

Africa shows a great deal of disparities in its level of urbanization. It is an ecologically, culturally, and historically diverse region. Table 6.3 shows the regional distribution of the world's population in "million-cities" and the location of the world's largest 100 cities in 1950 and 1990. The data show that the proportion of Africa's population that lived in "million-cities" increased substantially between 1950 and 1990, from 1.8 to 7.5 respectively. Among the regions of Africa, all show remarkable increases, especially the West African Region which started from a low base in 1950. Africa and its regions also showed a great deal of increase in their urban population as a proportion of the world's population. For example, the African proportion increased from 4.5 to 8.8 from 1950 to 1990 respectively. Among African regions, the greatest increase occurred in West Africa (from 0.9 to 2.6) and East Africa (0.5 to 1.7). Furthermore, the number of the world's 100 largest cities found in Africa increased from three (3) to seven (7) from 1950 to 1990 respectively. However, among the regions, only North Africa showed a substantial increase, from two (2) to five (5) during the same periods. Looking back at Table 6.2, it indicates that the highest urbanized country in continental Africa was Libya (82.4 percent), followed by Tunisia (54.9 percent), all in North Africa. The above figures are more than Africa's average of 31.7 percent. During the same period, the least urbanized country was Rwanda (5.6 percent), followed by Burundi (6.3 percent), all in East Africa. The rates of urbanization for these countries were below the continent's average.

Table 6.3: The Regional Distribution of the World's Population in "Million-Cities" and the Location of the World's Largest 100 Cities in 1950 and 1990

	Proportion of the World's Urban Population in Million-Cities				Number of the World's 100 Largest Cities in	
	1950	1990	1950	1990	1950	1990
Africa	**4.5**	**8.8**	**1.8**	**7.5**	**3**	**7**
East Africa	0.5	1.7	-	0.8	-	-
Middle Africa	0.5	1.0	-	0.8	0	1
North Africa	1.8	2.8	1.8	3.2	2	5
Southern Africa	0.8	0.9	-	0.8	1	0
West Africa	0.9	2.6	-	2.0	0	1
Americas	23.7	23.0	30.1	27.8	26	27
Asia	32	44.5	28.6	45.6	33	44
Europe	38.8	22.8	38.0	17.9	36	20
Oceania	1.1	0.8	1.6	1.3	2	2

Source: United Nations Center for Human Settlements (HABITAT), *An Urbanizing World. Global Report on Human Settlements, 1996*, (Oxford and New York: Oxford University Press, 1996) p. 20,

Since the past few decades, Africa and its regions have witnessed much-increased levels of urbanization, despite being the least urbanized continent of the world. The percentage of population living in urban areas, as well as the average annual urban growth rate in Africa, particularly its regions, has been increasing since the 1970s. Table 6.4 shows that in 1970, one in five persons lived in cities of Africa as against one in three in the whole world. In 1990, this rose to one in three persons in Africa with growth rate of about 5.0 percent which, indeed, is very high relative to other regions. For example, in 1990, the "first world" showed that three in four persons lived in cities with a declining growth rate of 0.8 percent.

Within continental Africa, the least urbanized region has the highest rate of urban growth while the highest urbanized region has the lowest rate. East Africa is the least urbanized with the highest rate of growth, followed by West Africa. Southern Africa is the highest urbanized with the lowest growth rate, followed by North Africa. Between 1970 and 1990, the least urbanized East African Region more than doubled its urban population. For example, in 1970, one in ten persons lived in cities in East Africa, but in 1990 the number was cut to one in five persons. At the same time, in the highest urbanized region, Southern Africa, the number was two in five in 1970 and one in two in 1990. The world also shown an increase, such that, in 1970 one in three persons lived in cities as against two in five in 1990, with the growth rate of 3.1 percent.

Africa has many large cities of international status, which are largely isolated from each other. These large cities play dominant role in their national internal urban systems, as well as centers of international interaction. The cities include: Dakar, Senegal; Abidjan, Cote d'Ivoire; Accra, Ghana; Lagos, Nigeria; Kinshasa, Democratic Republic of the Congo; Khartoun, Sudan; Addis Ababa, Ethiopia; Nairobi, Kenya; Dar es Salam, Tanzania; Lusaka, Zambia; Harare, Zimbabwe; and Maputo, Mozambique. These cities are strategic to economic globalization and integration because they are command points and global marketplaces, and production sites for the information economy and the advanced corporate service industries (Sassen, 1994, p. 124).

Table 6.4: Percentage of Population Living in Urban Areas by World's Regions, 1970-2010

	Average Annual Urban Growth Rate					Percentage Urban		
Region	1970	1980	1990	2000	2010	1965-70	1985-90	2005-10
Africa	**22.9**	**28.0**	**33.9**	**40.7**	**47.4**	**4.7**	**5.0**	**4.2**
East	10.3	15.2	21.8	29.0	36.0	6.2	6.8	5.1
Central	24.8	31.6	37.8	45.6	53.4	5.5	5.1	4.6
North	36.0	39.9	44.6	51.2	57.7	3.9	4.0	3.1
South	44.1	49.6	54.9	61.3	66.8	2.9	3.6	2.8
West	19.6	25.9	32.5	39.8	47.3	5.8	5.5	4.6
Third World	**25.5**	**27.3**	**37.1**	**45.1**	**51.8**	**3.6**	**4.5**	**2.9**
Latin America	57.3	65.4	71.5	76.4	79.9	4.0	2.9	1.9
Asia	23.9	26.3	34.4	42.7	49.7	3.0	4.5	2.6
First World	**66.6**	**70.2**	**72.6**	**74.9**	**77.9**	**1.8**	**0.8**	**0.7**
North America	73.8	73.9	75.2	77.3	80.2	1.6	1.0	0.9
Europe	66.7	70.3	73.4	76.7	80.1	1.5	0.7	0.5
World	**37.2**	**41.2**	**45.2**	**51.1**	56.5	2.7	3.1	2.3

Source: John D. Kasarda and Allen M. Parnell, Third *World Cities: Problems, Policies, and Prospects*. (Newbury Park, London, New Delhi: Sage Publications, 1993), pp. 4-5.

Data from the 2000 till 2010 are estimates.

THE FORCES OF URBAN GROWTH IN AFRICA

During the last few decades, most of the African cities have grown manifold. Not only that the largest cities have continued to grow but most of the medium-sized or intermediate-sized cities have been growing faster than the largest cities (HABITAT, 1996, p. 86; Aka, 1991, pp. 179-180). The rapid urbanization or over-urbanization creates the danger of disequilibria and strain in the urban socio-economic conditions.[2] The slow economic growth in the African region, combined with the continued increases in population growth has created over-urbanized cities. The absorption potential of the principal urban centers of the rural-urban migrants is unquestionably weak, which has left a majority of them socio-economically marginalized. According to Massignon

(1993), the demands to be met in these cities are huge and the policies, infrastructure and services to cope with them are not yet in place. Forces of urban growth in Africa include: rural to urban migration; natural increase or growth of the population already residing in the cities; policies of spatial decentralization by many African countries; and the annexation or incorporation of adjacent towns.

Rural to Urban Migration

The present major cities and urban systems in Africa are colonial inventions, although urban centers and urban civilizations had flourished in many parts of the continent prior to colonial rule, e.g. Benin City, Kano, Zaria, and Ife in Nigeria; Timbuktu (Djenne), Mali; Great Zimbabwe, Zimbabwe; Kumasi, Ghana; and Kampala, Uganda. Urban development during the colonial period was the development of coastal settlements which were outward looking serving the purposes of the colonizing countries. Most of them were new towns which became important and capital cities, such as Nairobi, Kenya; Harare, Zimbabwe; Abidjan, Cote d'Ivoire; Lagos, Nigeria; and Johannesburg, South Africa.

After political independence in most developing countries of Africa, rural to urban migration became the main component of growth of largest cities. The estimated migrant share of urban growth in Africa during the 1960-1970 decade averaged 40 percent. During the 1970-1980, migrant share of urban growth almost doubled, for example, in Kenya it was 64 percent; Senegal, 75 percent; Tanzania, 85 percent; and Tunisia, 77 percent (Kasarda and Parnell, 1993, pp. 14-15). In West Africa, rural to urban migration accounted for close to 60 percent of urban growth. For example, in Gambia it was 65 percent migrant share; Sierra Leone, 63 percent; Liberia, 60 percent; and Cote d'Ivoire, 59 percent (Zachariah and Conde, 1981).

The migration push and pull factors are largely responsible for the influx of rural migrants into the already overburdened cities. According to Massignon (1993), urbanization takes off some pressure on rural environment by putting ever-increasing pressure on the urban environment. The push factors include socio-economic, cultural and political factors that push migrants out of their rural homes, such as: rural-urban wage gaps in favor of urban areas, the desire to escape briefly from the social constraints of the extended family, short-term cash needs for bridal wealth, marital instability, birth order, and inheritance laws, as well as, urban bias government policies e.g. favorable disproportionate investment in social and physical infrastructure and terms of trade (Eicher at al., 1970; Becker et al., 1994; Gugler and Flanagan, 1978; Arthur, 1981). The pull factors include: the range of economic opportunities offered and wage differentials in favor of the urban areas, and social prestige and the psychological satisfaction of living in cities as depicted in Nigeria and Cote d'Ivoire (Todaro, 1969; Adepoju, 1983; Joshi et al., 1976).

In recent years women have become increasingly a major component of migrants leaving the rural areas for the urban areas in Africa. Evidence reveals that females who migrate to urban areas tend to be more educated, younger in age (20 to 29 years), and unmarried. Different studies show that, fertility, child mortality, education, ethnicity, age, and marital status affect female migrants (Becker et al., 1994; Brockerhoff and Eu, 1993; Mhloyi, 1987). Whether the rural migrants are male or female, they always maintain important and beneficial linkages with their villages or hometown. All African cities share this social linkage (Adepoju, 1983; O'Connor, 1983; Hoddinott, 1992) because of many reasons which include: the strength of family and kingship, the wish to retain land rights, and diversifying rural household income through income and cash remittances. Return migrants also contribute significantly to the development of farm and non-farm activities because they serve as innovators and agents of socio-economic and cultural change by introducing new varieties of crops, by employing new and improved techniques of production, and by encouraging education and innovation (Haggblade et al., 1989; Aryeetey-Attoh, 1997). Non-farm activities contribute significantly to the overall employment and development of the peripheral areas of Africa. Some rural development experts indicate that about 10-20 percent of the rural labor force is involved primarily in non-farm activities. The non-farm activities provide seasonal and part-time employment for an additional 7-30 percent of rural workers with a peak in the dry season immediately after harvest (Simmons, 1976b; King and Byerlee, 1977 and 1978; Chernichovsky et al., 1985; Norman et al., 1982; Hill, 1977; Okafor, 1983; Thomi and Yankson, 1985). According to Haggblade et al. (1989, p. 1174), non-farm activities include: "all economic activity other than crop and livestock production, encompassing services, construction, mining, commerce and manufacturing. . . . including also agro-industrial activities which store, process and market agricultural commodities."

Policies of spatial decentralization of many African countries which favor smaller cities in investment and planning decisions have contributed immensely to the growth of the medium-sized cities, and they have been growing faster than the largest cities. The growth of medium-sized cities is also aided by the steadily deteriorating conditions of infrastructure and public services in the largest cities. Rapid urbanization in large cities, with its attendant congestion and pollution, coupled with lack of resources, has disastrous effects on living conditions, such as squalid and overcrowded housing; scarcity of clean water; no proper sewage or drainage systems; and no provision of law and order whatsoever. Even, street children often fall prey to organized crime, drugs and prostitution (Massignon, 1993).

Presently in Africa, natural increase of the population residing in the cities, which is the difference between birth rate and death rate, has become a major component of urban growth. According to Aryeetey-Attoh (1997, p. 199), the United Nations estimates that natural population increases will be a dominant factor in the growth of urban centers in North and Southern Africa that are highly urbanized. Comparatively, rural-urban migration will continue to be the most significant urban growth component in West and East Africa that are the least urbanized of Africa's various regions.

Another factor of urban growth is the annexation or addition of adjacent towns which always results in the realignment of city boundaries. Nigeria is a typical example, where large cities have swallowed adjacent towns due to horizontal growth of informal housing, as well as, unplanned and less restrictive development e.g., in the cities of Lagos and Onitsha in the western and eastern parts of the country respectively.

AFRICAN URBAN MORPHOLOGY

The African city system exhibits a two-tier urban structure. The first-tier includes the primate cities and towns in their orbits, showing modern metropolitan characteristics and functions, while the second-tier includes small towns that are more traditional (Bruun and Williams, 1993, p. 267). Morphologically, a typical primate or largest city in Africa depicts urban internal dualism, depending on the site. Dualism is the juxtaposition of formal or modern sector to an informal or traditional sector, or a situation where the modern sector is superimposed on the traditional sector (Mabogunje, 1968). The colonial urban planning saw the partition of urban space into two zones, the "European" or "modern" area and the "indigenous" or "traditional" area. Before political independence in Africa, cities were overly regulated to reflect the colonial zoning influences and the needs of the colonial powers, but after independence, a new city emerged which tend to reflect the new African reality. According to HABITAT (1996, p. 86), the new urban morphology was termed the "self-help city" in the 1970s and the "informal-city" in the 1990s. Thus, the center of urban life has shifted from the Central Business District, with high quality shops and offices, of large and intermediate-sized cities to their peripheries where land is cheaper and much more easily accessible. Here, there are less harassment from the police and less restrictions of the formal planning.

The urban formal sector includes well structured public and private sector enterprises that are officially recognized, nurtured, and regulated by the government. Typically, enterprises with ten or more workers function within the formal sector (Aryeetey-Attoh, 1997, HABITAT, 1996, p. 90). The informal sector (economy) consists of those individuals and smaller enterprises that operate outside the mainstream of government activity, regulation, and benefits. Often, they operate without vendor's license. Informal activities are easy to enter, unregulated, predominantly family owned, small-scale, labor-intensive, many are held by women and immigrants, and they rely on indigenous resources. Nevertheless, the informal sector contributes to the formation of human capital by providing access to training and apprenticeships, generates surplus, employment and value-added of product per volume of investment (Aryeetey-Attoh, 1997). No wonder Sassen (1993, p. 121) calls the informal or traditional sector, the "de-valorized" sector. In other words, this is the "unsung" sector of the economy. Sassen sees the city as concentrating diversity—the immigrant community and the informal economy in conjunction with the dominant modern corporate culture constituting the "over-valorized" sector. According to Sassen (1993, p. 124), many of the devalued sectors of the urban economy actually fulfill crucial functions for the urban centers.

The main informal activities in a majority of African countries include artisans, basket weavers, goldsmiths, garment makers or textile and apparel manufacturing, carpentry and furniture production, tailoring, trade, vehicle and other repairs, metal goods fabrication, restaurants, construction, transport, footwear, and miscellaneous services. It also includes urban small-scale, residual/casual, and home production (HABITAT, 1996; Becker et al., 1994, pp. 159-60). According to Tinker (1997, p. 3), street food (which has been neglected) is a micro-enterprise of the informal sector, providing employment to a majority of women in most African countries. Street food is pervasive in different countries. For example, in Senegal there is "monie" (porridge made from millet and large calabashes) and large meat chunks made of beef; in Egypt, flat-bread sandwiches of foul and tamia, both made from dried beans; and in Nigeria, thick soup sauce served over farina or corn pudding sold from road-side stalls called "buka." Tinker indicates that street food enterprise, like most of the informal sector enterprises, includes mobile or ambulatory vendors, semi-mobile vendors, and residentially vendors. The vendors may roam the streets or rent regular stall space in markets.

Since the last two decades, the urban informal sector has become a powerful force for employment creation in most of the African cities because of the inability of scarce formal sector jobs to accommodate in-migrants. Estimates indicate that, since the mid-1970s in a typical African country, the informal sector employs about 60 percent of the urban labor force. For example, in Congo, the sector employs 55 percent; Senegal, 50 percent; Burkina Faso, 73 percent; Benin, 95 percent; Cote d'Ivoire, 44 percent; and Niger 65 percent. For individual cities, the figures were also high. For example, Abidjan, 44 percent; Nairobi, 44 percent; Kumasi, 65 percent; Lagos, 50 percent; Banjul, 42 percent; Lome, 50 percent; Brazzaville, 37 percent; and Djibouti, 20 percent

(HABITAT, 1966 p.90; UNDP, 1992; ILO, 1985; Charmes, 1990). In most African countries (except say Egypt, see Tinker, 1997, p. 5), whether by commission or omission, the interplay between vendors and governments does not exist. Despite the creative potentials and contributions of the informal sector, little effort has been made to integrate this sector into the mainstream of government regulations and benefits.[3] Such benefits include a potential source of badly needed (tax) revenue for African governments.

THE CONSEQUENCES OF URBANIZATION IN AFRICA

African countries are witnessing rapid and uncontrolled urbanization which has resulted to many problems including, among others, urban primacy, the increasing urban informal sector, mass unemployment, poverty, acute housing shortages and increasing number of informal housing, poor land management and infrastructure provision, deterioration in services, environmental pollution, and inadequate urban management (Ihonvbere, 1992; Kasarda and Parnell, 1993; HABITAT, 1996; Aryeetey-Attoh, 1997; Hardoy et al., 1993). Africa has been described as a "continent in crisis," a "region in turmoil," "on a precipice," and "suffering" (Ramsay, 1993; Herman, 1998). According to Ramsay, Africans today are suffering from the grinding poverty, pestilence, and in many areas, wars that afflict many lives. An average African is poorer today than at independence and the poverty is increasing. Almost all African governments are in debt; have low levels of industrial output which accounts for the continent's relative poverty; a majority engage in food production but still not producing enough food; have an overall population growth rate of 3.5 percent which is higher than the overall growth in the economy of 0.8 percent; and are plagued by debt per capita which is greater than income per capita, of which debt forgiveness might be the only solution (Griesgraber, 1998).

According to HABITAT (1996, pp. 84-85), the 1980s was a "lost decade" for Africa. Evidence indicates that, in East and Middle Africa, seven countries had decreases in per capita income between 1980 and 1990, with no growth in Tanzania and very small growth in Kenya. The seven countries were: Ethiopia, Madagascar, Malawi, Mozambique, Rwanda, Zimbabwe, and Cameroon. In North Africa, Algeria recorded a negative growth, while West Africa presented a similar picture of negative growth, such as in Cote d'Ivoire, Mali, Niger, and Nigeria (see HABITAT, 1996, p.85.). The above deplorable performances by African countries made them to score highly on the misery index (see Table 6.5). In 1993, among the 174 countries that made up the league of nations called the United Nations, the African countries scored poorly on the indicators of well-being which constitute the misery index[4] (Ramsay, 1997). Table 5 shows that South Africa which is highly urbanized and developed ranked 100, while Niger which is one of the least urbanized and developed countries of Africa ranked 174. The above performance reflects a stagnating or declining economy in the face of continuous rural-urban migration. For example, ten years later in 2002 and among 177countries, South Africa slacked to 119 position while Sierra Leone ranked 177 to come last. Between 1993 and 2002, human development index (HDI) worsened in most of the African nations (see United Nations Development Program, UNDP, 2004, pp. 139-142).

A major consequence of urbanization in Africa is the relative concentration of in-migrants in a few cities creating high primacy indices. The national system of cities is loosely integrated with a disproportionate amount of social, cultural, economic, and administrative resources concentrated in the primate or largest cities rather than in the secondary cities of at

Table 6.5: The Misery Index: United Nations Human Development Index, 1993 and 2002[*]

Country	Rank **1993**	Rank **2002**	Country	Rank **1993**	Rank **2002**
Mauritius	54	64	Central African Rep.	148	169
Seychelles	60	35	Mauritania	149	152
Botswana	71	128	Madagascar	150	150
South Africa	100	119	Rwanda	152	159
Swaziland	110	137	Senegal	153	157
Namibia	116	126	Benin	154	161
Gabon	120	127	Uganda	155	146
Cape Verde	122	105	Malawi	157	165
Zimbabwe	124	147	Liberia	158	
Congo	125	144	Guinea	160	160
Cameroon	127	141	Guinea-Bissau	161	172
Kenya	128	148	Gambia	162	155
Ghana	129	131	Chad	163	167
Lesotho	130	145	Djibouti	164	154
Equatorial Guinea	131	109	Angola	165	166
Sao Tome & Principe	132	123	Burundi	166	173
Zambia	136	164	Mozambique	167	171
Nigeria	137	151	Ethiopia	168	170
Comoros	139	136	Burkina Faso	170	175
Togo	140	143	Mali	171	174
Zaire (D.R.C., since 1997	141	168	Somalia	172	
Tanzania	144	162	Sierra Leone	173	177
Sudan	146	139	Niger	174	176
Cote d'Ivoire	147	163			

Source: Jeffress Ramsay, *Africa. Seventh Edition*. Global Studies, (Sluice Dock, Guilford, Connecticut: Dushkin/McGraw-Hill, 1997), p. 6.

1. Standings in a league of 174 countries in1993 and in a league of 177 countries in 2002.

For 2002 data, see United Nations Development Program (UNDP). *Human Development Report, 2004: Cultural Liberty in Today's Diverse World.* (New York/Oxford: Oxford University Press, 2004), Table 1, pp. 139-142.

least 100,000 and up, excluding the largest cities (Rondinelli, 1983). The primate cities sap the rural areas of vital human and natural resources, and at the same time create the existing large de-valorized informal sector found in large cities.

Housing shortages are endemic in most African countries, as well as, uncontrolled deterioration in social services such as in education, health and transportation. The African cities are characterized by a majority of the residents living in informal housing settlements including squatter housing[5]. Many informal housing settlements are concentrated in undesirable parts of the cities, especially on peripheral regions or on sites prone to natural hazards, such as flooding. The urban commercialized land markets often exclude the poorer groups from all possibility of developing housing on safe, legal sites (Hardoy, et al., 1993, p. 89). Ability to pay also denies most Africans the opportunity to own a home, because of the relatively low household incomes. According to the United Nations (1984), the estimates of informal settlements in African cities are as high as, 85 percent in Addis Ababa, 70 percent in Luanda, and 60 percent in Dar es Salaam. In the formal sector, most government housing expenditures are a very small percentage of their gross domestic products (GDP). Table 6.6 shows that in 1990 very few countries allocated more than one tenth of their gross domestic products on housing expenditure; the countries included, Burkina Faso, Central African Republic, Equatorial Guinea, Guinea Bissau, Libya, South Africa, Liberia, and Tanzania. Not only that more money is needed in the housing sector in different countries, but the state-run housing corporations are infested with many problems which include, mismanagement, corruption, and inefficiency (Aryeetey-Attoh, 1997).

Most of the African countries lack the basic infrastructures and services that constitute the underlying foundation and support structure of urban environment.

Table 6.6: Social Indicators and Physical Quality of Life Factors in Africa

	Housing Expenditure (% of GDP), 1990	Telephone #/100, 1991	School Enrollment[1]		Population per Hospital Bed		Population in Poverty Total (%), 1980-1990	H.D.I.[2]
			Primary	Sec.	1975	1990		
Algeria	6	3.4	99	59	352	400	23	0.609
Angola	8	0.8	91	12	368	771	-	0.304
Benin	-	0.3	66	12	851	684	-	0.224
Botswana	-	2.6	116	54	-	-	43	0.646
Burkina Faso	15	0.2	37	8	1750	3392	-	0.150
Burundi	-	0.2	69	7	890	1476	84	0.235
Cameroon	-	0.3	101	28	400	393	37	0.474
Central African Republic	11	0.2	68	12	542	1171	-	0.258
Chad	8	0.1	65	9	763	1373	54	0.157
Congo	-	0.7	-	-	218	-	-	0.395
Cote d'Ivoire	-	0.6	69	24	864	1260	-	0.393
Egypt	-	3.6	101	80	491	536	23	0.499
Ethiopia (former)	-	0.3	22	11	3500	4141	60	0.282
Gabon	1	1.8	-	-	101	800	-	0.525
Gambia	8	1.6	69	20	-	600	-	NA
Ghana	6	0.3	74	38	800	685	42	0.360
Guinea	9	0.2	42	12	562	1804	-	0.162
Guinea Bissau	12	0.6	60	7	572	562	-	NA
Kenya	-	0.8	95	27	800	623	52	0.481
Liberia	-	0.1	35	-	607	-	20	0.333
Libyan Arab Jamahirya	14	5.7	-	-	262	246	-	0.719
Madagascar	-	0.3	79	15	400	1140	43	0.440
Malawi	-	0.3	66	4	650	645	82	0.250
Mali	-	0.1	25	7	1400	-	54	0.143
Mauritania	-	0.4	62	15	2904	1278	-	0.208
Mauritius	-	6.0	106	54	300	300	8	0.788
Morocco	-	1.9	69	35	700	809	37	0.489
Mozambique	9	0.4	60	7	850	1280	59	0.239
Niger	-	0.1	29	7	1974	-	-	0.116
Nigeria	-	0.2	76	23	1799	599	40	0.322
Rwanda	-	0.2	77	10	805	602	85	0.304
Senegal	-	0.6	59	17	775	1385	-	0.274
Sierra Leone	-	0.4	48	16	1103	830	-	0.150
Somalia	-	0.2	11	7	845	1333	60	0.200
South Africa	13	8.8	109	71	-	-	-	0.731

Sudan	-	0.2	51	21	1000	959	-	0.255
Togo	9	0.3	111	23	700	686	-	0.337
Tunisia	-	4.1	120	49	400	516	17	0.657
Uganda	12	0.2	80	14	607	1248	-	0.354
United Rep. of Tanzania	-	0.3	68	5	677	938	58	0.413
Zaire (D.R.C.)	10	0.1	70	24	311	701	70	0.294
Zambia	-	0.8	92	20	300	-	64	0.481
Zimbabwe	-	1.2	119	47	300	1970	-	0.576

Source: United Nations Center for Human Settlements (HABITAT), *An Urbanizing World: Global Report on Human Settlements, 1996*, (New York: Oxford University Press, 1996), p. 526.

1. Gross Ratio
2. The Human Development Index (HDI) ranges from 0 (lowest) to 1 (highest). It is calculated by using index numbers for life expectancy at birth, adult literacy, and adjusted GDP per capita. The figures are from the United Nations' *Human Development Report, 1990*, (New York: Oxford University Press, 1991), pp. 128-129. Also, see Jan S. Hogendorn, *Economic Development*, 2nd edition, (New York, N.Y: Harper Collins Publishers, 1992), Chapter 2.

Inadequate public investment in urban infrastructure and services inhibit economic development, such as in Lagos, Nigeria; Dar es Salaam, Tanzania; Nairobi, Kenya; and Lome, Togo; among others. Table 6.6 also shows that, in the 1990s, a majority of the African countries had less than one telephone head per 100 people. Apart from South Africa and a few North African countries, such as Algeria, Egypt, and Tunisia, most countries that had more than one telephone head per 100 people were relatively small-sized. The majority of people live in non-serviced plots and housing, where telephone and electrical connections are scarcely available.

School enrollments in both primary and secondary level education during the 1990s were low, stagnating or declining in most of the African countries (see Table 6.6). Where enrollments were not declining, the existing schools were overcrowded with many students having minimal contact with their teachers (Aryeetey-Attoh, 1997). The declining or low rate of enrollment exacerbated the prevailing low literacy rates in most African countries, particularly those South of Sahara. In the face of the economic decline and stagnation of the 1980s and 1990s, many school-age children and individuals were generally disillusioned about educational careers, because a majority of the graduates were not absorbed into the labor market. As a result, in most African countries, there was the emergence of massive unemployment of educated individuals, thereby creating a class of the *lumpen intelligentsia*.

Table 6.6 indicates that health service delivery has deteriorated in a majority of African countries. Most countries were worse-off in the 1990s than they were in the 1970s. For example, between 1975 and 1990, population per hospital bed increased in most countries ,such as in Algeria, Angola, Burkina Faso, Burundi, Central African Republic, Chad, Cote d'Ivoire, Egypt, Ethiopia, Gabon, Guinea, Madagascar, Morocco, Mozambique, Somalia, Tunisia, Uganda, Tanzania, Zaire (D.R.C.), and Zimbabwe. Although during this period, Nigeria, for instance, showed a declining population per hospital bed, this was a glaring example of the serious problem of the unavailability of basic drugs in the clinics, and the difficulty of the poor and impoverished obtaining professional medical care. Also, in Nigeria, individual and public corruptions have led to the fraudulent use of corn or cassava starch as camouflage analgesic aspirins. Table 6.6 further supports the earlier statement that Africa is suffering from grinding poverty and many individuals and households incomes are below the poverty level. Between 1980 and 1990, the population in poverty in both rural and urban areas was high. For example, the percentage of total population in poverty was more than 50 percent in many countries such as: Burundi (84%), Chad (54%), Equatorial Guinea (67%), Ethiopia (60%), Kenya (52%), Mozambique (59%), Rwanda (85%), Somalia (60%), Tanzania (58%),

Zaire (70%), and Zambia (64%). The Human Development Index (HDI), which is calculated by using index numbers for life expectancy at birth, adult literacy, and adjusted GDP per capita, summarizes the levels of poor social conditions in Africa. According to Table 6.6, Niger had the lowest HDI (0.116), followed by Mali (0.143), and all of the rest of the countries south of Sahara. Except South Africa (0.731) and Mauritius (0.788) that had the highest, most countries south of the Sahara scored less than 0.500 on the index. Relatively, a majority of the relatively "developed countries" north of the Sahara scored more than 0.500 such as, Algeria (0.609), Libya (0.719), and Tunisia (0.657).

Major urban services in African countries have declined and deteriorated after political independence, especially in the areas of public transportation, water supply, waste management, and environmental quality. Most of these urban services are overburdened, inadequate, and inefficient. In the 1990s, analysis of the transport and transport infrastructure indicates that, in most countries, density (km/1000km^2) of railway and road network is low which causes congestion and traffic grid-lock to occur. A small percentage of urban roads are paved and drained, and the number of motor cars per thousand individuals is relatively small compared to other regions of the world. Inadequate and inefficient transportation systems contribute immensely to the lack of socio-economic development in most of the African countries. According to Brunn and Williams (1993, p. 481), faster and improved transportation systems facilitate and increase population and factor mobility, as well as facilitate regional and interregional transfer of commodities. Table 6.7 shows that railway and road network densities are relatively low in Africa, particularly in Africa South of Sahara. The data further show that less than 10 percent of the roads are paved in different African countries. For example, in Cameroon (5%), Central African Republic (2%), Chad (2%), Cote d'Ivoire (9%),

Gabon (8%), Guinea Bissau (9%), Namibia (8%), Rwanda (6%), Tanzania (4%), and Zaire (2%). By 1991, as Table 7 indicates, the population per thousand owning motor cars was also small, such as in Chad (2.7), Ethiopia (1.2), Mali (3.8), Nigeria (3.7), Somalia (1.6), Togo (1.1), Uganda (2.0), and Tanzania (3.8).

Table 6.7: Transport and Transport Infrastructure in Africa

	Density of Railway (km/1000 km²), 1991	Density of Road Network (km/1000 km²), 1991	Paved Road (%), 1991	Motor Cars (per thousand population) 1991
Algeria	1.7	32	59	48.3
Angola	2.0	59	12	17.7
Benin	5.1	87	11	7.3
Botswana	1.2	16	27	54.4
Burkina Faso	1.8	35	17	6.5
Burundi	-	202	16	4.9
Cameroon	2.5	148	5	7.4
Cape Verde	-	323	31	9.3
Central African Republic	-	40	2	5.2
Chad	-	21	2	2.7
Comoros	-	404	72	10.2
Congo	2.3	28	11	20.0
Cote d'Ivoire	3.6	154	9	20.5
Djibouti	4.3	157	10	18.3
Egypt	8.6	32	45	25.5
Equatorial Guinea	-	143	31	-
Ethiopia (former)	0.6	32	35	1.2
Gabon	1.2	32	8	26.8
Gambia	-	283	18	8.3
Ghana	3.9	154	23	8.3
Guinea	3.8	121	15	15.9
Guinea Bissau	-	115	9	7.7
Kenya	4.6	117	15	12.6
Lesotho	0.1	162	12	10.9
Liberia	5.0	62	39	14.1
Libyan Arab Jamahirya	-	45	78	169.4
Madagascar	1.8	87	10	8.2
Malawi	6.6	112	19	4.8

Mali	0.5	12	15	3.8
Mauritania	0.6	7	11	9.7
Mauritius	-	1134	86	63.7
Morocco	4.0	140	46	40.3
Mozambique	3.9	45	15	4.6
Namibia	2.9	8	8	-
Niger	-	16	22	6.3
Nigeria	3.8	121	28	3.7
Reunion	-	-	-	253.9
Rwanda	-	506	6	2.0
Sao Tome & Principe	-	250	42	26.1
Senegal	6.0	79	27	14.7
Seychelles	-	1079	70	78.6
Sierra Leone	1.2	124	19	12.8
Somalia	-	34	28	1.6
South Africa	19.3	160	29	137.6
Sudan	1.9	4	34	9.2
Swaziland	18.4	204	21	71.5
Togo	9.1	138	25	1.1
Tunisia	15.1	124	76	48.4
Uganda	4.7	122	15	2.0
United Republic of Tanzania	2.8	88	4	3.8
Western Sahara	-	-	-	-
Zaire (D.R.C)	2.2	63	2	5.1
Zambia	2.6	52	16	15.6
Zimbabwe	8.7	202	17	37.8

Source: United Nations Center for Human Settlements (HABITAT), *An Urbanizing World: Global Report on Human Settlements, 1996*, (New York: Oxford University Press, 1996), p. 522.

Many African countries are noted for overburdened public transportation systems, which affect the daily operations of urban residents and businesses. The role of formal public transportation has declined in most African cities that a new informal system has emerged, such as the use of private cars and motorcycles as taxis. The decline in public transportation is due to lack of fiscal, technical and administrative responsibility of African governments, e.g., frequent breakdowns of vehicles, inadequate spare parts, and chronic absenteeism of drivers who "moonlight" in the informal sector (Aryeetey-Attoh, 1997, p. 211). The obvious consequences are high transportation costs in terms of time and money, very congested traffic, and air and noise pollution. Thus, the maintenance and upgrading of urban infrastructure by different African governments to provide a healthy and self-sustaining urban environment cannot be overemphasized.

A small proportion of African cities' populations have direct access to clean, piped water, and regular garbage disposal mechanisms. Shortages in water supply, inequalities in the distribution of water, and inadequate treatment and disposal of wastewater plague most of the African cities.[6] Water and land pollution problems are pervasive in most African cities because many households and businesses are not adequately served by sewers, drains, and garbage collection. Several studies have emphasized the critical role water plays either in spreading disease or in avoiding contamination (Tinker, 1997, p. 4). According to Hardoy, et al (1993, p. 75), shortage of water adds greatly to the problem of disposing of wastes, especially from industries and sewage because large volumes of water dilute wastes and can render them much less dangerous, and also bacteria in the water breaks down organic wastes.

Serious environmental problems exist in most African cities because of inadequate and inefficient solid waste disposal systems. The problems of collection and disposal are so intractable that even toxic and hazardous wastes are disposed untreated in the streams or other nearby water bodies or on land sites without safeguards. More damaging today is the illegal dumping of dirty industries and toxic waste materials, in some African countries, by the more developed and highly industrialized countries of North America, Western Europe and Japan (Hardoy et al, 1993; Anderson, 1992; Castleman, 1987; Durksen and Leonard, 1980). Adequate solid waste disposal helps to maintain a sanitary and healthy environment and enhances one's socio-economic well-being (HABITAT, 1996; Aryeetey-Attoh, 1997; Hardoy, et al., 1993).[7] Environmental problems also plague intermediate-sized cities of less than one million people and smaller cities, because a significant proportion of urban dwellers live in smaller urban centers. According to Hardoy, et al (1993, p. 96), most of the environmental problems in most smaller centers arise from a lack of piped water supplies, or water sources used for human consumption being contaminated, lack of provision for drainage and for safe disposal of excreta and lack of provision for garbage collection and disposal. For example, as prevailing in Jinja and Kabele, Uganda; and Aliade, Igugh and Ugba in Nigeria (see Meekyaa, Ude James and Rakodi, Carole, 1990; and Amis, 1992). The deterioration of services and infrastructure is a consequence of rapid urbanization, whereby the available resources necessary for roads, sewers, water systems, schools and hospitals simply can not cope with the needs of the population.

Land management in most African cities is very problematic because many municipal governments are unable to efficiently issue, register, and maintain records of land transactions. As a result, many urban dwellers live in unplanned, informal, and illegal settlements on the outskirts of large cities or in more crowded and deteriorating high density areas in the city. As the proliferation of informal and illegal tenure arrangements abound, so also are bribery and corruption in obtaining them. For example, in Onitsha, Nigeria, a majority of the plots for housing in the peripheral growth areas are sold by touts, spivs, and chiselers, such that the same parcel of land could be sold to more than one person at the same time. In Cameroon, it is estimated that more than 90 percent of urban residents do not hold registered title on land they occupy (see Mabogunje, 1990).

GLOBALIZATION AND AFRICAN URBANIZATION

African urban development is inseparable from the on-going global development and integration process. Cities are strategic to economic globalization because they are the command point, global market place, and production sites for the information economy (Sassen, 1993, p. 124; and Kasarda and Parnell, 1993). Africa has major cities or world cities of international dimensions. These cities play a major role in the new global economy and integration. According to King (1991, pp. 83-84), the world is viewed as one through "Westernization," "modernization," "internationalization," "bourgeoisification," or "globalization," of the world major cities in the form of modern architecture, skyscrapers, the automobile society, Western high technology, especially in transportation and telecommunications. Distance as a barrier to interaction is virtually non-existence due to telephone and other telecommunication devices, airplanes, and computers with internet connections as one of its functionaries (Brunn and Williams, 1993, p. 480). Globalization is further defined as a combination of much freer trade in goods and services with free capital movement (Brittan, 1998).[8] In other words, globalization conveys the notion of economic integration, a trend which is likely to benefit both developing and industrial world (World Bank, 1998).

The cities are sites for international financial flows, especially for the transactions of financial markets, advanced corporate service firms, banks, and the headquarters of transnational corporations. The African cities that are integrated into a global urban network include, among others: Lagos, Nigeria; Cairo and Alexandria, Egypt; Tripoli, Libya; Algiers, Algeria; Casablanca, Morocco; Abidjan, Cote d'Ivoire; Kinshasa, Congo (DRC); Nairobi, Kenya; Addis Ababa, Ethiopia; Dakar, Senegal; Accra, Ghana; and Johannesburg, South

Africa (HABITAT, 1996, p. 84). Some characteristics of global cities include: center of transnational corporations; seat of international banks; location of world renowned universities; location of major world or regional summits and conventions (e.g., Lagos, world conference of city mayors in 1997; Population Summit, the International Conference on Population and Development in Cairo in 1994; and African Union (AU) meetings in Addis Ababa); and large proportion of non-resident (foreign) population (e.g., the 1990 population estimate of Abidjan of 2.5 million consists of 750,000 foreign residents, which is 32 percent of the total population; and according to the 1989 population census of Nairobi of 827,775 people, 183,818 were without Kenyan nationality, which is 22 percent of the total population (Sassen, 1993, pp. 126-127).

Undoubtedly, millions of people in Africa are currently drawn into a genuinely unified world economy. The consequence is that, African countries are playing greater role in global economies, politics, and policies. African cities are assuming a greater part in global decision making as the traditional European world cities, such as Rome, Stockholm, Paris, London, and New York. Nonetheless, the longevity and sustainability of "world city" functions by African cities are relatively doubtful, because of the prevailing urban crisis. Such urban crisis include: stagnating and declining economy; high unemployment rate; increasing informal sector which is largely devalorized; deterioration of urban infrastructures; and deterioration in service delivery, especially water supply, solid disposal, public transportation, and environmental quality. The success of African countries in the present globalization and integration process is also going to be jeopardized by the fact that almost all African governments are in debt, and debt per capita being greater than income per capita, as well as dollar debts exceeding the foreign exchange reserves of the countries concerned (see *The Economist*, 1993, pp. 7-12; *Developing World*, 95/96, pp. 42-45). In most of the African countries, debt burdens are more than their exports which create balance of payment problems and budget imbalance (see Table 6.8). The African domestic debt crisis is likely, in the near future, to contribute to recessions in the lender industrial countries, such as the United States of America, Britain, France, Germany, and Japan. Table 6.8 indicates that, within ten years— between 1980 and 1991—, debt as percent of export more than doubled in most African countries. The Table further indicates that during debt peak years, debt as percent of export reached more than 1000 percent in Mozambique, Sao Tome and Principe, Sudan, Tanzania, and Uganda, and more than 3,000 percent in such countries as, Guinea Bissau and Somalia.

The above factors will really slow down national and urban economic development and globalization in Africa. After more than five years after the dawn of the 21st Century, Africa's globalization processes remain relatively weak and bleak. According to the World Bank (1998), the downside of the globalization trend is that the benefits are not evenly distributed and some developing countries, especially African countries, are lagging further behind.

LOOKING AHEAD: AFRICAN URBAN FORMS AND PROBLEMS IN THE FUTURE

According to Kasarda and Parnell (1993, pp. 97-100), between 1950 and 1990, economically active population (labor force) in Africa more than doubled from 99.2 million to 243.The projection for 2000 was 318 million people. The labor force will grow to nearly 650 million by the year 2025. They also noted that between 1950 and 1990, the percentage of labor force in nonagricultural occupations in Africa has also doubled from 18.2 percent to 36.8 percent respectively, and should triple to 55.5 percent in the year 2025. Further, at the turn of 21st century, 42.5 percent of the population

Table 6.8: Debt as Percent of Exports in Selected African Countries, 1980-1991

Country	Year		
	1980	Peak (year)	1991
Algeria	128.6	313.2 (1987)	199.3
Angola	102.4	242.9 (1991)	242.9
Burundi	180.1	925.7 (1990)	758.9
Congo (DRC)	163.7	444.5 (1986)	424.4
Cote d'Ivoire	159.4	509.6 (1991)	509.6
Egypt	214.9	547.3 (1987)	280.0
Equatorial Guinea	511.5	618.6 (1991)	618.6
Ethiopia	136.2	635.2 (1991)	635.2
Ghana	108.3	384.5 (1991)	384.5
Guinea-Bissau	927.9	3463.7 (1986)	3086.9
Kenya	170.4	329.6 (1987)	313.7
Liberia	111.8	389.4 (1987)	389.4
Madagascar	242.4	853.4 (1988)	795.9
Mali	227.5	508.6 (1986)	473.4
Mauritania	306.7	458.2 (1991)	458.2
Morocco	223.8	400.5 (1985)	255.5
Mozambique	1209.0	1731.0 (1987)	1287.2
Nigeria	31.8	427.8 (1988)	257.1
Sao Tome & Principe	100.7	1779.8 (1990)	1779.8
Sierra Leone	153.5	765.7 (1990)	765.7
Somalia	253.5	3572.0 (1988)	2594.7
Sudan	504.7	2742.6 (1991)	2742.6
Tanzania	370.3	1118.7 (1990)	1118.7
Uganda	221.6	1298.3 (1991)	1298.3
Zaire (DRC)	201.0	442.4 (1987)	438.9
Zambia	201.0	773.8 (1986)	503.4

Source: *Developing World, 95/96,* Annual Edition, (Sluice Dock, Guilford, Connecticut: The Dushkin Publishing Group, Inc, 1996.), p. 44.

should engage in nonagricultural occupations, leaving about 60 percent of the labor force engaged in agriculture. The above continental conditions call for: more numerical growth in the number of future urban settlements; growth in size of the existing settlements; and filling-in of the open spaces between large cities. The participation in economic globalization and changes in labor force in different African countries may bring about some new and different functional orientations of cities in the future. The question is whether the technological, economic, political, and ideological environment of the "New World Order of Globalization" and integration will strengthen the traditional forces, making for continued inequality and misery (Herman, 1998, p. 52).

As long as the informal sector continues to increase in the face of debilitating economic conditions, the importance of the African governments in providing basic needs and services will continue, and the appearance of future cities will still be dispersed and horizontal rather than clustered and vertical. The basic needs and services include: affordable and sound housing, potable and running water, available and accessible healthcare, schools to improve literacy, model farms and marketing systems, and rudimentary transportation and communications systems (Brunn and Williams, 1993, p. 488). As long as economic growth rate continues to lag behind population growth rate, the problems of adequately satisfying and providing basic human needs will continue to persist in all African cities.

The future urban problems in Africa are likely to be multi-faceted, which include economic, social, political, administrative, and environmental problems. The tide of rural to urban migration will likely to continue, with the expansion of the peripheral settlements, hence the morphologically dispersed and horizontal settlements. Public resources to service them are likely to continue to contract unless the countries will adequately and vigorously address the issues of grinding poverty, pestilence, immiseration and wars that create economic and political instabilities and refugees.

Adjustment problem will occur in many cities as they move from pre-industrial to industrial and post-industrial economies. New economic, political, cultural, and social forces will likely shape the cities, pattern urbanization, and create new physical and spatial forms of the built environment. How to maintain economic growth with sound environmental management will be problematic, especially on how to balance intergenerational equity with pro-growth policies.

BEYOND THE URBAN AND SOCIAL MALAISE: SOME POLICY RECOMMENDATIONS

African urbanization is not an expression of capitalist industrialization, as witnessed in the more developed countries (MDC's) of Western Europe and North America, where industrialization kept pace with urbanization. African urbanization is an expression of rapid population concentration characterized by urbanization running ahead of industrialization; slow or declining economic growth; and the imbalance between industrial, social, administrative infrastructure and the demands and expectations of the in-migrants.[9] The results have been a debilitating and devastating urban crisis which include, among others, urban primacy; massive unemployment; deterioration in urban infrastructures and services; rapid increase of the informal sector activities; environmental problems; and the uncertainty of the role of African cities in the globalization and integration of world economy. Response by many African governments, especially after political independence, had been inadequate and ineffective.[10] According to HABITAT (1996, p. 88), the response failed to capture the speed and direction of growth, especially in the peripheral areas, and in some cases never supported by the level of capital expenditure necessary to implement their infrastructure projections. Others saw it as lack of fiscal, technical, and administrative responsibilities on the part of African governments, and the absolute inability of policy makers and development experts to address the issues.

Most of the large cities in Africa which were founded by the colonists have outgrown their sites, which were considered safe and convenient centuries ago (see Hardoy et al., 1993, p.89; Aryeetey-Attoh, 1997). Thus, the policy recommendations should address the above problem issues. First, African urbanization is characterized by increasing high primacy index reflecting the concentration of population in one or two large cities with a loosely integrated urban system. In most African countries, development efforts, such as investments, are in favor of urban areas, especially the large cities, thereby creating a pronounced rural-urban dichotomy. Plans and programs should be implemented to decentralize urban activities, especially to small- and intermediate-sized centers. African governments should make these alternative growth centers more attractive by more of the investments being in their favor. This will help stem rural to urban migration or capture a large number of rural migrants going to already overburdened large cities, since migration is step-wise in a majority of African countries (see Aka, 1991). The process is also likely to stem the ever increasing unemployment and underemployment in the primate cities.

Second, unemployment is very pervasive in many African countries that even the university-educated professionals have great difficulty finding secured employment, talk less of the unskilled labor pool. As long as fertility rate is high in most countries, the economically active population or labor force will be increasing with high unemployment, especially in the urban areas. Undoubtedly, more and more urban dwellers should be working in the burgeoning informal, small-scale, and unregulated sector, which barely provides for their basic needs. Consequences include (HABITAT, 1996, p. 90): continued growth of spontaneous, popular housing areas; increasing number of ambulant hawkers and food-sellers inside the cities; increase in the number of open-air markets; pervasive small-scale, privately owned public-transport vehicles; and virtual explosion of small trades and services dealing with every facet of life in the cities. As African countries struggle for development, efforts should be made to increase their levels of industrial output, coupled with adequate family planning policies and strategies to slow down the natural increase of the population. The combined effort of high level of industrialization and low fertility rate are likely to have direct and indirect effects in the economy. For example, the effort may lead to a development state when economic growth will keep pace with urban growth; when basic needs and services will be adequately provided; and when a substantial increase in personal and national income will occur, such that debt per capita should be less than per capita income.

Third, urban dualism is a major feature of African cities, depicting the coexistence of formal and informal sectors in the economy. The informal sector of the economy is largely neglected in terms of government services and benefits, unregulated, and non-valorized by most of the African governments, despite their aforementioned contributions to the city and national economies. The informal sector comprises of vendors of different goods and services. Efforts should be made by different African countries to integrate the informal sector into the mainstream of government regulations and benefits. With adequate and appropriate government regulations, the informal sector is a potential source of much needed revenues for African city governments. There should be an interplay between vendors and governments about the methods by which they should be organized and regulated, and about the types of services the vendors need. For example, small-scale credit or micro-credit lending by government financial institutions not only will reduce poverty but promote other development goals (Yunusi, 1998). More efforts will be directed toward the extension of public services to this valuable sector of the economy.

Fourth, African cities are characterized by infrastructure and service deterioration, especially in solid waste disposal; public transportation; education, health and social services; and in the provision of adequate housing, piped water, electricity, sewerage and roads. Inadequate services and infrastructure, as well as proliferation of informal and illegal tenure arrangements are more acute in the ever-expanding peripheral settlements of the African urban areas. With the present horizontal and dispersed growth of a majority of African cities, and the public resources to service them continue to dwindle, a new approach to the planning and management of these cities have to emerge if they are going to be viable social entities in the new millennium. Despite the efforts towards city planning, most African city government should emphasize more on city mending. It is essential, therefore, for governments to maintain and upgrade the infrastructure to provide a healthy and self-sustaining urban environment.

Fifth, since public transportation problems in African cities are a result of a lack of fiscal, technical, and administrative responsibility on the part of African governments, the governments should seek alternative measures to ease congestion and pollution, such as transportation demand management (TDM) that encourages bike paths, pedestrian walkways, car/van/bus pooling through the high occupancy vehicle (HOV) lanes. Another measure that would conserve available scarce resources and improve accessibility is transportation system management (TSM), which tends to maintain the existing facilities without major construction activities, such as, the provision of stop signs where necessary, and synchronization of traffic lights. Since a majority of African city governments are disengaging from the responsibility for providing a whole range of local services, a new balance should emerge between private and public activities. For example, a potential exists for private investment to substitute for public investment through the privatization of some services, such as urban transport, airport services, non-piped water services, and waste collection and disposal (World Bank, 1994, p. 115). Nonetheless, all African countries should invest in education, health, and essential infrastructures, such as roads and telecommunications facilities, which will make the accessibility and mobility of factors of production a lot easier, as well as, quicken the overall national socio-economic development.

Sixth, environmental problems are very serious in most of the African countries which are aggravated by the lack of effective planning and regulation systems. As a matter of fact, very few governments have shown much interest in controlling industrial pollution of air, land, and water (Hardoy, et al., 1993, p.64). Inefficient heaters, cookers (especially using solid fuel), very congested traffic, inefficient and poorly maintained engines in most road vehicles add greatly to air pollution. The most devastating is the transfer, to African countries, of dirty industries, dangerous industrial equipment, outdated industrial technology, and toxic wastes themselves from North America, Western Europe, and Japan, among others (Hardoy, et al., 1993, pp. 68-69; Durksen and Leonard, 1980; Castleman, 1987; Mackenzie and Mpinga, 1988; Consumer Information and Documentation Center, 1988; Kone, 1988; Phantumvanit and Liengcharernsit, 1989; Anderson, 1992).[11] The combustion of fossil fuels used by the industrial processes, for heating and electricity generation, and by motor vehicles contribute to outdoor pollution in urban areas, to major health hazards, to acid rain and to ozone depletion. Serious water pollution is from non-point sources since large proportion of households and businesses are not served by sewers, drains, and garbage collection. The poorer groups of the urban dwellers bear most of the environmental costs since many of them live on sites prone to natural hazards. All African governments should take measures to control air pollution at the source, as well as promote and encourage efficient fuel use, such as the use of the least polluting fuels e.g., natural gas rather than coal with high sulfur content for domestic and industrial use, and unleaded petrol for motor vehicles (World Bank, 1992). The illegal dumping of toxic wastes and industrial wastes in African countries by the more developed Western and Far Eastern countries should be stopped posthaste. People's health should be of primary concern than economic profits.

Seventh, all African countries should embark on a comprehensive sewage and storm system which makes it much easier to control non-point water pollution, since the wastes collected by the system can be treated before being returned to rivers, lakes, estuaries and the sea. Adequate and constant provision of water, especially in the urban areas, is essential in the disposing of wastes, especially liquid wastes from industries and household sewage. Good governance and a stable and prosperous economy are needed by all African countries to enable them control industrial pollution and occupational exposure, and to promote environmental health. Most local environmental problems need local institutions, such that a competent representative local government is necessary for the long-term solution to any city's environmental problems (Hardoy, et al., 1993, p. 207).

Eighth, as we are in the era of time-space convergence and the world has become increasingly interconnected by a vast array of communications and transportation networks, the "world cities" of Africa must prepare themselves to partake in the globalization activities. A city that is "globally" conducive for business and conventions should be literate, politically stable, and environmentally friendly and dynamic. These conditions are required of all African governments. Free trade and capital flows or economic globalization and integration may help African cities emerge from the misery of socio-economic underdevelopment and modernization.

Therefore, African national and urban development strategies should be inseparable from global economic policies and development processes.

CONCLUSION

African urbanization is rapid, erratic, intractable, non-sustaining, and contradictory. For example, a gap exists: between the industrial, social and administrative infrastructure, on the one hand, and the demands and expectations of the population, on the other; between urban population growth and the pace of economic growth; and between urban primacy and environmental response. Rapid urbanization coupled with declining or stagnating economic performance of many African countries have created many urban problems, including but not limited to urban primacy, deteriorating infrastructure and services delivery system, inadequate urban management and land management, the increasing urban informal sector which is greatly non-valorized, acute housing shortages and proliferation of squatter settlements, unguided urban sprawl which creates more dispersed and horizontal urban form, and environmental degradation and pollution. These problems are likely to continue in the African urban future, unless adequate and countervailing measures are taken, such as those recommended.

After political independence, most of the African governments responded to the above urban problems without success. The reasons for their failure include, among others, the lack of financial capital; the inability of the African policy makers and development experts to articulate and capture the speed and direction of growth, especially in the peripheral areas; and the unwillingness and inability of the policy makers to implement urban policies and programs. African leaders are perplexed and confused about how to fund and plan for the basic needs in the face of rapid population growth, increasing indebtedness, and conflicting development goals and priorities.

The urbanization process in Africa should not be viewed in isolation from the much larger world system. Many African large cities are "international" or "world" cities, which are likely to play major roles in the on-going globalization and its attendant economic integration processes. The nexus of urbanization and socio-economic development in the 21st Century Africa should go beyond the traditional increase in economic growth rates. The relationship will also consider, according to Kasarda and Parnell (1993, p.2), a broader range of development goals, such as equity, welfare, political instability, quality of life, efficiency, and environmental quality and protection. If African cities of the new millennium should play their expected role as major centers of production for industry, services and trade, and so generate resources and jobs, then African urbanization ought to curb population growth through targeted family planning and full employment of the economy. For African countries to succeed, they must invest in human capital by providing greater access to education and health care, pursue economic reform, increase savings, and reduce the endemic private and public corruption (see Kristof, 1998). Presumably, African countries will then reach a development stage where urbanization is running behind industrialization, and urban economic growth keeping pace with or ahead of urban population growth.

Notes

1. Internet. ABC News.Com, June 4, 1997. Copyright 1997 Associated Press, by Angus Shaw. The statement was made during the First Free-Trade Zone Meeting of the African Leaders on Tuesday, June 3, 1997, in Harare, Zimbabwe at the OAU meeting to inaugurate the African Economic Community.
2. Over-urbanization is the process of rapid urbanization which is characterized by urbanization running ahead of industri-

alization. The result is that the industrial, social, and administrative infrastructure cannot accommodate the demands and expectations of in-migrants (see Aryeetey-Attoh, 1997; Breese, 1966).

3. Street food vendors organizations, such as the one in Minia, Egypt, which the composition of its governing board includes both vendors and local decision makers (see Irene Tinker, *Street Foods: Urban Food and Employment in Developing Countries,* (New York, Oxford: Oxford University Press, 1997), p. 5.
4. Indicators of well-being can be divided into two components (HABITAT, 1996, p. 99): (a) the constituents of well-being e.g., health, life expectancy, civil and political rights; (b) the main determinants of well-being e.g., income, housing quality, and accessibility of schools, health care services and other social facilities (see also, Partha Dasgupta, and Martin Weale, "On Measuring the Quality of Life," *World Development*, Vol. 20, No. 1, 1992, pp. 119-31).
5. Informal housing settlements include: (i) slum housing in which physical features violate minimum standards; (ii) invasion housing in which dwellers occupy the land illegally regardless of standards; and (iii) squatter housing which violates both the legality of land occupancy and physical standards. (See G. Lim, "Housing Policies for the Urban Poor in Developing Countries," Journal *of American Planning Association*, Vol. 53, No.2, 1987, pp. 176-185.
6. Shortages are due, in part, to insufficient foreign and local revenues for local governments to enable them purchase imported chemicals to treat and purify water and acquire spare parts to maintain existing water lines. (see R. Stren, "Administration of Urban Services," in R. Stren and R. White (eds.), *African Cities in Crisis.*, (Boulder, CO: Westview Press, 1989), pp. 247-275.
7. For more detailed information on environment and well-being, see also, B. Schaeffer, "Home and Health on Solid Foundations?" *World Health Forum*, Vol. 11, 1990, pp. 38-45; Solvig Ekblad et al., *Stressors, Chinese City Dwelling and Quality of Life*, D12, (Stockholm: Swedish Council for Building Research, 1991); and David Bradley, et al, *A Review of Environmental Health Impacts in Developing Country Cities,*

Urban Management Program Discussion Paper, No. 6, World Bank, UNDP and UNCHS (HABITAT), (Washington, DC., 1991).

8. The economic case of globalization is that, it has enabled countries with high rate of savings and relatively low returns on investment to lend to others with low savings but a higher return on capital. In the International Monetary Fund's (IMF) words, a great benefit from globalization is, "world level fluctuations would be damped owing to the lack of synchronization of disturbances across national economies and a partial absorption by external imbalances." This statement is in light of the (1997/1998) Asian financial crisis (involving Indonesia, Korea, etc.) in which case there could be a need for timely "monetary easing" in the developed world "to arrest an escalating downturn," among the Asian Tigers (see Samuel Brittan, "Who's Afraid of Globalization?" *Financial Times, London*, World Business Newspaper, Thursday, January 8, 1998, p. 11.
9. In Britain, U.S., and Japan, industrialization was closely tied-in with the development of artisan industry, which filled niches not adequately supplied by factories and provided a technological base important to future industrial development. In developing countries, especially African countries, urbanization and national development are characterized by "international demonstration effect," whereby national surpluses of relatively poor countries are frittered away in elite purchases of fashionable foreign consumer goods rather than being used to stimulate domestic industry or provide investment funds for indigenous development. Despite indications of growth in many developing countries, the benefits continue to be skewed in favor of socio-economic elite. Furthermore, the costs associated with this growth fall disproportionately on the poorest segments of society. (see Herman, 1998, p. 50).
10. The responses to urban crisis and the contradictions in most African countries after political independence have included urban master planning; series of national development planning schemes, including town and country planning efforts, and large-scale government sponsored construction of resi-

dential dwellings, through slum clearance and public housing programs.

11. The dirty industries and toxic wastes themselves are transferred, with little or no consideration of possible consequences for local population, through multinational corporations avoiding the costs of meeting workplace safety and pollution standards. For example, asbestos-related industries—arsenic production, lead refining, battery manufacture, metal smelters and biocide production. Export of toxic wastes has affected African states like Nigeria, Benin, and Guinea Bissau.

References

Adepoju, A. (1983). "Issues in the Study of Migration and Urbanization in Africa South of Sahara." In P. Morrison, ed., *Population Movement: Their Forms and Functions in Urbanization and Development.* Liege, Belgium: Ordina Editions.

Aka, E.O. (1991). "The Functions of Intermediate-Sized Cities in Innovation Diffusion and National Socio-Economic Development in Developing Countries." *African Urban Quarterly.* Vol.6. Numbers 3 and 4, (August and November), pp. 175-184.

Amis, Philip (1992). *Urban Management in Uganda: Survival Under Stress.* The Institutional Framework of Urban Government: Case Study No. 5. Development Administration Group. INLOGOV, University of Birmingham, Birmingham.

Anderson, Ian (1992). "Dangerous Technology Dumped on Third World," Report of a Paper by Nabiel Makarim, presented at a Conference on the Trade in Hazardous Machinery or Technology, Melbourne, Australia, *New Scientist,* March 7, quoted in Jorge Hardoy, Diana Mitlin and David Satterhwaite (1993). Environmental Problems in Third World Cities. London: Earthscan Publications.

Arthur, J.A. (1991). "Interregional Migration of Labor in Ghana, West Africa: Determinants, Consequences, and Policy Intervention." *The Review of Black Political Economy.* Vol. 20. No. 2, pp. 89-103.

Aryeetey-Attoh, Samuel (ed.) (1997). *Geography of Sub-Saharan Africa*. Upper Saddle River, New Jersey: Prentice-Hall.

Becker, C., A. Hamer and A. Morrison (1994). *Beyond Urban Bias in Africa: Urbanization in an Era of Structural Adjustment*. Portsmouth, N.H: Heinemann.

Bradley, David et al (1991). A Review of Environmental Health Impacts in Developing Countries' Cities. Urban Management Discussion Paper No. 6. World Bank, UNDP and UNCHS (HABITAT). Washington DC.

Breese, G. (1966). *Urbanization in Newly Developing Countries*. Upper Saddle River: Prentice-Hall.

Brittan, Samuel (1998). "Who's Afraid of Globalization?" *Financial Times, London*. World Business Newspaper, http://www.FT.com. Thursday, January 8. p. 11.

Brockerhoff, M. and H. Eu (1993). "Demographic and Socio-economic Determinants of Rural to Urban Migration in Sub-Saharan Africa." *International Migration Review*, Vol. 28. No.3, pp. 557-577.

Castleman, Barry I. (1987). "Workplace Health Standard and Multinational Corporations in Developing Countries," in Charles S. Pearson (ed.), *Multinational Corporation, the Environment and the Third World*. Durham, USA: Duke University Press, pp. 149-172.

Charmes, J. (1990), "A Critical Review of Concepts, Definitions and Studies in the Informal Sector." In D. Turnham et al (eds). *The Informal Sector Revisited*. Paris: OECD Development Center.

Chernichovsky, Dov, Robert E.B Lucas and Eva Mueller (1985). *The Household Economy of Rural Botswana: An African Case*. World Bank Staff Working Paper No. 715. Washington, DC: The World Bank.

Consumer Information and Documentation Center (1988). *Consumer Currents*. March-April. International Organization of Consumers Union, pp. 5-6.

Dasgupta, Partha and Martin Weale (1992). "On Measuring the Quality of Life." World Development. Vol. 20. No. 1, pp. 119-131.

Duerksen, Christopher and Leonard, Jeffrey (1980), "Environmental Regulations and the Location of Industries: An International Perspective." *Columbia Journal of World Business*, Summer, pp. 52-58, quoted in Jorge Hardoy, Diana Mitlin and David Satterthwaite (1993). Environmental Problems in Third World Cities. London: Earthscan Publications, Ltd.

Economist. The (1993). "Debtors Prison." *The Economist*. September 25. pp. 7-12. Distributed by the New York Times Special Features.

Eicher, Carl et al (1970). *Employment Generation in African Agriculture*. Report Number 9. Institute of Agriculture, Michigan State University, East Lansing.

Ekblad, Solvig et al (1991). Stressors, Chinese City Dwelling and Quality of Life, D12. Stockholm: Swedish Council for Building Research.

Griesgraber, Jo Marie (1998). "Forgive Us Our Debts: The Third World Financial Crisis." In Developing *World, 98/99*. Annual Editions. Sluice Dock, Guilford, Connecticut: Dushkin/McGraw-Hill, pp. 54-60.

Gugler, J. and Flanagan, W. (1978). *Urbanization and Social Change in West Africa*. Cambridge: Cambridge University Press.

Haggblade, Steven, Peter Hazell, and James Brown (1989). *Farm-Nonfarm Linkages in Rural Sub-Saharan Africa*. World Bank Reprint Series, Number 450. Reprinted with permission from *World Development*, Vol. 17. No. 8, pp. 1173-1201. Published by Pergamon Press, Great Britain.

Hardoy, Jorge, Diana Mitlin and David Satterthwaite (1993). *Environmental Problems in Third World Cities*. London: Earthscan Publications Ltd.

Herman, Edward S. (1998). "Immiserating Growth (2): The Third World." In *Developing World, 98/99*. Annual Editions. Sluice Dock, Guilford, Connecticut: Dushkin/McGraw-Hill, pp. 49-53.

Hill, Polly (1977). *Rural Hausa: A Village and Setting*. Cambridge: Cambridge University Press.

Hoddinott, J. (1992). Modeling Remittance Flows in Kenya." *Journal of African Economies*, Vol. 1. Issue 2, pp. 206-232.

Ihonvbere, Julius O. (1992). "The Third World and the New World Order in the 1990s."In Robert J. Griffiths (ed.) *Developing World, 1997/98*. Sluice Dock, Guilford, Connecticut: The Dushkin Publishing Group, Inc., pp. 6-15.

International Labor Organization (ILO) (1985). *Informal Sector in Africa.* Jobs and Skills Program for Africa. ILO, Addis Ababa, pp. 13-15.

Joshi, H. et al (1976). *Abidjan: Urban Development and Employment in the Ivory Coast.* Geneva: International Labor Organization.

Kasarda, John D. and Allan M. Parnell (eds.) (1993) Third *World Cities: Problems, Policies, and Prospects.* Newbury Park, London, New Delhi: Sage Publications.

King, Anthony D. (1991). *Urbanism, Colonialism, and the World-Economy: Cultural and Spatial Foundations of the World Urban System.* London and New York: Routledge.

King, Robert P. and Derek Byerlee (1977). "*Income Distribution, Consumption* Patterns *and Consumption Linkages in Rural Sierra Leone.*" African Rural Economic Paper, No. 16. East Lansing, MI: Michigan State University, Department of Agricultural Economics.

King, Robert P. and Derek Byerlee (1978), "Factor Intensities and Locational Linkages of Rural Consumption Patterns in Rural Sierra Leone." *American Journal of Agricultural Economics.* Vol. 60. No.. 2, (May), pp. 197-206.

Kone, Sidiki (1988), "Stop Africa from Becoming the Dumping Ground of the World." *The Siren*, No. 31, pp. 2-3.

Kristof, Nicholas D. (1998), "Why Africa Can Thrive Like Asia," in *Developing* World, *98/99*. Annual Editions. Sluice Dock, Guilford, Connecticut: Dushkin/ McGraw-Hill, pp. 70-73.

Lim, G. (1987). "Housing Policies for the Urban Poor in Developing Countries." Journal of American Planning Association. Vol. 53. No. 2, pp. 176-185.

Mabogunje, Akin L. (1968). *Urbanization in Nigeria.* New York: Africana.

Mabogunje, Akin L. (1990). *Perspective on Urban Land and Urban Management Policies in Sub-Saharan Africa.* Washington, DC: World Bank.

Mackenzie, Deborah and James Mpinga (1988). "Africa Wages War on Dumpers of Poisonous Waste." *New Scientist.* June 23. pp. 30-31.

Massignon, Nicole (1993). "The Urban Explosion in the Third World." In Robert J. Griffith, (ed.). *Developing World, 95/96.* Sluice Dock, Guilford, Connecticut: The Dushkin Publishing Group, Inc., pp. 203-207.

Meekyaa, Ude James and Carole Rakodi (1990), "The Neglected Small Towns of Nigeria." *Third World Planning Review.* Vol. 12. No. 1, pp. 21-40.

Mhloyi, M. (1987), "The Proximate Determinants and their Socio-Cultural Determinants: The Case of Two Rural Settings in Zimbabwe." *The Cultural Roots of African Fertility Regimes.* Proceedings of the Ife Conference, Ife: Obafemi Awolowo University, pp. 125-149.

Norman, David W., Emmy B. Simmons and Henry M. Hays (1982). *Farming Systems in the Nigerian Savanna: Research and Strategies for Development.* Boulder, CO: Westview Press.

O'Connor, Anthony (1983). *The African City.* New York: Africana Publishing Company.

Okafor, Francis C. (1983), "Rural Employment Diversification in Anambra State, Nigeria: Its Nature and Implications for Development." *Labor, Capital and* Society. Vol. 16. No. 2, pp. 226-239.

Phantumvanit, Dhira and Liengcharernsit, Wanai (1989), "Promoting Clean Technologies in Developing Countries." *Environment and Urbanization*, Vol. 9. No. 1, pp. 31-39.

Ramsay, Jeffress F. (ed.) (1993). *Africa.* Fifth Edition. Sluice Dock, Guilford, Connecticut: The Dushkin Publishing Group, Inc.

Ramsay, Jeffress F. (ed.) (1997). *Africa.* Seventh Edition. Annual Editions Publication. Guilford, Connecticut: Dushkin/McGraw-Hill, p. 6.

Rondinelli, D. (1983). *Secondary Cities in Developing Countries.* Beverly Hills: Sage Publications Ltd.

Sassen, Saskia (1994). *Cities in a World Economy.* Thousand Oaks, London, New Delhi: Pine Forge Press.

Schaffer, B. (1990). "Home and Health on Solid Foundation?" World Health Forum. Vol. 11, pp. 38-45.

Stren, R. (1989). "Administration of Urban Services." In R. Stren and R. White (eds.). African Cities in Crisis. Boulder, CO: Westview Press.

Tinker, Irene (1997). *Street Foods: Urban Food and Employment in Developing Countries.* New York, Oxford: Oxford University Press.

Thomi, W.H., and P.W.K. Yankson (1985). *Small Scale Industries and Decentralization in Ghana: A Preliminary Report on Small Scale Industries in Small* and *Medium Sized Towns in Ghana.* Frankfurt and Accra. Institut fur Wirtschaft and Sozialgeographie/Department of Geography.

Todaro, M. (1969). "A Model of Labor Migration and Urban Unemployment in Less Developed Countries." *American Economic Review.* Vol. 59. No. 1, pp. 138-148.

United Nations (1984). *Land for Human Settlements.* Nairobi, Kenya. United Nations Center for Human Settlements.

United Nations (1995). *World Urbanization Prospects: The 1994 Revisions.* Population Division, New York.

United Nations Center for Human Settlements (HABITAT), (1996). *An Urbanizing World. Global Report on Human Settlements, 1996.* Oxford, New York: Oxford University Press.

United Nations Development Program (1992). *Human Development Report.* New York: Oxford University Press.

United Nations Development Program (2004). *Human Development Report, 2004. Cultural Liberty in Today's Diverse World.* New York, Oxford: Oxford University Press.

World Bank (1992). *World Development Report, 1992.* New York: Oxford University Press.

World Bank (1994). *World Development Report, 1994: Infrastructure for Development.* New York: Oxford University Press.

World Bank (1998). "Economic Trends in the Developing World." In *Developing* World, *98/99.* Annual Editions. Sluice Dock, Guilford, Connecticut: Dushkin/ McGraw-Hill, pp. 49-53.

World Population Prospects: The 2004 Revision. Population Database. *World Population Prospects: The 2004.*

Revision and World Urbanization Prospects: The 2003 Revision. Population Division of the Department of Economics and Social Affairs of the United Nations Secretariat. http://esa.un.org/unpp. Accessed Online on 10/02/07.

Yunus, Muhammad (1998). "Empowerment of the Poor: Eliminating the Apartheid Practiced by Financial Institutions." In *Developing World, 98/99.* Annual Editions. Sluice Dock, Guilford, Connecticut: Dushkin/McGraw-Hill, pp. 61-64

Zachariah, K. and J. Conde (1981). *Migration in West Africa: Demographic Aspects.* New York: Oxford University Press.

Chapter 7

The Tragedy of the African Environment

F. Wafula Okumu

INTRODUCTION

The environment in Africa is in a critical state. The destruction of the ecosystems and depletion of non-renewable resources has accelerated to an alarming level: the land has been degraded; the forests are disappearing; the biological diversity of the fauna and flora is declining at an alarming rate; natural resources, such as freshwater, are being misused; the soil, water, and air are being polluted; garbage is an eyesore in virtually all the urban centers; and the health of the people is threatened by hazardous and toxic waste dumping, lack of food and safe drinking water, and exposure to numerous health hazards. These, and many other indicators, point to the sad reality that "Africa is on the verge of ecological collapse" (Forje, 1984, p.573). Unless drastic actions are taken to reverse the tragic trends of environmental abuse, misuse and neglect, Africa's future survival might be imperiled.

This chapter seeks to address three major interrelated issues. First, it traces the history of the environmental tragedy confronting Africa. Second, it examines some of the most challenging environmental issues facing the continent. Third, it then offers some solutions to these problems.

THE HISTORY OF THE TRAGEDY OF THE AFRICAN ENVIRONMENT

The tragic state of the African environment can be traced to various sources, but specifically the policies and practices of colonial and post-colonial states, superpowers, and international financial institutions. The Berlin Conference of 1884-1885 is the landmark event that triggered the merciless and massive exploitation of African resources. Indeed, the partition of Africa among European powers is a clear reflection of how the resources of Africa were identified and exploited. For instance, Zambia and Ghana were created as mining colonies, Malawi and Burkina Faso as labor reservoirs, and Zimbabwe and Kenya as settler colonies.

Colonialism contributed to the tragedy of the African environment in a number of ways. Europeans established and administered colonial states in Africa to serve as sources of agricultural products such as coffee, tea, cocoa, sugar, cotton, bananas, peanuts, and sisal; and minerals such as copper, gold, silver, and diamonds. These resources were not only exploited with impunity but also with total disregard to the impacts of these activities on the environment. In the most fertile places, the European colonialists introduced large-scale commercial farming which mainly focused on high-intensity crops that extracted more nutrients and required heavy use of chemicals. To make room for plantations and dairy farms, large tracts of land were cleared.

Since its "discovery" and occupation to the present time, many Europeans and Americans have gone to Africa on adventurous safaris to hunt elephants, lions, buffaloes, leopards, and other exotic animals roaming the savannas of East, Central and Southern Africa. Even those who had settled in Africa regularly indulged in wildlife hunting as a favorite pastime. In the eyes and minds of Europeans and Americans, there has existed an image of Africa as a land of ferocious wild animals and rugged terrain that need to be tamed. This impression has led to the allure of Africa as a land of adventure and big game hunting. This perception of Africa has been boosted and glorified in books, movies, television series such as *Tarzan*, and magazines such as the *National Geographic*. Both Winston Churchill's *My African Journey* and Theodore Roosevelt's *African Game Trails* evoke an Africa that Bonner calls (1993) "still in the Pleistocene era." Ernest Hemingway was to build on these views of Africa in *The Green Hills of Africa* and *The Snow of Kilimanjaro*, which was latter made into a movie starring Eva Gardner and Gregory Peck. Other movies that have portrayed Africa as a land of adventure are *Mogambo* starring Clark Gable and Eva Gardner, *Out of Africa* starring Meryl Streep and Robert Redford, *Gorilla in the Mist* about Dian Fossey's life with mountain gorillas in Rwanda, and Michael Douglas' *The Ghost and Darkness*.

Africa's highly mineralized ancient metamorphic rock contains some of the most coveted minerals by the industrialized countries. Among Africa's rich metallic ores are bauxite, cobalt, copper, diamond, gold, magnesium, silver, tin, titanium, and uranium. In 1990, Africa possessed 20 percent of the world's reserves of bauxite, chromium, cobalt, copper, iron, lead, lithium, manganese, molybdenum, nickel, tin, titanium, tungsten, vanadium, and zinc (World Resource Institute, 1992, p.322). Africa is also endowed with 14 percent of the world's offshore oil proven reserves and 16 percent of offshore proven gas reserves. Africa's oil, particularly Nigeria's, is both ecologically and strategically desirable to America because it is unusually sulfur-free and "it represents diversification from Middle Eastern sources (Cohen, 1998, p.1)."

It is this rich resource base that attracted Europeans such as Cecil Rhodes and Ernest Oppenheimer to establish large mining conglomerates that still survive to this day. The preferred method of mining was open- earth, which excavated large tracts of land to extract minerals needed in European industrial production. Today, while flying over some parts of Africa, one cannot fail to notice gaping holes and painful scares that are testimony to what the continent has endured as its coveted minerals were extracted.

A large labor force was needed to grow the cash crops and extract the minerals. This led the colonialists to consciously promote policies that increased population to get cheap labor that was needed to excavate the mines and till the plantations. Excessive taxation was one of the methods that was used to force Africans into employment in mines and plantations, where low wages meant all the able-bodied members of the family had to be engaged in employment. The bigger the family, the more hands were available to earn the meager and measly pay that was used to pay taxes and buy European goods. The need for bigger families became more pronounced when Africans were allowed to engage in limited cash cropping. Again, the urge to generate wealth led to the need for bigger families. Henceforth, the assumption that big families were sources of income has persisted to the present time.

When colonial rule came to an end in most of Africa, the former colonies were transferred into the hands of a comprador bourgeois class that continued, unabated, to practice colonial policies. Most of the new leaders promised their subjects immediate development and the same good living as that led by the colonialists. President Kwame Nkrumah of Ghana is widely quoted to have told one of his followers that "an elephant has been slaughtered and there was enough meat for everyone." This has come to symbolize the mentality of the leaders who have seen African resources as plentiful and inexhaustible. Consequently, these leaders have adopted economic and agricultural policies, similar to those practiced during colonialism, of extracting as much resources as they can so that they can export to earn money for development projects such as schools, hospitals, and roads.

By adopting the classical Western development paradigm that essentially ignored ecological issues in the broad sense by assuming that the environment had the capacity to absorb the burden of development, these African leaders made an egregious mistake. They had no understanding that Africa had reached its natural carrying capacity. It is unfortunate that today "the significance of the environment in the development process is still not properly grasped by the policy makers (Forje, 1984, p.568)." Consequently, according to Forje, "concrete corrective measures have not been taken to protect natural resources in order to improve the human environment (Forje, 1984, p. 568)."

The prevailing official mentality and development paradigm is to increase the quantities of export products. By exporting more minerals and agricultural products, the assumption, now aggressively promoted by international financial institutions such as the International Monetary Fund (IMF) and the World Bank, is that more foreign currency will be earned to acquire Western symbols of development (Bayalama, 1992). But this dependence on the export of primary products and fluctuating international prices has meant "that nations are motivated to exploit their resources to the fullest, (which in turn) exerts pressure on the natural carrying capacity of resources and, of course, leads to the abuse and exhaustion of limited resources" (Forje, 1984, p. 569).

After four decades of exporting raw materials from Africa, the continent is distinct for its pervasive poverty and economic stagnation. The common explanation for Africa's pathetic state of underdevelopment has been that it lacks resources. However, Forje argues that "there is minimal correlation between natural resources and the level of economic development in Africa; the existence or non-existence of natural resources does not immutably determine the economic development of a nation" (Forje, 1984,p. 572). According to Forje (1984, p. 572), unlike the Danes and Japanese,

> who do not have a natural resource base... African countries center their process of development purely on the abundance of natural resources. The problem, however, is that even with the abundance of natural resources, policy makers in Africa have not ploughed back achievements or profits from the exports of agricultural products to further development. . . . (Thus, the argument that) underdevelopment is necessarily associated with the lack of resources simply do not stand up to scrutiny.

Sachs and Warner (1995) whose study demonstrates that countries that are rich in natural resources have on average performed poorly in economic terms compared to those that are resource-poor also back this view.[1] Even worse and contrary to a multinational investment pitch, mining activities have created fewer jobs in poor countries (Daniel, 1992).

Africa is faced with the challenge of converting "some of its natural resources into knowledge, skilled labor and knowhow" (Forje, 1984, p. 573). So far, the African countries "have not been able to trade their resources in the proper way to build a solid stock of human knowledge and capability to protect its environment and prolong the natural carrying capacity of individual nation states" (Forje, 1984,p. 573).

Countries with rich natural resource base, such as Angola, Cameroon, Congo (Kinshasa), Cote d'Ivoire, Gabon, Nigeria, and Zambia, are underdeveloped because they lack "the knowledge, organizational skill, and trained manpower in converting natural resources into finished products which are then exported" or consumed by their populations. Forje (1984, p. 573) argues that,

> African policy makers and political leaders have not fully appreciated the "interdependence of natural resources and technical process," but have rather fallen prey to the conceptual orientation of technical progress and international trade and capital which are out of their control. So far, policy makers have not developed any mechanism that enables them to dictate, control and influence the pattern of international trade. To develop such a control mechanism requires considerable political will, interest and planning.

It is also notable that policy makers in Africa are subscribers to an anthropocentric notion that assumes that natural resources are inexhaustible and are there to be exploited for the benefit of human beings. This notion that has been reinforced by the Western liberal ideology that fosters materialism, consumerism, and capitalism has energized the exploitation of nature rather than supported a "harmonious balance between the environment and exploitation of resources" (Forje, 1984, p. 575).

Western liberalism also favors economic values such as capital accumulation, enhanced trade, and economic growth over ecological values that protect nature. Thus, capitalism requires that the market becomes the determining force of ecological and social justice considerations. This ideology is imbedded in the Lockean thought that legitimizes virtually endless accumulation of material goods and equates the process of accumulation with liberty and the pursuit of happiness. Locke also contends that with ingenuity, human beings can go beyond the fixed laws of nature, adhering only to whatever temporary laws they establish for themselves while in the process of pursuing their happiness. Furthermore, he promotes the idea that happiness is only achievable through each person's pursuit of private gain, and that there will always be enough for those willing to work.

In the aftermath of the Cold War, a missionary zeal has evolved among the Western capitalist nations to spread "free and liberalized markets" in every corner of the globe. Adoption of capitalist economies and the nurturing of consumer populations are now primary conditions for disbursing aid to those countries in need. However, what is being overlooked is the fact that the survival of capitalism depends on a "consumer class." And this is the class that is wreaking havoc on the environment by contributing to the release of virtually all ozone depleting chemicals; two-thirds of the greenhouse gases and pollutants that are causing acid rain; radioactive waste; and other environmentally harmful chemicals and products.

The tragedy of the African environment can also be traced to superpower policies during the Cold War and the structural adjustment programs and lending policies of international financial institutions such as the IMF and the World Bank. Africa was for more than three decades used as a playground for superpower geo-political games. Superpower rivalry was played on the continent through arming of allies and proxies to promote the respective superpower's strategic and ideological interests on the continent. The victims of this rivalry are strewn all over the continent from the Cape of Good Hope to the Horn of Africa and the far-western end of the Continent. These superpowers propped up or coddled dictators who flagrantly violated the rights of the people and cared less about the environment. Many used the forests to destroy human life and to harvest their resources. The brutal practices of dictators such as Idi Amin of Uganda, Jaffer Numeiri of Sudan, Siad Barre of Somalia, Mengistu Haile Miriam of Ethiopia, and Samuel Doe of Liberia forced millions of Africans to seek refuge in other countries.

The World Bank and the IMF have contributed to the destruction of the African environment by funding development programs and implementing structural adjustment policies that are ecologically unfriendly. The World Bank has funded "development projects" such as dam construction, roads leading to mines or markets, and ports for export of raw materials. The IMF's structural adjustment program contains conditions that promote increased exploitation of natural resources to bolster export earnings. In view of this history, policies, and practices, it is no wonder that Africa at the dawn of a new millennium is facing the most challenging environmental problems faced by any other continent. In the following section, I explore the most prominent challenges facing the African environment.

THE MAJOR CHALLENGES FACING THE AFRICAN ENVIRONMENT

The Organization of African Unity (now the African Union), United Nations Environmental Program (UNEP), and United Nations Economic Commission for Africa (UNECA) have identified the following as Africa's major environmental concerns: degradation and desertification of the land; lack of protection and unsustainable use of forests; mismanagement and destruction of biological diversity; inefficient management of water resources; pollution; demographic changes and population pressures; urban waste disposal; and dumping of toxic waste and hazardous chemicals. The first environmental problem facing Africa is the degradation of the land. Because of its age and long exposure to the tropical sun and rain, Africa is a very fragile continent. As a result, the original top surface has been eroded, leaving bare, poor and infertile soils. The rich and fertile soils found in a few places such as the Niger delta and the Kenya highlands have been devoted to cash crop farming of coffee, cocoa, tea, wheat, and horticultural products. Subsistence farming, which has to compete with other cash crops such as sugar cane, tobacco, cotton, and sisal, takes place in the less fertile areas. In 1990, Africa had an estimated 3 billion hectares of land, of which 6.2 percent was cropland, 29.7 percent permanent pasture, 22.9 percent forest and woodland, and 27 percent wilderness (World Resource Institute, 1992, p. 262).

Africa has "the world's largest expanse of drylands, covering roughly 2 billion hectares of the continent or 65 percent of (her) total land area" (Global Environmental Outlook, 1997, p. 25; UNEP, 1991, p. 262). These drylands, which are inhabited by more than half of the continent's population and a third of which are hyper-arid deserts, have recurrent droughts (Darkoh, 1994; Toulmin, 1997). These droughts have severely affected subsistence farming and pastoral activities, caused famine, malnutrition and death, and increased desertification (Thomas and Middletown, 1993; Ohlsson, 1995; Dahlberg, 1994).

Although the extent of land degradation, particularly clearance of vegetation cover and soil erosion, has not been fully and precisely determined due to lack of data, the Global Assessment of Soil Degradation estimated in 1990 that "about a half-billion hectares in Africa are moderately to severely degraded." This corresponded "to one third of all cropland and permanent pasture on the continent" (Global Environmental Outlook, 1997, p.26) According to Thomas and Middleton (1993), soil degradation is mainly caused by overgrazing; extensive clearance of vegetation for agriculture; deforestation; extensive cultivation of the marginal lands; the use of inappropriate technology; poor management of arable lands; land shortages; marginalization of subsistence farming due to agricultural modernization; and droughts (Thomas and Middletown, 1993). The consequences of these factors and activities are depletion of soil fertility, water and wind erosion, salination, and food insecurity and insufficiency (Global Environmental Outlook, 1997, pp. 25-26).

Land degradation is further undermining agricultural production by stripping the soil of key nutrients, such as phosphorus, which is essential in the production of biomass. The surface crusting has, in turn, affected water infiltration and retention capacity of the Africa soil. The danger posed by this land degradation is being felt most in agricultural production on which most of the African countries are heavily dependent for their Gross Domestic Product (GDP) (Global Environmental Outlook, 1997, p. 26). The rate at which land is being degraded in Africa is not only alarming, but it is also posing a grave danger to agricultural production. Since most African farmers cannot afford enough fertilizers, they are essentially mining the soils for nutrients "three to four times faster than they are replaced" (Brown, 1998, p.101). This degradation of the land, according to a 1995 World Bank report, cost Africa's land about 20 percent of its productivity in the 1980s. Consequently, Africa has become more and more reliant on foreign food aid as illustrated by the increase of food (cereal) aid from about 3.5 million metric tons in 1977-1979 to 5.7 million metric tons in 1987-1989 (World Bank, 1995).

The second environmental challenge facing Africa is the protection and sustainable use of forests. A forest resources assessment carried out by FAO in 1990 found out that approximately 38 percent of Africa's total land area is covered by forests and other woods. Of the 1.14 billion hectares of forests and wooded land, about 530 million hectares are tropical forests (Global Environmental Outlook, 1997, p.26). Africa's rain forests are being depleted at an annual rate of 0.7 percent. According to a 1994 UNEP report,

Africa's forests "are the most depleted of all the tropical regions" (Global Environmental Outlook, 1997, p.26). And a 1995 FAO *Forest Resource Assessment* report pointed out that between 1980 and 1990 temperate forests decreased by 0.9 percent (Ruffins and Coleman-Adebayo, 1992).

Although there are many causes of deforestation in Africa, the major one is forest clearance for agriculture, fuel, and timber trade (SARDC, 1994; United Nations Economic Commission for Africa, 1992). A study conducted in 1992, by World Conservation Monitoring Center, found out that cultivation accounted for 70 percent of the deforestation in sub-Saharan Africa. And a 1993 SADC report pointed out that 70 percent of the total energy consumed and 90 percent of the household energy in sub-Saharan Africa is derived from wood fuel (SADC ELMS, 1993). Cote d'Ivoire's economy that flourished in the 1960s and 1970s in large part because of the export of timber has seen its export earnings from timber products plunge to nearly zero because "the timber was harvested on a unsustainable basis" (Brown, 1998) Nigeria that was once an exporter of tropical hardwoods is now an importer of forest products. Uncontrolled logging and forest clearance by other human activities have stripped forest covers. The shrinking of the forest cover has increased rainfall runoff, which in turn has contributed to flooding and soil erosion. Thus, deforestation is exacerbating aquifer depletion by reducing the amount of water that percolates downward to recharge aquifers.

A third environmental challenge facing Africa is how to effectively manage and protect its bio-diversity. Africa is endowed with very high species diversity of flora and fauna (James, 1993). This biological diversity ranges from endemic species found in the Indian Ocean islands, to the exotic wildlife roaming the Savanna plains or inhabiting the rain forests, and rare plant species and migratory birds found in the wetlands. The Savannas, which are the most extensive ecosystem in Africa, "are the richest grassland regions in the world, with a high incidence of indigenous plants and animals and the world's greatest concentration of large mammals" (Global Environmental Outlook, 1998, p. 28).

Africa's biological resources—its species, habitats and ecosystems—are facing significant threats from development, tourism, pollution, grazing, poaching, over-harvest of plants and trees, fire, nature, and inadequate or insufficient management and protection (World Resource Institute, 1992, p.302). Most game sanctuaries are either terribly mismanaged or have become playgrounds for bandits. In some countries where wildlife park employèes ran poaching syndicates, the population of game animals has been significantly depleted. For example, Kenya's elephant population plummeted from 160,000 to only 16,000 between 1975 to 1990. Over the same period, the number of rhinos declined from 20,000 to less than 500; that is a 97 percent disappearance (Sunday Nation, 1998). The African red Colobus monkey, whose habitat ranges from Kenya to Senegal, is now classified by the International Union for the Conservation of Nature and Natural Resources (IUCN) as "near-threatened" due to hunting and habitat loss (Brown, 1998, p. 47).

In Gabon, a burgeoning wild game and ivory trade is threatening the traditional livelihood of the Bongon pygmies' the same way as the tropical forest is being threatened by an expanding logging industry. Besides subsistence hunting, there is also a thriving commercial "bushmeat" industry that is threatening gazelles, elephants, iguanas, and lowland gorillas, harming the environment, and profoundly changing the lives of the Bongons (New York Times, 1998).

Human activities, such as cultivation and animal grazing, are also depriving wildlife of its habitat land. The African vegetation, which has some of the world's rarest flora and fauna species, is being foraged by 22 percent of the world's sheep and goats and 14 percent of the world's cattle (World

Resource Institute, 1992, p. 276). Since only 18 percent of the grains produced in Africa are fed to livestock, these animals have to forage the earth and in many places they have to compete with wildlife for grass and scarce water. These activities are not only stressful to the land but have also contributed to the "loss of medicinal and aromatic plants of high value" (Global Environmental Outlook, 1998).

In South Africa, indigenous trees, such as the *fynbos*, have been destroyed by the black wattles, Port Jackson trees and Australian myrtle, which are not only alien to Africa but are also sucking up Africa's most precious resource: water. As such, the South Africans have launched an environmental movement targeting alien species of trees. The Ministry of Water Affairs and Forestry has created a public works program employing 40,000 people to clear watershed areas of alien trees and brushes (McNeil, 1998).

Whereas the wildlife habitats have been dwindling due to expropriation of the land by growing human populations, the "wetlands are under threat from conversion (draining and filling), overuse, pollution from farm runoff and untreated urban and industrial effluents, and unplanned development" (Global Environmental Outlook, 1998). Coastal ecosystems are also being threatened by erosion, pollution from construction of harbors and industrial plants, expansion of tourist resorts, and the growth of human settlements (Global Environmental Outlook, 1998). This threat will increase as more people settle close to the coast. For instance in 1980, population in coastal urban agglomerations stood at 43 million but stood rose to an estimated 112 million in 2000 (World Resources Institute, 2001).

Although only 4 percent of Africa's natural areas were protected in 1990, a number of African countries have taken various steps to conserve their biodiversity (World Resource Institute, 2001). There were, for instance, 727 protected terrestrial areas in Africa (World Resource Institute, 2001) and 112 protected marine areas in 2001 (Global Environmental Outlook Yearbook, 2007). Namibia, South Africa, Botswana, Zimbabwe and Kenya have launched aggressive ecotourism programs aimed at protecting the wildlife and generating revenue from tourism (Bonner, 1993). By setting aside and protecting land exclusively for wildlife, 40 species of "megafauna" in East and Southern African "that would otherwise almost certainly be sliding into extinction" have been conserved (Brown, 1998). However, protected areas need to be expanded to all areas of high biological diversity. As of 1991, there were only 82 botanical gardens with rare and threatened plants (World Resources Institute, 1993, p. 306). The African countries, with the assistance of environmental organizations such as the World Wide Fund for Nature and the World Conservation Union, need to map out "ecoregions" where future protected areas will be located (Brown, 1998, p.56).

A fourth environmental challenge facing Africa relates to water resources issues, particularly the problem of water scarcity and efficient water management. Water, in particular rainfall, is a crucial factor in the lives of the people and nation-states. Most of the agricultural production in Sub-Saharan Africa is dependent on the rain. But due to fluctuating rainfall, falling below the mean level since 1968, Africa has had frequent droughts with devastating outcomes (United Nations Environmental Program, 2005). Agricultural chemicals, industrialization, land degradation and deforestation are also adversely affecting water quality and aquifer levels (World Bank, 2007).

Although Africa has 23 of the world's major lakes (World Resources Institute, 2005) and receives 4 trillion cubic meters of renewable water annually, only 4 percent is used (World Resources Institute, 2005). Due to poor infrastructure, lack of technical know-how, and meager financial resources, Africa has not been able to effectively use its water resources (United Nations Environmental Program, 2005). The underground water, 15 percent of the renewable water resources and a major source of supply, is being overexploited and deteriorating in quality due to lack of proper assessment and management (Global Environmental Outlook Yearbook, 2007).

All the African countries rely on water sources such as rivers that flow from neighboring countries and aquifers or share one or more river basins for their water needs. There are at least 54 rivers or water bodies that not only cross or form international boundaries on the continent but there are also a number of lakes that are shared by many countries. There is a growing concern, and this is also a potential source for serious conflict, that few of these rivers and lakes are effectively managed jointly. Whereas rivers such as the Nile, Zambezi, Volta, and Niger and lakes such as Victoria and Tanganyika can be used for cooperation and economic integration, they also have the potential to create serious conflicts as well (Global Environmental Outlook, 2002).

The region of Africa where conflict is brewing over the use of water resources is the Northeast. In this region, water is not only a scarce commodity but it is also a vital one, as it is needed for agricultural irrigation, industrial expansion, and human consumption (Global Environmental Yearbook, 2007). Since underground water supplies, or aquifers, can only be drawn once and will eventually run out, the Nile River remains the only reliable source for renewable water supplies in the Nile Basin (Global Environmental Outlook, 2002). Although six of the nine states which share the Nile's water are experiencing acute water shortages, Egypt and Sudan have already defined access to the Nile as a vital national priority. This means these two states are willing to go to war over access to the Nile's waters.

The overuse and misuse of the Nile River has led to serious consequences. An example of the misuse of the Nile was the construction of the Aswan Dam and Lake Nasser. The former has caused severe environmental damage by interfering with the silt from the river that for millennia has fertilized Egypt's cropland as it flowed down the river. Now chemicals have to be used to fertilize the land. The banks and the deltas have also been eroded and are not being replenished by the silt that used to be carried down the river. Since there is increased evaporation in Lake Nasser, the Nile water is now saltier when it gets to the fields. Another danger posed by the misuse of the Nile is in the delta area where the barriers protecting the low lands are being eroded, making the coastal land vulnerable to rising sea level. Further competition over freshwater is arising from individual consumption, agricultural activities, fishing, industrial activities, power supply, livestock and wildlife use, recreation, and watershed protection. As this competition intensifies there is increased potential for local, national and regional conflicts.

But the factors that are putting most pressure on water resources, both in terms of quantity and quality, are "rapid population growth, urbanization, industrialization, and the drive for food security." As a result, "domestic wastewater, industrial effluents, and agrochemicals are polluting both freshwater and coastal resources causing health hazards, eutrophication, and stress on aquatic and marine ecosystems (Global Environmental Outlook Yearbook, 2007). Consequently, the people are being exposed to water-related diseases such as malaria, river blindness, schistosomiasis, onchocerciasis, and filariasis. According to the World Health Organization (WHO), in its 1995 *The State of World Health Report*, Africa has the highest percentage, 58 percent, of people without access to safe drinking water. Furthermore, the poor water supply has aggravated the inadequate sanitation thus creating conditions for the spread of infectious diseases such as cholera. Cholera, a serious "threat to human health posed by environmental deterioration," has become pandemic in Africa particularly West Africa where "more than 45,000 cases and nearly 3,500 deaths" were reported in 1991" (World Resources Institute, 1993)

A fifth environmental challenge facing Africa arises from pollution problems, particularly those affecting the air quality, land nutrients, freshwater resources, and coastal and marine areas. Africa contributed 3 percent of the carbon dioxide emitted in the atmosphere in 1989 from industrial production. However, 80 percent was produced by five countries, which were also ranked among the "50 countries with the highest industrial emissions of carbon dioxide" (World Resources Institute, 1993). In 1989, Africa emitted 7 percent of the other greenhouse gases emitted into the atmosphere by all continents in the world (World Resources Institute, 1993). The 23 percent of the carbon dioxide that African countries emitted from land-use activities were only surpassed by South American countries that emitted 28 percent (World Resources Institute, 1993).

Africa's vast coastline, with "open ocean, near-shore waters, beaches, lagoons, sand dunes, mud, and sand flats, rocky cliffs, sea grass beds, coral reefs, and mangroves," has one of "the richest fishing grounds in the world and contain great wealth" (Global Environmental Outlook, 1997, p.33) But these coastal areas are being adversely affected by, among other factors, pollution. Pollution is mainly caused by untreated and unchecked sewage and effluents, which are discharged in rivers, lakes, seas, and the oceans.[2] Pollution is seriously damaging aquatic life and coastal ecosystems. Another serious source of marine pollution is oil spillage.

On January 12, 1998, a pipe from one of Mobil's 57 offshore wells in the Niger Delta snapped and spilled 40,000 barrels of oil, or roughly one-sixth of what the giant Exxon Valdez spilled in Alaska. On June 27, 1998, a ship sank at the Kenyan port of Mombasa while unloading its cargo of chemicals and fuels. As fuels created an oily surface, it also mixed with water to emit "foul odor and toxic fumes" that engulfed the port and choked many in the vicinity (Pan-African News Agency, 1998).

A sixth environmental challenge facing Africa is the impact that demographic change and population pressures are having on natural resources and urban areas. In 1950, Africa had 222 million people, that was 8.8 percent of the world's total population then. By 1990, Africa's population, which has been growing at an annual rate of about 3 percent, had almost tripled to 642 million or 12 percent of the world's population and reached 747 million in 1995. With an annual growth rate of 2.9 percent and a doubling time of 20-30 years, Africa's population is projected to be 1.6 billion by 2025 (World Resources Institute, 1993, p.246). Since 1975, 45 percent of Africa's population has consistently been below 15 years of age (World Resources Institute, 1993, p. 248).

Although 65 percent of Africans live in rural areas, urbanization is increasing at a very rapid rate. Whereas in 1960 only 18 percent of the population lived in urban areas, there were 83 million living in urban areas in 1970, and in 1990, the numbers soared to 206 million (Global Environmental Outlook, 1997, p. 35) In the 1990s, Africa's urban population grew at an annual rate of 5 percent. According to Hinrichsen and Marshall (1991, p. 18), a number of factors contributed to Africa's high level of urbanization. These are "rapid population growth, natural disasters, ethnic tensions, armed conflict, prospect of jobs and higher incomes, poverty and lack of land in rural areas, and declining returns from agricultural commodities" (Hinrichsen and Marshall, 1991, p.18).

African towns and cities lack basic environmental services, such as proper garbage disposal, sewer treatment, clean water, proper sanitation, and pollution abatement. This has increased urban health problems such as respiratory infections and diarrheal diseases. Lagos, like most African cities, is dotted by garbage dumps, which during the rainy season are washed into the drainage system, creating environmental and health problems for the inhabitants.

Garbage collection in African cities is hamstrung by lack of equipment, vehicles, and refuse incinerators. For instance, the city of Cotonou, Benin, with a population of more than one million that disposes 140,000 tons of garbage annually, "has only four tractors and one dump truck for household waste collection and disposal operations" (Idrissou, 1997, p.1) A study on waste management in Benin, conducted in 1995 by Adrien Affogbolo, found out that the government's poor mechanism for waste collection, disposal and treatment was worsened by the city's inhabitants who had developed habits of littering streets and undeveloped plots of land.

Although air pollution levels are still low in most African urban areas, in the major cities it is neither monitored nor controlled. Besides exhaustion from automobiles and emission from factories, the burning of grasslands and forests also pollutes the air in Africa. The harmful effects of this pollution are felt most by the children and the poor who cannot afford basic health care. In March 1996, a University of Michigan team issued a report that showed that most children in African cities had blood-lead levels high enough to cause neurological damage. The team also reported that more than 90% of children suffered from lead poisoning.

Intra- and interstate conflicts, which are usually caused by differences over resource distribution, are significantly altering the spatial distribution of Africa's populations. These conflicts have not only made 7 million Africans refugees but have also internally displaced 17 million. Consequently, Africa has gained a distinction as a continent with "the largest number of people in the world forced to leave their homes" (Global Environmental Outlook, 1997, p.35). Interstate and civil wars have played a major and harmful role in destroying the African environment. Wars in the Lake region, the Horn of Africa, Southern and Central Africa, and in West

Africa have degraded the environment by creating millions of environmental refugees, destroying wildlife, overexploiting natural resources, and directly destroying forests by logging trees or making them inhabitable for rebel forces. Environmental refugees, those fleeing from degraded lands that can no longer sustain human populations, are growing at an alarming rate.

Refugees and their animals that have a high demand for food, firewood and grass usually strip the land of crops and vegetation where their camps are located. But there are also cases where the environment has been targeted in armed conflicts. In Angola, Jonas Savimbi, whose rebel force the National Union for the Total Independence of Angola (UNITA) waged a protracted civil war from 1975-2000 ostensibly to topple the Angolan government, financed his guerrilla activities by poaching elephants and selling their tusks. During the Ethiopian- Eritrean war in the 1980s, the Mengistu government's air force deliberately destroyed forests "to deny shelter to rebel forces."

Environmental deterioration in Africa is intricately linked to rapid population growth and poverty. These two factors have combined to accelerate deforestation and the expansion of agriculture into marginal areas, leading in turn to land degradation," which in turn has exacerbated "food insecurity, loss of biodiversity, decline in water quality, and decrease in health status. However, the African Common Position on Environment and Development downplays the high population growth by urging that the source of Africa's problems is the maldistribution and underexploitation of its resources. It further states that slowing population growth "will not necessarily minimize or eliminate existing levels of poverty, unemployment, and unevenness in income distribution" (United Nations Economic Commission for Africa, 1992, p.1).

The seventh environmental challenge facing Africa is the dumping of toxic waste and the prevalence of hazardous chemicals. The legal and illegal dumping of toxic wastes from overseas is regarded, by Ruffins and Coleman-Adebayo (1992, pp. 5-6), as "one of the most pernicious ecological threats facing Africa." Toxic waste from western Europe and the United States has been deposited in Benin, Equatorial Guinea, Gabon, Guinea (Conakry), Guinea Bissau, Nigeria, Sierra Leone, Somalia, South Africa, and Zimbabwe. Ibrahima Niang, Chairman of the African Network for the Promotion of Exchanges and Environmental Protection, expressed concern that asbestos manufacturers have turned the continent into a dump for their cancer-causing roofing material. Chrysotile, the most commonly used type of asbestos in the African construction industry, has been determined to contain carcinogenic properties, which cause cancer in humans.

Toxic waste has been dumped illegally in some African countries "because local authorities were bribed, deceived or lacked the technical expertise to accurately assess the toxicity of the imported material" (Ruffins and Coleman-Adebayo, 1992, pp.5-6). Ruffins and Coleman-Adebayo (1992, pp. 5-6) narrates the following incidents of toxic dumping in Africa:

> In the mid-1980s, Benin signed contracts to accept industrial waste containing asbestos and cyanide. In February of 1988, Guinea-Bissau signed a five-year contract to accept 15 million tons of European industrial waste in exchange for $120 million a year, an amount nearly equal to that nation's gross national product of $150 million. One Norwegian firm dumped 15,000 tons of 'raw materials for bricks' on a resort island owned by Guinea. After trees and plants there started dying, an investigation revealed that the material

> was really incinerator ash originally from Philadelphia containing lead and other heavy metals. An Italian firm deposited 10,000 steel drums in an empty lot in the small Nigerian town of Koko. Reportedly the company paid $100 a month to rent the lot and hired workers for $2.50 a day to unload the drums, which were later found to contain toxic and nuclear wastes.

An Algerian researcher at Oran University, Kadhem Amoudi, conducted a desert animal study in 1998 that found out that nuclear wastes buried in the Algerian Sahara Desert during French colonial rule and in Somalia by Americans during the Cold War were "causing adverse environmental effects" (Pan-African News Agency, 1998, p.2). The study also points out that these wastes have had a negative impact on desert wildlife, increased the mortality of camels, led to the extinction of certain African desert animals, and introduced "serious diseases such as cancer, which were historically non-existent in the Arab-African region" (Pan-African News Agency, 1998, p. 2).

When President Siad Barre was ousted from power in 1989, Somalia was thrown into a state of anarchy. As a series of warlords waged a senseless war against each other, firms that specialize in the disposal of hazardous waste took advantage of the prevailing anarchy and dumped several thousand tons of toxic waste in Somalia and off its coastal waters. In December of 1991, Achair Partners, a Swiss firm, and Progresso, an Italian firm, entered into an $80 million agreement with Nur Elmy Osman, a former health official in the Barre government to build a 10 million-ton storage facility for hazardous waste (Inter Press Service, 1992). Somalia's environmental problems were made worse when a storage facility in the northern part of the country filled with pesticides was destroyed during the war spilling chemicals and poisoning the few sources of drinking water. Due to the chaotic state of the Somali Republic, no trade protection measures are effective at this time. It is also worth reiterating that Somalia has still not signed the Basel Convention or the Bamako Convention, which bans the import of hazardous waste in African States.

In June 1998, the Namibian government denied the city of Walvis Bay permission to construct a waste-to-power project using 100,000 tons of waste imported annually from New York. The rationale given for this denial was that it would contravene the constitution that bars toxic dumping in the country. The Organization of African Unity passed a unanimous resolution in 1988 that asked African nations to cancel all agreements they had entered into to import nuclear or hazardous waste.[3] Nigeria has not only enacted laws making toxic and hazardous dumping a crime punishable by death, but has also spearheaded a regional program called "Dumpwatch" to monitor dumping in the region in the aftermath of the Koko dumping.

A common source of hazardous material is the presence of, and reliance on, chemicals such as Polychlorinated Biphenyls (PCBS), sulfur and cyanide. The United Nations Environment Program International Register of Potentially Toxic Chemicals has identified PCBS as among the 12 persistent organic pollutants (POPS) on the list of industrial, consumer and agricultural chemicals. PCBS, which are used as pesticides or in industrial productions, are highly stable compounds that persist in the environment for a long time before breaking down. They can accumulate in the tissue of man and animals through drinking, eating and breathing contaminated water, food and air.

In June 1997, Mozambique's environment minister, Bernardo Ferraz, admitted to the existence of large quantities of abandoned agro-chemical products in ports and farms countrywide (Pan African News Agency, 1997). These chemicals that had been abandoned in deficient storage conditions, were contaminating soil and water. The minister also acknowledged the existence of radioactive materials, which had been used in mining, in the provinces of Tete and Nampula. Also, in 1997 Zambia disposed of about 100 metric tons of obsolete toxic agricultural chemicals which had been abandoned in various parts of the country by national agricultural agents. The materials were shipped in March to Germany for incineration at a cost of 1.2 million U.S. dollars (Kayaya, 1997). In 1998, Ethiopia sought financial help to get rid off some 1,500 metric tons of expired pesticides that had been stored in various places across the country for 30 years. These chemicals, which were a potential threat to humans, animals and the environment, constituted, according to Yibra Tetemke, a senior expert on pesticides with the Ministry of Agriculture, the largest known amount of toxic waste concentration anywhere in Africa. Ethiopia lacked not only the money but also the technology and expertise in handling chemical waste disposal. In South Africa, the processing of the country's mineral riches of gold, diamonds, coal, and chrome is generating toxic waste products from harsh chemicals such as sulfuric acid and cyanide that are leaching into the soil and water.

The United Nations Environmental Program (UNEP), which is charged with spearheading the global campaign to eliminate toxic and potentially dangerous chemicals, estimated that in 1997 there were between 10,000 and 12,000 brands of toxic chemicals on the international market (Kakaya, 1997). Experts say these chemicals pose a serious threat to both human health and the environment. In view of the lack of storage capabilities and technical expertise to dispose them, African countries should unilaterally ban the manufacture and use of hazardous chemicals such as PCBs, as South Africa did in 1997.

The tragedy of the African commons can be summed up as a litany of failures and missed opportunities. One area where Africa has failed miserably is in controlling the astronomical population growth that was fostered during the colonial period. This was accompanied by the failure to invent technology that wisely uses natural resources to benefit the population. Instead Africans have either continued to use technology introduced during the colonial period or obsolete technology imported from the West. There has also been a failure to realize that maximizing economic development cannot be done without protecting the environment or replenishing used resources. African countries are faced with the problem of balancing accelerated development without degrading the environment. This is an act that involves balancing economic values and ecological values. Unfortunately, most, if not all, of these countries have sacrificed the latter for the former.

Finally, there has also been a failure by African countries to reduce their debilitating and spiraling foreign debt. In 1979, African countries' external debt was $93 billion; it was $14 billion in 1984; and $247 billion in 1989;and in 1994 it stood at $313 billion, "equivalent to 234 percent of export income and 83 percent of GDP" (World Bank,1995) The World Bank noted in 1995 that Sub-Saharan African countries were spending an average of $43 per capita to service their foreign debt as compared to $35 spent on health and education (World Bank, 1995). According to a World Bank debt payment criterion, 24 African countries "will continue to face an unsustainable debt burden well into the twenty-first century" (Global Environmental Outlook, 1997, p. 37). To stem the declining export earnings and ease the debt burdens; many governments are boosting their cash crop production and timber sales. However, this has only done more damage to the environment and marginalized more people and lands.

Consequences of unchecked exploitation of resources and the destruction of the environment in Africa are already being felt. As the environment rapidly deteriorates, the continent is witnessing more social and political conflicts related to the environment. More than ever before, there is a dire need to halt the destruction of the African environment. As we approach the end of the first decade of the new millennium, substantial and comprehensive solutions must be found and implemented. In the next section, I propose a number of solutions that will go a long way, if implemented, in reversing the environmental tragedy facing Africa.

TACKLING THE ENVIRONMENTAL LACUNAS: SOME PRESCRIPTIONS

For the African environments to experience significant improvement, attention must be paid to the following factors. First, Africans must change the anthropocentric attitude that has led to senseless destruction of the African commons. Since colonialism there has persisted a callous attitude that regards natural resources as being inexhaustible and there to be exploited for the benefit of human beings. The best means to change this attitude is through the incorporation of environmental education in the curriculum and emphasizing it as a core subject. Brown (1998) recommends that environmental education programs be built into school curricula (preferably beginning at an early age) to help people understand the complexity and intrinsic value of natural commodities.

Second, ways must be found to reduce and eliminate poverty on the continent. UNECA attributes environmental degradation in Africa to the scarcity of financial resources needed to initiate, stimulate, promote, and sustain development. According to the World Bank, the poorer the people are, the more at risk they are from environmental damage, regardless of the cause.[4] Since most of the African economies are based on natural resources, the degradation of their environments severely reduces the productivity of the poor and increases their susceptibility to extreme weather, economic and civil events, and environmental health threats.

Unless poverty is reduced, some desperate African governments, such as Mozambican, will continue sacrificing the health of their people by allowing toxic waste to be dumped in their countries in exchange for a few million dollars. Reduction of poverty will entail reducing the debilitating foreign debt burden and eliminating endemic corruption and gross mismanagement of the economies. There must also be internal restructuring of these countries' economic systems by freeing the banking systems from state control; eliminating endemic corruption; and privatizing state-run corporations which have been havens for corruption and hemorrhages of the national economy. Public expenditures must also be re-prioritized to cut the fiscal deficits, which are severely draining the national economies.

Third, African countries must also stabilize and ultimately reduce the astronomical populations that are unsustainable on a continent with dwindling resources. Failure to do this will not only severely endanger the environment but will also lead to more intra- and inter-state conflicts. Africans must also avoid the creeping materialistic and consumer culture that is systematically destroying the environment in the industrialized countries.

Fourth, there must be democratization and restructuring of African states. This will entail nurturing civil society, respecting human rights, promoting social justice, and encouraging popular participation in decision-making processes. It is notable that the state and the environment are decaying simultaneously in Africa. The protection of the environment can only be done by states that are stable, democratic, and well functioning. The governments that will steer Africa in the new millennium must respect environmental rights, promote environmental justice, guarantee a safe and clean environment as a right, and empower people at the grassroots level to be caretakers of the Mother Earth.

Fifth, there must be an improvement in communication and information access and exchange. In many parts of the continent, there is inaccessibility to basic information on hygiene, birth control, and environmental protection. By teaching, instilling, and encouraging behavioral changes of how to adapt to changing environmental conditions, humans can play a significant role in minimizing the natural climatic changes. For example, by caring for the soils, by increasing its nutrient (phosphorous) content, organic matter and water infiltration and retention capacity, agricultural production will be significantly enhanced. More research needs to be carried out to establish causal links and the relationships among the various factors responsible for Africa's environmental problems. Findings from these studies should then be used to formulate sound policies that will protect the African commons for the next generations to enjoy them.

Sixth, African governments must initiate conservation programs to replant drought-resistant trees in arid areas; and convert peanut shells, corn husks, and animal dung into cooking charcoal rather than trees. They also need to introduce technology that is environmentally friendly such as cooking stoves that use less wood to cook and support grassroots conservation organizations such the Greenbelt in Kenya; and to conduct environmental impact studies before embarking on "development projects."

Seventh, there must be greater efficiency in Africa's material and energy use. To effectively use their resources, African governments must merge policy planning, mass participation, and the general perceptions of natural resources. Policy planners must incorporate factors that contribute to high misuse of resources in poverty stricken areas and include the masses in policy planning and implementation. In working together toward this goal, both the policy planners and the masses will change their relationship to the environment. Such "a combined package of policy, participation, attitudinal change, and planning" will greatly enhance "the proper use of resources" (Forje, 1984, p.574)· In this regard, policy makers must come up with

> . . . practical, culturally sensitive development initiatives . . . that can help local people make a living from nature without permanently damaging it. Well-planned ecotourism projects can play such a role . . . as can "biodiversity prospecting"-the search for species that might yield new chemicals, drug precursors, genes, or other beneficial products (Brown, 1998, p.57).

Biological diversity and social diversity can benefit from each other if long-established communities can be allowed to protect forests, mountains, and rivers that are traditionally regarded as sacred and ceremonial sites. This is important since members of these communities "have an abundance of knowledge about these places: they know how the local weather works; they know which organisms produce powerful chemicals; they know what grows where" (Brown, 1998, p.57).

African countries also need to adopt integrated policy packages and development input mechanisms, which incorporate "political leadership, duty consciousness, attitude change, (and) perception of policy strategy of developed nations" (Forje, 1984, p. 574). African policy makers should know that they "have a special obligation to stand on the side of the future, by halting the destruction of natural resources and the pollution of the environment" (Forje, 1984, p. 574). Furthermore, environmental issues must be included in the national development agendas, political debates and decisions, and economic plans.

Eighth, the protection of the environment must be spelled out in law. Unlike the human beings who can stand up for, or advocate for protection of, their rights when they are trampled upon, the environment and its species cannot speak for themselves or seek protection from an authority that exists to protect it from degradation. But if human beings are aware that a pristine environment is essential for the enjoyment of all their rights, particularly the right to life, then they will be motivated to protect the environment. Human beings should know that their lives are dependent on the environment in a number of ways. First, through the web of life, which we are just part of. Destruction of a species, regardless of its size, will eventually affect human life. And second, without the natural resources human life would be miserable and even impossible to flourish. This symbiotic relationship must be recognized, respected and valued.

Environmental protection must be stipulated in the constitution as a primary duty of a government. The environmental rights must also be protected and a clean environment should be enshrined as a right that human beings are entitled to so that they can enjoy other rights. African countries should follow the Namibian example by stipulating in their constitutions measures that protect the environment.

Ninth, more effective management and wise use of joint resources such the atmosphere, oceans, lakes and rivers. Treaties need to be entered into to prevent future conflicts and assign responsibilities in the care of these commons. Most African countries have signed and/or ratified the African Hazardous Waste Convention, African Conservation Convention, and UNEP Regional Agreements, and are also contracting parties and signatories to major global conventions on the atmosphere and hazardous substances. African countries are also signatories or contracting parties to major global conventions protecting wildlife and habitat, and the oceans. In view of the level of environmental destruction that has taken place in Africa, there is an urgent need to rigorously enforce the letter and the spirit of these treaties. These treaties must also be incorporated in respective national laws and their enforcement assigned to a special environmental police.

CONCLUSION

The chapter has attempted to address three major issues. First, the chapter examined the evolution of the environmental tragedy that has engulfed Africa. The central argument it that colonial conquest and subsequent plunder set the stage for the destruction of the continent's environment. Obsessed with the profit-making motive, the colonial powers and their economic enterprises pillaged Africa's economic resources and inflicted incalculable environmental damages in the process. With the advent of the independence era, the hope was that African governments would have designed and implemented policies to protect their respective states from the marauding practices of multinational corporations. Unfortunately, African states reneged on this crucial responsibility. Hence, the assault on the continent's environment continued unabatingly as multinational corporations pillaged the continents vast natural resources.

In view of the foregoing, the study identified and discussed some of the major environmental challenges confronting Africa: soil erosion, pollution, the dumping of toxic waste, sustainable use of the forests and biodiversity. Again, these challenges are powered principally by the callous attitudes of multinational corporations and the acquiescence of the ruling African elites. That is, as I have argued, the failure of multinational corporations to balance their economic activities with the imperatives of environmental protection has been the principal source of the various environmental problems plaguing the continent.

Finally, the chapter offers some ways in which African states could address the vexing environmental problems. One of the major steps is the formulation and implementation of environmental education. This would be designed to educate the populace of various African states about sustainable development. Another measure must be the urgent development of a plan to fight poverty on the continent. Such a plan must transcend the superficiality of the so-called "poverty reduction strategy" currently being promoted by the champions of neo-liberalism. Alternatively, it must seek to identify and address the root causes of mass abject poverty on the continent. Also, steps must be taken by African states to address population explosion and its attendant impact on the environment. One other measure must be the promotion of information flow and exchange about various issues relating to the environment. Overall, there is the urgent need to engage in the restructuring of the state in Africa, so that meaningful and substantive democratization can be promoted. This would mean, among other things, that the current liberal state restructuring project presently underway must be transcended. In other words, state restructuring must go beyond political procedures, rights and freedoms and include meaningful social and economic rights that are indispensable to human survival.

References

Bayalama, Sylvain (1992). "The Environmental and Structural Adjustment Programs in Africa." *TransAfrica Forum*. Vol. 9. No.3, pp. 88-99.

Bonner, Raymond (1993). *At the Hands of Man*. New York: Alfred A. Knopf.

Brown, Lester (1998). *State of the World*. New York: W.W. Norton.

Churchill, Winston (1990). *My African Journey*. New York: W.W. Norton.

Cohen, Roger (1998). "High Claims in Spill Betray Depth of Nigerian Poverty." *New York Times*. September 20, p.1.

Dahlberg, A (1994). *Contesting Views and Changing Paradigms: The Land Degradation Debate in Southern Africa*. Uppsala, Sweden: Nordiska Afrikainstitutet.

Daniel, Philip (1992). "Economic Policy in Mineral Exporting Countries: What Have We Learned?" In John E. Tilton (ed). *Mineral Wealth and Economic Development*. Washington D.C.: Resources for the Future.

Darkoh, M.B.K (1994). "The Deterioration of the Environment in Africa's Drylands and River Basins." *Desertification Control Bulletin*. No. 24, pp. 35-41.

Forje, John W ((1984). "Th e Misuses, Destruction, and Exhaustion of Natural Resources in Africa." *Alternatives*. Vol. 10 No.3, pp. 565-579.

Global Environmental Outlook (2002). Nairobi: United Nations Environmental Program.

Global Environmental Outlook (1998). Nairobi: United Nations Environmental Program.

Global Environmental Outlook (1997). Nairobi: United Nations Environmental Program.

Global Environmental Outlook Yearbook (2007). Nairobi: United Nations Environmental Program.

Hemingway, Ernest (1995). *The Snow of Kilimanjaro*. London: Scribner.

Himrichsen, Don and Alex Marshall (1991). "Population and the Food Crisis: Lower Population Growth Rates, Along With Better Management of Land and Water resources, is Necessary to Avert Food Shortages." *Populi*. June 18, pp. 24-34.

Idrissou, Ali (1997). "The Ordeal of Waste Disposal in Cotonou." *PANA*. August 18.

Inter-Press Service (1992). "Somalia: European Firms Dumping Toxic Wastes: UNEP Probe." September 10.

James, Valentine Udoh (1993). *Africa's Ecology: Sustaining Biological and Environmental Diversity of a Continent*. Jefferson, NC: McFarland.

Kayaya, Musengwa (1997). "South Africa Bans Hazardous Chemicals." *PANA*. December 8.

New York Times (1998)."Africa's Environmental Challenges." July 6.

McNeil, Donald G. (1998). "South Africa's New Environmentalism." *New York Times*. June 15.

Ohlsoson, Lief (1995). *Water Security in Southern Africa*. Stockholm: Publications on Water Resources.

Pan-African News Agency (1998). "Cargo Ship Sinks." June 29.

Pan-African News Agency (1997).Mozambique Worried By Contaminated Agro-Chemical Products. June 9.

Ruffins, Paul and Marsha Coleman-Adebayo (1992)." Poverty, Politics, and Ecology in Africa: Expanding Deserts, Deforestation for cash, and Imported Toxic Waste Combine With War and Poverty to Threaten the African Environment." *Focus*. January 20, pp. 5-6.

Sachs, Jeffrey and Andrew Warner (1995). *Natural Resource Abundance and Economic Growth*. Cambridge, MA: Harvard Institute for International Development.

SADC ELMS (1993). *Splash-Newsletter*. September-December.

SARDC (1994). *The State of the Environment in Southern Africa*. Johannesburg: Penrose Press.

Sunday Nation (1998). "Africa's Environmental Woes." January 4.

Thomas, D.S. G and N.J. Middletown (1993). "Salinization: New Perspectives on a Major Desertification Issue." *Journal of Arid Environments*. Vol. 24. No.2, pp. 95-105.

Toulmin, Camilla (1997). "Pastures Lost." *Geographical Magazine*. Vol. 6. No. 9, pp. 54-60.

United Nations Economic Commission for Africa (1992). *Africa Common Position on the Environment and Development*. Addis Ababa: UNECA.

United Nations Environmental Program (2005). *State of the Marine Environment: West and Central African Regions*. Nairobi: UNEP.

World Bank (2007). *Making the Most of Scarcity: Accountability for Better Water Management Results in the Middle East and North Africa*. Washington D.C.: The World Bank.

World Bank (1995). *Toward Environmentally Sustainable Development in Sub-Saharan Africa*. Washington D.C.: World Bank.

World Health Organization (1995). *The State of the World Health Report*. Geneva: WHO.

World Resources Institute (2001). *World Resources*, 2000-2001. New York: Oxford University Press.

World Resources Institute (1993). *World Resources*, 1992-1993. New York: Oxford University Press.

World Resources Institute (1992). *World Resources*, 1991-1992. New York: Oxford University Press.

Chapter 8

Civil Wars in Africa

Augustine Konneh

INTRODUCTION

Since the dawn of the post-independence era in the 1960s, several African states have been plagued by civil wars. Civil wars have occurred in a number of countries, including the Sudan, Ethiopia, Angola, Mozambique, Democratic Republic of Congo (formerly known as Zaire), Rwanda, Somalia, Sierra Leone, and Liberia. The Western media's usual portrayal of "tribalism" as the major culprit in these conflicts is frequently an oversimplification of complex realities. Rather, regionalism, inequities in the provision of services, political demands by those without power, and outside intervention (especially encouragement from the superpower blocs during the days of the Cold War) often contributed to the outbreak of civil wars (Deng and Zartman, 1991).

Against this background, using various case studies, this chapter examines the following questions: 1) What were the causes of civil wars in these African states; 2) what was the impact of civil wars on these affected African states; 3) what were the ramifications of these civil war for stability on the continent?; and 4) what steps can be taken to minimize the occurrence of civil wars in Africa during the new millennium?

THE ETHNIC MODEL: A REVIEW OF THE LITERATURE

The dominant theoretical framework for explaining the root causes of civil conflicts in Africa is the ethnic model. This section of the study reviews some of the scholarly literature pertaining to it.

Ellis (1995) argues that the conflict in Liberia can be traced to the Americo-Liberian ethnic group's hegemony, especially during its heyday under the Presidency of William V. S. Tubman (1944-1971), and its political vehicle, the True Whig Party. He further maintains that while the regimes of both Tubman and his predecessor, William R. Tolbert, amid the crisis of legitimacy, recruited office holders from among the various indigenous ethnic groups of Liberia, the major criterion for appointment was the attachment of selected indigenes to one of the Americo-Liberian families. In the case of Samuel K. Doe's regime, he argues that the Krahn, Doe's ethnic group, replaced the Americo-Liberian as the new hegemon (Ellis, 1995, p. 174).

Liebenow (1986) claims that divisions among ethnic groups in Africa resulted from "tribes" having their own economic, political, and social orientation. Being diametrically opposed to each other, these competing "tribal" agendas are prone to cause conflict.

Gurr (1993) asserts that group mobilization is relevant to political violence and revolution in Africa. He argues that ethnic groups are formed primarily for the purpose of exploitation. That is, as a particular ethnic group gains political power, it uses such power to eliminate others or to deny them access to services and resources. This denial and monopolization of goods and services by one group often leads to conflict.

Another assumption of the ethnic model is that competing ethnic interests and agendas eventually lead to civil conflict. Thus, Foltz (1995) maintains that ethnic diversity in Chad fostered a chain of conflict-laden antagonisms: factionalism in political and military organizations; the "North versus South" regional divide; and personal rivalries among the principal factional leaders—Habre, Weddeye, and Debey—each representing an ethnic regional bloc.

AN ALTERNATIVE MODEL: THE INTEGRATIVE MODEL

This study uses an integrative model in assessing the roots of civil conflicts in Africa. For example, the overarching premise of the model is that while ethnicity may be a factor in African civil conflicts, it is not the only factor. Any claim to the contrary neglects the significance of the political, economic, and social discontent of African peoples. It is not tribal alliance as such that matters but, rather, inequity of opportunities. Only within the context of political, economic, and social discontent can the emergence of ethnic antagonism be explained; only with the anger fueled by such discontent can governments mobilize ethnic tensions and employ scape-goating to achieve their own selfish goals.

By attributing every civil conflict in Africa to ethnicity, the ethnic model negates the broader range of issues that tend to divide African peoples. Therefore, to conduct a thorough examination of the roots of civil conflicts in Africa, the integrative model explores two major categories of causal factors: contingent and necessary.

The Contingent Factors

The contingent or the base factors that contribute to the occurrence of civil conflicts in Africa arise fundamentally from the nature and character of the state in Africa. For example, all African states, with the exceptions of Ethiopia and Liberia, are the products of colonialism (even in the cases of Ethiopia and Liberia, their evolutions were similar to that of their sister African states). Accordingly, it is the process of state formation of African countries that has sown the seeds of discontent that flourish today. These seeds germinated by the way in which power was used; the self-serving motives of the leaders; and the violation of historical realities during the period of state formation. For example, it is important to note that many of these countries were already in the process of state formation when Europeans and other foreigners usurped it. The destruction of the African process of state formation and the legacies that emerged from the European version have left a plethora of unresolved pathologies, such as a predisposition toward violence, predominant repression, the manipulation of cleavages by the state, and a dependent economy based primarily on the export of cash crops (Boahen, 1987).

At the structural level, the discussion of conflicts often overlooks or underplays the role of the state in the generation and reproduction of contradictions and coalitions that culminate in conflicts. For instance, the construction of a violent, undemocratic, and highly interventionist state under colonialism suffocated civil society, underdeveloped indigenous entrepreneurship, and divided the people. Subsequently, this repressive state was transferred intact to the new leaders as countries gained their independence. Lacking economic power, these leaders exercised only limited control over their territories. They could not promote growth, much less development, and were thus unable to fulfill the glossy and rosy promises of the nationalist struggles. Within a few years (in some cases, months), the neo-colonial state was confronted with challenges from a variety of groups, most notably peasants, women, workers, and the unemployed. Finding themselves in a rather defensive position, the state's leaders easily resorted to the manipulative, exploitative, and repressive tactics, institutions and politics of colonialism. Consequently, the state became increasingly delegitimized and drove the opposition into exile, jail, or underground. Many recent political upheavals in Africa are mere manifestations of this longstanding contradiction between the state and civil society (Ihonvbere, 1998).

The Necessary Factors

Although the contingent factors associated with state formation constitute the basis of civil conflicts in Africa, they are not sufficient to explain the widespread eruptions that have practically engulfed the continent. Rather, certain necessary factors—ethnic, religious, and economic disparities; racial discrimination; and regional differences—must be considered as intermediaries in triggering the occurrence of civil conflicts. These proximate causes of conflict are discussed in the following sections.

The Ethnic Factor

Ethnic domination is a contributor to the conflict in Africa. The monopolization of political and economic power by one ethnic group excludes others from participating in affairs of the state. Such conditions result in discrimination by the limitation of access to public goods and services, inequitable distribution of economic resources, marginalization in the political arena, denial of land and territory, and genocidal elimination (ethnic cleansing) of groups based on ethnic origins.

In addition, the perception of the government as belonging to a particular group creates problems in government-controlled arenas such as the military, public educational institutions, and the judiciary. This attempt by one group to dominate resources— and the counter demands for power by other groups— often result in conflict as seen in the cases of Rwanda, Sudan, and Liberia (Rothchild, 1991, pp. 195-196; Horowitz, 1985).

The Religious Factor

Religion is another contributor to civil conflicts in Africa. In countries such as Sudan, Uganda, and, to some extent, Nigeria, religious factors have become vehicles not only for economic advancement but also for the acquisition of political power. For example, because of Islamic influence in northern Sudan, the political rulers are, by and large, Muslims. The imposition of Islamic law (the Sharia) as the governing legal code is perceived by southern Sudanese and the non-Islamic segments of the international community as targeting Christians and other non-Muslims. These religious differences contributed to the political upheaval and resultant protracted civil war in which the South was struggling to secede from the country (Anyang-Nyango, 1991, pp. 109-110).

The Economic Factor

Because of its direct impact on the daily lives of peoples, economics play a pivotal role in fostering conflict in Africa. Economic disparity manifests itself in two prominent ways: discrepancies in income levels and inequitable distribution of wealth and resources.

First, there are marked differences within individual income levels as well as between the income levels of groups that are in power versus groups that are virtually "powerless." Discrepancies in individual income are often directly attributable to political affiliation and favor. For example, during the 1990s, the average annual incomes for Africans ranged from $210 to $2,500. For example, in Sierra Leone, the average individual monthly income was less than $50, while in Mozambique it was $80 (Mbaku, 1998). In many African countries those groups which occupy the upper echelons of urban society receive higher salaries than rural dwellers who perform the same jobs. This geographical economic disparity is epitomized in Liberia, where in the 1970s, those in rural areas earned an average annual income of $70 compared to $600 earned by those in the urban areas (Kieh, 1999).

Second, the distribution of wealth or resources is often based upon virtually the same premise as discrepancies in income levels. That is, those in power determine how resources are allocated both within the controlling group and within the country as a whole. For example, in The Democratic Republic of Congo, before the overthrow of Mobutu, 3 percent of the population controlled 70 percent of the country's wealth or resources; and in Liberia, before the civil conflict, 5 percent of the population controlled 75 percent of the country's wealth or resources (Kieh, 1996a, pp. 44-46). Thus, as in many economies a small percentage of the population controls the greatest percentage of resources or wealth (Mbaku, 1998). The old adage, "To the victor belongs the spoils," is quite evident when it comes to the impetus for conflict in the economic arena in Africa.

The Regional Factor

Often a conflict that has its genesis in one African country may for sundry reasons spill over into neighboring countries, thereby sparking similar conflicts in those countries. For example, many of the refugees from Rwanda who sought sanctuary in Uganda joined Yoweri Museveni's National Resistance Army that eventually overthrew the second Milton Obote regime. In Sierra Leone, the rebels of the Revolutionary United Front (RUF) led by Foday Sankoh were trained in Liberia by Charles Taylor, who constantly provided assistance to the RUF against the government of Joseph Momoh as a means of punishing him for giving support to the Economic Community of West Africa Monitoring Group (ECOMOG), the West African peacekeeping force during the first Liberian civil war (1989-1997). Similarly, Ethiopian assistance to the Sudanese People's Liberation Army (SPLA) and the Sudanese government's aid rendered to the Eritrean resistance are other cases of the willingness of neighboring states to lend assistance to dissident forces. Among other things, these states' provision of arms and training led to regional instability (Newbury, 1995, p. 13; Anyang-Nyongo, 1995, pp. 105-106).

THE CASE STUDIES OF CIVIL WARS IN AFRICA

This section of the study depicts some of the major civil conflicts in Africa within the broader context of the fundamental and contingent factors that precipitated them.

Sierra Leone

The conflict in Sierra Leone can be partially attributed to the impact of colonial state formation; that is, the way in which ethnicity has been used for the control of state power, personalization of authority, and extension of state control into virtually every sector of the society. The establishment of political parties on the basis of ethnicity instead of ideologies has resulted in ethnic competition for power.

From the end of the nineteenth century until Sierra Leone was granted its independence by the British government on April 27, 1961, the Creoles, who were considered Western elites by the major indigenous groups (Mende, Temne, and Limba), dominated the political and economic arenas of the country. They rejected the notion of political parity with the indigenous groups, instead considering themselves superior to the latter. The persistence of this condition over time led to resentment by the indigenous groups. The resulting polarization produced rifts that still persist today—especially among the Mende of the South and the Temne of the

North, on the one hand, and the Limba of the Northeast on the other. Membership in political parties reflected these divisions with the Sierra Leone Peoples Party (SLPP) being composed primarily of Mende; the United People's Party (UPP), of Creole; and the All Peoples Congress (APC), of Temne and Limba (Kandeh, 1992).

Since independence, the struggle for power has been mainly between the Mende and Temne ethnic groups, who were formerly allied against the Creoles. The APC defeated the SLPP in a general election held in 1967. This brought Siaka Probyn Stevens, the party's leader, to power. Ten years after Stevens assumed leadership, his government still faced many challenges. The growing economic difficulties of the country, coupled with his banning of opposition parties, prompted demonstrations from students, workers, and women. In January and February of 1977, students of Fourah Bay College, joined by other citizens, mounted a series of demonstrations against the APC-led government. Although unable to dethrone the APC, these acts of protest did expose Stevens' inability to resolve Sierra Leone's economic and political problems (Kpundeh, 1995).

In 1985 Stevens retired, transferring power to his handpicked successor, Joseph Momoh, in a staged election. Unfortunately, President Momoh inherited the state's problems. Also, he was not able to end the private control of Sierra Leone's wealth that many of Stevens' cronies enjoyed. Momoh's inability to provide necessary state services such as salaries for workers, drugs for hospitals, and adequate roads prompted many Sierra Leoneans to seek better living conditions elsewhere.

In March 1991, a rebel threat emerged along the country's eastern border with Liberia. Liberian warlord, Charles Taylor, had used the guerrilla Revolutionary United Front (RUF), a group of Sierra Leonean dissidents, as a proxy to control economically viable areas of Sierra Leone so that he could buy arms and pay his own rebels. The RUF became a homegrown insurgency under the auspices of Foday Sankoh, a former military officer who had been imprisoned for his alleged role in a 1971 coup plot (Reno, 1997, pp. 227-228).

Despite his efforts to bring in Guinean soldiers and to expand the Sierra Leonean military, Momoh was unable to repel the rebel invasion. Causalities continued to mount in the eastern province. In addition, due to the growing budget deficit, Momoh lacked sufficient funds to finance his expanded army. As a result, on April 29, 1992, 26 years old Army Captain Valentine Strasser and several other officers marched to Freetown, the capital city, and overthrew Momoh.

However, the young president soon faced more dire straits than his predecessors. He, too, was unable to deal effectively with the rebel situation despite using 75 percent of the country's revenues toward that end. Not only did his action worsen the financial posture of the country, but it also invoked international condemnation and delayed critically needed aid from overseas.

In desperation, Head of State Captain Strasser called in the Executive Outcomes (EO), a mercenary group that was trained in South Africa. The EO arrived in April 1995, and within two weeks had managed to dislodge the rebels from the Freetown area. Working in partnership with the Kamajos, a unit trained by a British-based firm, the EO seized control of the main diamond mines. The EO's primary role was to provide security for foreign firms that gained concessions in the mines (Reno, 1997, pp.228-229).

To prevent Captain Strasser from running as a presidential candidate in the upcoming elections, Brigadier-General Julius Maada Bio, a hard-liner in the Sierra Leonean Military and the Vice Chair of the ruling military junta, removed Head of State Strasser from office in a palace coup in January 1996. However, the change did not alter the relationship between the EO and the government in Freetown. In March of the same year, nationwide elections brought to power Ahmed Tejan Kabbah, the SLPP presidential candidate. In an attempt to resolve the rebel situation, the RUF's leader Sankoh and President Kabbah signed a peace treaty in Abidjan, Cote d' Ivòire on November 30, 1996. However, the "Abidjan Peace Accord" failed to end the civil war. Not only did the fighting continue but also clashes escalated among the Kamajos, EO, and the Sierra Leonean Army (Reno, 1997, pp. 229-230). In order to end the war, ECOWAS brokered the Conakry Peace Agreement between the Sierra Leonean Government and the RUF. Again, the accord failed to end the war.

Consequently, the country's deteriorating military situation coupled with its declining economic conditions culminated in a coup led by Major Johnny Paul Koroma in May 1997. Major Koroma had been previously jailed on allegations of his role in an attempted coup. The then Organization of African Unity (now the African Union)mandated the sub-regional institution, the Economic Community of West African States (ECOWAS), to intervene. ECOWAS organized and undertook a peace enforcement operation through ECOMOG, its ad hoc military force. The operation was designed to restore President Kabbah to power. In 1998, ECOMOG defeated the military junta-RUF alliance, and restored President Kabbah to power. In order to monitor ECOWAS' campaign to disarm the RUF rebels, the United Nations stationed an observation mission in Sierra Leone (UNOMSIL). However, the restoration of the Kabbah regime to power did not end the civil war. So, again, under ECOWAS' auspicies, the Kabbah regime and the RUF signed the Lome Peace Accord in 1999. Thereafter, the United Nations raised its observation mission to that of a full-fledged peacekeeping force. However, the accord was violated recurrently by the RUF. So, the war continued for another three years until 2002, when it finally ended with the holding of elections. Also, RUF forces were disarmed (Cole and De Blij, 2007, p. 349).

Finally, despite the end of the civil war and the holding of multi-party elections in 2002, Sierra Leone is still faced with major obstacles in the implementation of its post-conflict peace-building agenda. Kieh (2005, p. 177) identifies the major obstacle to post-conflict peace-building in Sierra Leone as "…the failure to deconstruct, rethink and democratically reconstitute the neo-colonial Sierra Leonean State." In essence, Sierra Leone needs to reconstruct the state so that it can serve the interests of the majority of Sierra Leoneans.

Liberia

The two civil wars in Liberia are by-products of the formation of the state. Liberia was not colonized like other African countries. Rather, it was established for repatriated peoples of African descent returning from the United States. Nevertheless, the historical and political conjecture that emerged from the settlement, particularly relationships between the returnees (commonly known as Americo-Liberians) and the indigenous Liberians produced familiar colonial conditions, such as exploitation, inequity, and monopolization of power and resources. These factors generated deep contradictions, conflict, and suspicion not only between the Americo-Liberians and the indigenes, but also within the various class levels. Thus, the nature of Liberia's settlement made the degeneration of the state into authoritarianism almost inevitable.

Therefore, it came as no surprise when divisions and contradiction within the military itself were revealed (Kieh, 1996b). Samuel Doe's manipulation, execution, corruption, mediocrity, ineptness, pretentious politics, reliance on violence, and the creation of ethnic strife generated overt and covert opposition within and outside Liberia. For example, in August 1984, Sergeant Doe jailed Amos Sawyer, Dean of the College of Humanities and Social Sciences, and George

Klay Kieh, Jr., Lecturer of Political Science. This action inspired students at the University of Liberia to protest. In response, Sergeant Doe sent approximately 200 soldiers from his Presidential Guards to storm the campus, injuring hundreds of people and killing an undetermined number. Also, the invading soldiers beat, raped, and assaulted administrators, faculty, staff and students. Additionally, records, books, equipment, and laboratories were destroyed. Millions of dollars in damage were done in this chaotic three-hour spectacle (Liebenow, 1987).

The proverbial "straw that broke the camel's back" was Sergeant Doe's manipulation of the process that culminated in the October 1985 general elections. Disregarding the newly approved constitution, he banned two prominent political parties, the United People's Party (UPP) led by Bacchus Mathews and the Liberian Peoples Party (LPP) headed by Amos Sawyer, from participating in the elections. However, under the guise of fairness and democracy, he did permit three other parties— the Liberian Action Party (LAP), the Liberian Unification Party (LUP), and the United Party (UP) to participate in the elections and "oppose him." Of course, none of these parties posed any real threat to Doe's determination to civilianize his military regime.

While Doe restricted opposition political parties from organizing, he formed his own political party named the National Democratic Party of Liberia (NDPL). As it became clear in early counting that Doe was losing badly, he ordered the ballot boxes collected and taken to the outskirts of Monrovia, the capital city, where his handpicked "counting committee did the counting. To no one's surprise, the "counting committee" announced that Sergeant Doe won 51% of the vote, with Jackson Doe (no relation) of the Liberian Action Party coming in second. With the perpetuation of this fraud, Doe's remaining minuscule credibility vanished completely.

The fraudulent election was immediately followed by an attempted coup in November 1985, led by Thomas Quiwonkpa, one of the prominent leaders of the 1980 coup that had brought Doe to power. However, the coup was foiled, and Quiwonkpa was subsequently murdered. Moreover, about 2,000 people were killed by Doe's troops in the reprisals that followed the abortive coup. The reprisals were particularly severe in Nimba County, Quiwonkpa's home area. Because Doe viewed the Mano and Gio ethnic groups as some of his major adversaries (and because Quiwonkpa was a Mano), many were killed. Additionally, hundreds of Mano and Gio soldiers were summarily executed on the grounds of the Executive Mansion and hundreds of other people were detained, starved, and mistreated. Ethnic violence had erupted throughout a country where ethnic tensions had always been minimal prior to 1980 (Liebenow, 1987, pp.300-302).

During the Doe regime, ethnicity and "tribe" defined the central principles of the Liberian government. This new development specifically connected to the drastically altered circumstances of Doe's overthrow of longstanding Americo-Liberian dominance. However, it should be emphasized that even though Doe made ethnicity central in his policymaking, much of the Liberian society continued to operate on other principles. For instance, many members of the Krahn ethnic group (Doe's ethnic group) did not benefit from his rule and complained about it like anyone else (Gibson, 1994).

Sergeant later President Doe completely dominated the "Second Republic" (1986-1989), as the era that was ushered in by President Doe's "election" and the subsequent formal end of military rule was known. During his brief tenure, President Doe hired and fired ministers without explanation and surrounded himself with a coterie of lieutenants principally from his Krahn ethnic group. For example, Edward Taye was the Commissioner of Immigration; G. Alvin Jones, Minister of State for Presidential Affairs; George Boley, Minister of

Education; and General Henry Dubar, Chief of Staff of the Armed Forces of Liberia . President Doe's signature effort was to "ethnicize" the Armed Forces of Liberia by stacking the officer corps and key units with Krahns. In the manifold upheavals of his decade-long rule, Krahn soldiers responded to repeated protests, plots, and coups by widespread murdering, raping and pillaging (Kieh, 1996b).

President Doe also ravaged the Liberian economy. It is estimated that during the ten years of his presidency, he and his principal lieutenants siphoned approximately $300 million from the public coffers, an amount roughly equal to half the anemic gross domestic product of their final year in power. Liberia's distinctive American panache (the United States dollar remains legal tender) helped him to establish a lucrative money-laundering racket. President Doe amassed a personal fortune of about $200 million that he kept in various banks abroad (Kieh, 1996b) Also, the prices for basic commodities soared without end, while schools, hospitals, and other institutions experienced collapse. The Doe government depended almost entirely on aid from the United States to stay afloat (Kieh, 1996b).

The struggle to end this brutal and visionless military cum civilian dictatorship culminated in the first civil war in 1989 initially between the Doe government and the National Patriotic Front of Liberia led by Charles Taylor. The first civil war claimed the lives of over 250,000 people; destroyed properties; brutalized the consciousness and assaulted the spirituality of citizens; and pushed Liberia back almost into the "Dark Ages." Also, the first war promoted and consolidated a general culture of violence, intolerance, and destruction and the promotion of undemocratic attitudes. Rampant opportunism among the various groups, their inability to reach accommodation, and the use of children as soldiers nurtured to kill is not the way to build a democratic and accountable future for Liberia or any other country (Konneh, 1997).

Several valiant attempts were been made to restore peace to Liberia. The most prudent effort was that of July 1996, when heads of state of ECOWAS met again (this time in Abuja, the capital city of Nigeria), to make arrangements for restoring stability. They developed an aggressive timetable that included deadlines for disarmament, encampment, and the holding of elections. However, these activities were partially completed before the country's elections that were held on July 19, 1997. Taylor won the election by an overwhelming margin: Of the approximately 751,000 registered voters, he garnered over 75% of the vote; his closest opponent, Ellen Johnson-Sirleaf (currently the President of Liberia), received only approximately 10%. The voting eligibility requirements restricted participation to only those Liberians who were residing in the country at the time of the elections. This meant that Liberians, who were refugees in other countries, and other Liberians, who were residing abroad were not allowed to vote.

However, barely three years into the Taylor Presidency, Liberia was plunged into a second civil war. The war commenced in 1999, when a group operating under the name "Liberians United for Reconciliation and Democracy (LURD)" launched an armed insurgency from neighboring Guinea against the Taylor regime. Realizing the grave threat the insurgency posed to his hold on power, President Taylor responded with all of the military might he could marshal. Consequently, Liberia degenerated into its second civil war. For most of its duration, the war was confined to the western and northwestern portions of Liberia. However, in February 2003, LURD scored series of military victories against Taylor's military forces, thereby placing it within striking distance of Monrovia, the capital city. One month later, the war took an interesting turn with the emergence of the Movement for Democracy in Liberia (MODEL), a second insurgency group, which operated from southeastern Liberia, especially, the areas bordering Cote d'Ivoire. By April 2003, the war escalated as LURD launched indiscriminate attacks against Monrovia, and MODEL attacked from the eastern and southeastern regions of Liberia. With the intervention of the international community under the leadership of the Economic Community of West African States (ECOWAS), a peace deal was brokered that included President Taylor's resignation after the expiration of his term of office in August 2003 and his departure into exile in Nigeria; the termination of the war and the establishment of a transitional government consisting of the representatives of LURD, MODEL, the remnants of the Taylor regime, political parties and civil society. The interim government, which was headed by Charles Gyude Bryant, ruled the country for a little over two years (October 2003-January 16, 2006). In October 2005, multi-party presidential and legislative elections were held. Later, in November 2005, the 'run-off presidential election" was held between George Weah, the top vote getter during the first round of the presidential race, and Ellen Johnson Sirleaf, the runner-up. Ellen Johnson Sirleaf was declared the winner of the presidential election with about 60% of the votes to about 40% for George Weah (Elections Commission of Liberia, 2005). On January 16, 2006, Ellen Johnson Sirleaf was inaugurated as the first elected female President in the history of the African Continent. The Sirleaf regime is now faced with the tasks of providing the requisite leadership for peace-building in Liberia.

The Democratic Republic of the Congo

The conflict in The Democratic Republic of Congo was not unique as far as African countries are concerned. With a shrinking economy and a plethora of contending and polarized ethnic groups, the struggles for political and economic power were typical.

The conflict's history can be traced to both its colonial and neocolonial roots. During colonialism the control of agriculture was vested in centralized institutions; market mechanisms were not utilized. As a result, rural Congolese (and urban ones, when necessary) were used simply as cheap laborers for the benefit of the large colonial enterprises. That is, native Africans were not allowed to develop either agrarian capitalism or a peasant economy. They were trapped in a virtual "no man's land." Sadly, independence did not improve the situation. President Mobutu Sese Seko's regime did little to benefit the peasantry, the only class that could play a central role in the resolution of the agrarian crisis. Instead, control of agriculture was merely shifted from the colonial ruling powers to a small nucleus of the Congolese bourgeoisie. With external financial support, this nucleus embarked on a process of privatization of land, with most of the money from the state's budget being spent on projects that benefited large corporations (Rosenblum, 1997, p.200).

Thus, ordinary people had to develop their own strategies for survival. One such strategy was the complete avoidance of the state. The people undertook activities that exerted considerable influence on their daily lives outside of the sphere of state action. Such activities included smuggling and other types of participation in the underground economy as well as seeking employment opportunities in a neighboring country. This type of parallel existence was necessary to enhance their long-term interests and survival. Catherine Newbury describes various forms of strategies that ranged from individual attempts to secure livelihood to group political action. They included the creation of social networks for mutual support and the emergence of collective solidarity that could be channeled into more direct forms of resistance and confrontations, thus helping ordinary people preserve a sense of self-respect. This rise in civil society, the informal economy, the activism of churches, and the efforts of local human rights groups and development organizations played major roles in helping the Congolese people survive (Newbury, 1995, pp. 13-15).

However, the tragedies of Rwanda and Burundi that began in the early 1990s, served to deter progress. Old rivalries flared as local politicians took advantage of the situation to "get even" with members of the refugee population. The international community did nothing. Laurent-Desire Kabila, the rebel leader at the helm of the rebellion, was welcomed hesitantly by fellow Congolese, who disliked having their country viewed as a receptacle for refugees. Subsequently, one of the principal strategies employed by President Mobutu for holding onto power was the fostering of rivalries among the political and military elites, who had turned against him. However, the emergent rivalries prevented the elites from unifying in their own self-interests.

Interestingly, President Mobutu made one last attempt to divide his enemies by using the regional and ethnic loyalties of the country's two most popular political leaders. He named Etienne Tshisekedi as Prime Minister to replace Leon Kengo wa Dondo. At the same time he reinstated Kyungu wa Kumwanza, Tshisekedi's greatest antagonist. Both leaders feared Laurent Kabila. The tactic worked; an undercurrent of resistance and conflict was set off within the populace (Rosenblum, 1997, pp. 202-2003). However, President Mobutu's desperate effort did not yield the desired benefit, as his regime continued to experience an avalanche of pressure from diverse sectors of the Congolese state. By 1997, the demise of the Mobutu regime became imminent as the insurgency led by Laurent Kabila under the banner of the Alliance of the Democratic Forces for the Liberation of the Congo (ADFLC) had virtually taken control of the country. Finally, in May 1997, Mobutu's regime was toppled, and replaced by a government headed by Laurent Kabila. Former President Mobutu took refuge in France and subsequently in Morocco, where he died. President Kabila and the ADFLC were assisted in their insurgency against the Mobutu regime by Rwanda and Uganda. As Lumumba-Kasongo (2005, p. 33) argues, "[Rwanda and Burundi's support for Kabila and the ADFLC was informed by]…a proposition that in search for the national security formulas in their common and long borders with the DRC, given the size of the Congo and long borders with [them], if Kabila captured Kinshasa, their security problem was likely to be solved militarily once and for all."

Interestingly, the alliance between President Kabila, on the one hand, and Rwanda and Uganda, on the other hand, was short lived: After major quarrels, the alliance was terminated. The major resultant effect was the decision by Rwanda and Uganda to support anti-Kabila forces for the purpose of removing President Kabila from power. Consequently, the Congo degenerated into a second civil war between the Kabila government on the one hand, and various militias supported by Rwanda and Uganda. Later, the war expanded with the military interventions by several countries, including Angola, Namibia and Zimbabwe, in support of the Kabila regime. In January 2001, President Kabila was assassinated by one of his body guards (Lumumba-Kasongo, 2005). President Kabila was replaced by his son Joseph Kabila. However, the change in leadership did not end the civil war. To the contrary, the war became even more complicated with the emergence of several new militias, including the disintegration of existing armed factions into splinter groups. However, on December 16, 2002, after several efforts by the international community to end the war, the Congolese government and the warring factions signed the "Global and Comprehensive Agreement on Transition in the Democratic Republic of the Congo" in Pretoria, South Africa. Under the peace accord, the war formally ended and a transitional government of national unity headed by President Joseph Kabila was established. The interim regime assumed power on April 7, 2003. Importantly, the United Nations intervened with a peacekeeping force as the anchor of the transitional security arrangements. On July 30, 2006, multi-party presidential and parliamentary elections were held. In the presidential race contested by 33 candidates, Interim President Joseph Kabila, the incumbent, and Jean Pierre Bemba, one of the transitional Vice Presidents, were the top two vote getters—Kabila garnered 44.8% of the votes to 20.8% for Bemba. Since, none of them garnered the required absolute majority, a "run-off" election was held on October 29, 2006, between the top two vote getters in the first round. According to the results, the incumbent, President Joseph Kabila won with 58.05% of the votes, to 41.95% for his rival Jean-Pierre Bemba, the former warlord. After the results were announced, Bemba rejected them. This emboldened some of his supporters to engage in acts of violence against state property as a way of expressing their disagreement with the results of the second round of the presidential election.

Clearly, the formal end of the Congolese civil war and the installation of a new government constitute major steps forward in the arduous journey to building a peaceful, stable, democratic and prosperous new society based on pluralism and peaceful co-existence. Undoubtedly, the Congo has the natural resources that could constitute the financial anchor for spurring socio-economic development. However, several major changes need to be made, if Congo is to make the transition not just from war to peace, but from the perennial crises of underdevelopment to development for the benefits of all of the Congolese people. At the center of the agenda for change, according to Baregu (2006, p.70), must be the imperative of addressing "structural obstacles, which arise from the structure of power and interests..."

Rwanda

For four months in 1994 (April through July), the world looked on in horror as the Habyarimana government waged a massive campaign of genocide in Rwanda. However, what many people in the international community viewed as mindless tribal violence was really a series of planned and calculated actions. The central goal was the elimination of the members of the Tutsi ethnic group and moderate Hutus, who were seen as opposed to the Habyarimana government.

However, the conflict in Rwanda should not be viewed simplistically as a single act of genocide. Rather, its roots can be found in the social, economic, and political conditions (both internal and external) of history. Among the multiplicity of contributing factors were the: (1) nature of the postcolonial state and the changing configuration of regional, class, and ethnic divisions; (2) growing militarization of state and society; (3) emphasis on political liberalization and multipartyism and the neglect of the concerns of ordinary citizens; (4) sharply deteriorating internal economic conditions; (5) heightened anxieties fostered by the Arusha Peace Accords of 1993; and (6) increased fears and insecurities caused by events in neighboring Burundi. All of these factors operated in a climate created by the intersection of multiple pressures (Newbury, 1995, pp. 12-17).

Although Rwandan society is generally divided into three groups consisting of Hutu (85%), Tutsi (about 14%), and Twa (less than 1%), they all speak the same language and hold common membership within a set of state structures. During European colonialism, the high offices under the monarchy that ruled Rwanda were dominated by a Tutsi minority. Colonialism exacerbated the situation by relegating the vast majority of Hutu to the lower levels of society and by actively favoring Tutsi in all forms of access to jobs and education. As a result, by the time colonialism ended, most of the wealthy and powerful people were Tutsi. However, the Revolution of 1959 resulted in the ascension to power of the Hutu and the killing or exile of thousands of Tutsi (Newbury, 1995, p. 12).

Within the post-colonial state, relations between the two groups changed; and during the regime of Juvenal Habyriamana (particularly during the mid-1980s), there were serious economic and political problems. The main conflict, based on region and class, was primarily among Hutu factions. However, in an effort to maintain power, inter-ethnic group conflict was used quite effectively fueled by the history of such strife between Tutsi and Hutu. Thus, resources that should have been used to combat economic difficulties were diverted to war efforts (Newbury, 1995, p. 13).

In addition to ethnic conflict, the declining economy of Rwanda had devastating social consequences. With the reduction in coffee production, the country's main export, peasant growers as well as traders and merchants were impacted. Also, the currency was devalued; and citizens were required to pay higher fees for public services such as primary school education, health care, and even access to water. Most important politically was the social impact on the country's youth. With no jobs, little education, and no hope for the future, their path to social adulthood was blocked.

Little changed for the better with the adoption of the new constitution in June 1991, and the legalization of multiparty competition in July of that same year. The linkages between political parties and organizations in civil society were weak. Most rural dwellers expressed minimal interest in the government's activities because they had no strong voice to present their concerns. Additionally, there were widening splits among leaders in the major opposition parties. Political tensions escalated over several major issues: the makeup of the new government, the merging of the two armies and the accommodation of soldiers (jobs and subsistence) who were displaced by the merger, and the right of refugees to return home. No mechanism was put into place to effectively deal with any of these issues. On April 6, 1994, the conflict took the turn for the worse, when Presidents Habyarimana of Rwanda and Cyprien Ntaryamire of Burundi were killed in a plane clash as the consequence of an act of sabotage by disgruntled members of the Rwandese Military. The death of President Habyarimana unleashed a "wave of genocide" engineered by Hutu-based militias referred to as "Interahamwe" against Tutsis and Hutu moderates. The resultant murderous campaign broke the fragile peace and re-plunged the country into another round of civil war, as the forces of the Tutsi-based Rwandan Patriotic Front (RPF) took countermeasures designed to end the genocide. Even more tragic was the inaction of the international community. Western governments sent troops to evacuate their citizens, while leaving those most affected to the mercy of the murderers. In fact, United Nations troops often stood passively as thousands of innocent civilians were killed right in front of them (Newbury, 1995, pp. 16-17). In spite of empirical records to the contrary, the West persisted in viewing and portraying the conflict in the media as just another "African tribal war." Finally, in July 1994, the "wave of genocide" ended with almost a million people dead. The RPF defeated the remnants of the Rwandese Military and assumed control of the state machinery.

Unfortunately, it did not take a long time before the post-genocide regime (currently headed by President Paul Kigame) under the Rwandan Patriotic Front (RPF) returned Rwanda to the era of authoritarian governance. Since 1995, the RPF-led government has waged a campaign of repression against various sectors of the society, including some of its former supporters. Reyntjens (2006, p. 18) aptly refers to the phenomenon of political repression as "the shrinking political base." Specifically, since its inception—both during the interim period and now—the Kagame regime has imprisoned political opponents, forced others into exile and closed newspapers. In effect, the post-genocide era has not ushered in a new dawn anchored on political pluralism, respect for human rights, the sanctity of the rule of law, accountability and transparency. Even the 2003 elections have not set into motion a process of democratization. Instead, the Kigame regime has used the results of the fraudulent elections as so-called "mandate" to re-institutionalize state terror. Clearly, if Rwanda is to transition from its sordid past to a new era of peace, stability, democracy and development, then the Kagame regime must provide the requisite leadership that is exigent for constructing a democratic post-genocide society.

The Sudan

The origin of conflict in Sudan can be traced to Britain's strategy of "divide and rule," using religion and ethnicity as their primary initial instruments—an Arab-Muslim North versus an African non-Muslim (Christian) South. Britain further promulgated this division by fostering the notion of Northern superiority versus Southern inferiority with Northerners viewing Southerners as "pagans." Further, Britain encouraged the proliferation of Christian missionaries in the South to promote this division.

Moreover, Britain attempted to solidify the fragmentation of Sudan by fueling internal conflict within the Arab-Muslim communities. Using clan and religion as the major vehicles, Britain manipulated the historically based division between the Ansar Muslims led by Mahdi, and the Khatmiyya led by the Mirghani family, to its ultimate imperial advantage. This long-standing intra-community rivalry continued to permeate every facet of life in Sudan, including politics and allegiances within the army (Ayang-Nyongo, 1991, p. 105).

In the past, despite the overt efforts made by the ruling political parties (whose constituents originate from both the North and South) to marshal the social forces needed to develop Sudan based on principles of justice, equality, peace, and democracy, the covert aim was not peace but the continued pursuit of means of bringing the South under Islamic rule (Ayang-Nyongo, 1991, p. 105). Among others, the civil war resulted in the tragic loss of lives of both military personnel and civilians. In addition, the loss of human potential in terms of the refugees, who constantly fled to other African countries, was phenomenal. Of course, there can be no socio-economic progress without the human resources to bring it into existence.

After decades of warfare and its associated violence, death, destruction and displacement, the parties to the Sudanese civil war, including the government, finally heeded the recurrent calls and associated efforts from the international community to end the continent's longest running civil war. Finally, after 72 failed peace agreements (Nasong'o and Murunga, 2005, p. 67), in January 2005, the seemingly endless civil war ended with the signing of the Nairobi Comprehensive Peace Agreement (CPA). As Nasong'o and Murunga (2005, p. 73) note, "There is no doubt that the Comprehensive Peace Agreement is ground-breaking in the manner it tackles the most contentious issues in the Sudanese Conflict." However, it is left to be seen if the operational modalities would be developed and brought to bear on these critical issues.

Although, the war has formally ended, there is an ongoing war in Sudan's Darfur Region among various armed militias, including the Jinjinwa militia, which is being supported by the Sudanese government. The war has caused the deaths of thousands of Sudanese living in the region and has caused one of the worst humanitarian crises in the world. In an effort to end the war, the African Union (AU) intervened with a peacekeeping force. However, due to various reasons—logistical, operational, etc. —the peacekeeping force has not been able to end the fighting, a major prerequisite for peacemaking efforts. Given the shortcomings of the AU's peacekeeping force, the United Nations has made the determination to send a peacekeeping force to replace the one from the

AU. However, the Sudanese government has consistently expressed opposition to the intervention of a UN peacekeeping force. Accordingly, Darfur has degenerated into a genocidal war as reflected in the wholesale massacres of civilians by various armed groups, especially the state-sponsored Jinjinwa Militia. Clearly, Sudan cannot begin the process of post-conflict in earnest, unless the war in its Darfur Region is resolved.

Somalia

Somalia remains one of the poorest countries in Africa. Its impoverished conditions can be traced to several factors, the major one being the long history of the country's domination by the colonial powers of Britain, France, and Italy. Using the age-old strategy of "divide and rule," these colonialists worked diligently to play Somalia's six major clans and several sub-clans against each other, leading to fragmentation of the people and the underdevelopment of the political economy. Another major factor has been the gross inability of post-colonial Somalia governments to stem the tide of disintegration, mediate class and clan contradictions, and promote growth and development of the country.

The leadership of Siyaad Bare decimated the country. In addition to the terror his regime inflicted on the people, he was insecure in his abilities and had no concept of what programs needed to be implemented to ensure the success of the country. His government mismanaged scarce resources, allowing the country to be used as a pawn in the hands of the superpowers. Thus, Somalia, like all African nations, reaped no benefits from the Cold War. In advancing their own interests, the superpowers were more than willing to provide guns instead of bread. That is, the country was patronized and provided some of the most dangerous and destructive weapons of the 20th Century. Placing such weapons in the hands of a largely poverty-stricken and backward populace (along with fueling of the fires of ideological differences) was homicidal. Also, the Somalia's leaders exacerbated the conflicts between and among clans by politicizing them. As a result, their focus was on defense and security rather than reconstruction and development (Ihonvbere, 1994, pp. 9-10).

By 1988, the Barre regime's grip on power began to slip, as Somalia was plunged into the inferno of civil war. The Barre regime was consumed by the civil war on various fronts, as the multiple armed militias attacked. Consequently, the Barre regime was unable to repel the multi-frontal attack from the various insurgency groups, who were united in their desire to oust Barre from power. Finally, the Barre regime collapsed. However, rather than forming a government of national unity that could have laid the ground work for building a post-Barre democratic society, the various factions turned on one another, thereby beginning another civil war. As Murunga (2005, p. 144) asserts, "Once Barre was ousted, the coalition entered a new phase of intense suspicions, factionalism and conflict." As Somalia degenerated into an orgy of violence, the international community was consumed by the "Gulf War." Hence, Somalia was neglected. The slowness, reluctance, and neglect of the United Nations, especially the United States, in responding to the Somali situation led to a deepening of the crisis. The UN and the USA's actions may have been attributed to the perceived uselessness of Somalia in the servicing of American interests as far as resources. Perhaps their rationale may be summed up in the words of an American soldier, who was a part of the failed peacekeeping efforts in Somalia: According to the soldier (1992), "There is nothing over here worth dying for."[1] Anyway, in 1991, with the approval of the United Nations, the United States intervened. However, the United States deviated from the locus of the intervention into attempts to impose on Somalia an American vision of a post-Barre order. One of the major strategies used by the United States was the effort to remove

Mohammed Farrah Aideed, the major warlord, from the Somali power calculus. The result was a conflict between the United States and General Aideed. Interestingly, an appreciable amount of the Somali people became sympathetic to the Aideed faction. Subsequently, some American soldiers were captured and killed; their bodies were paraded through the streets of Mogadishu. Frustrated by its failed peacekeeping and nation-building efforts, the United States withdrew its peacekeeping force. Thereafter, the war continued as various factions angled for strategic advantage. Various efforts were made by the Intergovernmental Authority on Development (IGAAD) to help resolve the war. In part, the peacemaking efforts led to the formation of various interim governments. However, these arrangements failed to end the war and create the conditions for addressing the problems that underlie the country's civil conflict. To make matter worse, Ethiopia, with American support, intervened militarily in Somalia in early 2007. The intervention witnessed a "min-war" between Ethiopia and the forces of the Union of Islamic Councils. In addition, the United States launched military strikes against what it termed "terrorist targets" in Somalia. Despite these military interventions, Somalia remains in a state of war.

Finally, what will it take to resolve the long Somalia civil war and restore the country to peace and stability? Undoubtedly, there are no easy recipes that can be drawn from a "cook book." However, several major steps need to be taken in helping to create the conditions for peacefully resolving the war. These measures should include the disarming, encamping and demobilization of the various clan-based forces; the establishment of a broad-based interim government of national unity with effective authority to govern the totality of the country; the drafting of a new constitution; the holding of democratic elections; the reconstruction of the infrastructure; the repatriation and re-settlement of internally displaced Somali and refugees; and the provision of basic human needs—housing, food, etc. Ultimately, the success of these and other proposals would depend upon the willingness of Somalia's warlords, their followers and the totality of the political class to put the supreme interests of their country and people above their own. The Biblical admonition of "beating swords into plowshares," rather than the converse, may be the definitive answer to Somalia's crisis.

Mozambique

The conflict in Mozambique can be attributed to four major factors: (1) the suffering and aftermath of four centuries of Portuguese colonization, (2) a thoughtless decolonization process, (3) the regional impact of Cold War tensions and an aggressive South Africa, and (4) the extension to Mozambique of the struggle against white minority rule in Rhodesia (Hume, 1994).

Unlike in other African countries, the genesis of conflict in Mozambique stemmed not from the issue of national identity but rather from disagreement over who should govern and how. That is, Mozambicans have always had a sense of who they are as a people. Thus, although the conflict has international and regional implications, it is essentially a domestic one.

The roots of Mozambique's current conflict can be traced to the issue of foreign governance. Starting with the actions of Spain in the late fifteenth century when Pope Alexander VI mediated the Treaty of Tordesillas (which in essence placed Mozambique under Portugal's domination for over four centuries), the subjugation of the country continued with the Berlin Conference of 1885's decision to use it as a bulwark against German expansion and to protect the British colony of Rhodesia. In particular, during the early years of the twentieth century, Mozambique became attractive as a natural outlet to the sea for the gold mines of South Africa and southern Rhodesia (now Zimbabwe) as well as a source of labor for the mines.

With the arrival of fascism in 1932, the Salazar government asserted control over Portugal's African colonies to provide an outlet for Portugal's emigrants and a domain for Lisbon's enterprises. No thought was given to the day when Mozambique would gain its independence. However, in 1962, former liberation groups from throughout the country merged to form the Front for the Liberation of Mozambique (FRELIMO) which was led by Eduardo Mondlane. FRELIMO's organized resistance to the colonial government made it untenable for colonialism to continue to exist. Ultimately, in 1974 Lisbon authorities decided that it was no longer feasible to remain in the country and beat a hasty retreat, leaving Mozambique in shambles (Hume, 1994, pp. 5-6).

Mozambique's troubles continued after independence in 1975. When South Africa implemented a forward defense based on its ability to project power beyond South Africa's borders, it relied on local insurgent forces and its own troops to implement the strategy, first in Angola, another Portuguese colony. In January 1975, Portugal signed an agreement with three Angolan liberation groups for elections to be held before independence. The groups began to fight among themselves, and the subsequent arrival of a huge contingency of Cuban military advisers and combat troops led to the intervention of the South African Defense Forces.

Also, Mozambique's independence was severely affected by the armed struggle against white rule in Rhodesia. Military operations included areas of the country where some members of the Zimbabwe African National Union had taken refuge. In addition, many Zimbabweans, including Robert Mugabe, the leader of the Union, are members of the Shona ethnic group, which extends across the border into central Mozambique (Hume, 1994). In retaliation for Mozambique's support of Rhodesia's liberation struggle,

Ian Smith, the Prime Minister, created RENAMO (The National Resistance Movement of Mozambique), a shadowy "anti-Marxist" guerilla movement, as a destabilizing force which waged war directly against FRELIMO. Supported by South Africa, the United States, and Portugal, RENAMO played an integral part in the anti-Communist Cold War strategy of the United States and its allies.

After decades of violence, death and destruction, the civil war ended in 1996. Thereafter, multi-party elections were held; they were won by FRELIMO. So, Joachim Chissano became the first President in the post-conflict era. Since, then, Mozambique has held two elections. The country has developed and is seeking to implement a post-conflict agenda that is designed to set Mozambique on the path to democracy and development.

CIVIL WARS IN AFRICA: THE RAMIFICATIONS FOR STABILITY AND DEVELOPMENT

Civil wars in Africa have resulted in a number of problems. First, they have weakened the control exercised by the state. Clearly, civil wars affect the ability of a state to exercise full control over the body politic. For example, it is difficult for the state to collect taxes, due to the migration of people in search for safety. Also, it is impossible for the state to enforce "law and order" in the affected areas of the war.

Second, an anarchical environment void of security usually emerges. As a result, the civilian population becomes vulnerable to violent crimes, particularly murder, as evidenced in the various cases covered in this chapter. For example, in the case of Rwanda, the emergent state of anarchy provided the conditions for the commission of acts of genocide.

Third, the high death tolls exacted in these civil wars have severely reduced the sizes of the affected countries' labor forces. For instance, during the Rwandan civil war of 1994, approximately 500,000 men, women, and children lost their lives (Kieh, 1996a, p. 44). Similarly, during the first Liberian civil war than 150,000 people were killed (Kieh, 1996a, p. 45).

Fourth, the spillover effects of these wars in terms of the plight of refugees, who seek safety in neighboring countries, are incalculable; although, estimates indicate that approximately one-half of the world's refugee population is African. These large groups of people (millions) are the poorest, most vulnerable, and least able to contribute productively to the economies of their respective countries. Instead, they exert tremendous pressure on the meager resources of their host countries for food, shelter, and other services (Obasanjo, 1991, p. xviii).

Fifth, civil wars adversely affect productive economic activities. Evidence shows that many of the African countries that have been engulfed in civil wars were simultaneously poor economic performers. For example, during their respective civil wars, the Sudan, Mozambique, and Somalia registered negative growth rates. Of course, there is no security of property rights, an important element in the determination of saving. Without saving, there can be no capital formation (Mbaku, 1998, p. 25).

Sixth, civil wars damage or destroy national infrastructures. Such infrastructures include roads, railways, telephone and telegraph installations, public health facilities, educational institutions, airports, bridges, irrigation systems, and electrical power plants. The disruption of services leaves the economic system incapable of meeting the basic needs of the people (Mbaku, 1998, p. 27).

Seventh, civil wars result in capital flight. African countries in conflict are most risky for investment. As a result, many international corporations, companies, and businesses abandon them for more stable countries. This lack of sufficient capital substantially hinders or inhibits the countries' potential for economic growth (Mbaku, 1998, p. 28).

BEYOND CIVIL WARS IN AFRICA: SOME PRESCRIPTIONS

Although, it is impossible to eliminate the factors that cause civil conflicts in Africa or any other place in the world, it is possible to control civil conflicts so that they do not degenerate into civil wars. In other words, conflicts are inevitable, because they are integral parts of human existence. However, mechanisms can be developed to help ensure that these conflicts do not become wars. Based on the case studies in this chapter, several suggestions can be made. Certainly, no one solution can help prevent the escalation of conflict into war; hence, it is better to use a synergistic approach First, the political systems of African states need to be democratize. This should include the respect for human rights; the sanctity of the rule of law; "checks and balances," especially the curtailing of presidential powers; the institutionalization of the "rules of politics;" the inclusion of all sectors of the society in the political process as stakeholders; the development of a strong and functioning civil society that is national in scope and practices internal democracy; the holding of regular, free and fair elections; the importance of merit as the basis for recruitment to the public sector; accountability in the conduct of the business of the state; and transparency in the administration of public affairs..

In the economic realm, attention should be given to those factors that create inequalities in a society. These should include job creation; the equitable allocation of national resources; the equitable distribution of wealth; the re-investment of the profits from the investments of foreign corporations in the local economy; the development of an industrial base; and the diversification of the economy.

In the social area, the investment in education would have to be the top priority, given the imperatives of the new millennium. Specifically, all African states need to give the highest priority to the expansion and improvement of their educational systems. This must include the construction of more schools; the provision of books, supplies and equipment; the development of a strong vocational educational sector; investment in the development of the naturals sciences; and emphasis on research and development. Also, public investments would have to be made in the provision of quality national health care; public housing; public transportation; sanitation; and safe drinking water.

Another major realm is religion. It is important for African states to promote religious pluralism based on tolerance and respect. Also, it is critical for all of the citizens of the various countries to have the freedom to practice their religious beliefs, as long as they do not violate the rights of others. Importantly, the state should not be used to privilege one religion over the others.

Culturally, ethnic diversity must be respected. That is, all of the various ethnic groups should be encouraged to respect and be sensitive to the cultures of the others. One of the major functions of the state in this regards is to encourage pluralism and peaceful co-existence by not giving any ethnic group advantage over the others in terms of the allocation of state resources.

CONCLUSION

This chapter has discussed some of the major causes of civil wars in Africa. It identified the nature of colonial state formation as the common underlying element. The case studies of Sierra Leone, Liberia, Rwanda, the Democratic Republic of Congo, Somalia, Sudan and Mozambique exemplify this phenomenon.

In the discussion of the various cases, the findings indicate that certain contingent or base factors play pivotal roles in laying the foundation for civil conflict and wars. The specific roles of these factors vary from country to country. For example, in Sudan economic and political classifications assumed ethnic characteristics; in Liberia, socioeconomic and political malaise led to conflict; and in Rwanda, the domination of power by one ethnic group over other groups precipitated a nightmare of genocide rarely witnessed in modern times.

Also, several proximate factors triggered civil wars in Africa: the colonial legacy of divide and rule; religious differences, micro-economic discontent; the domination of power by one group to the exclusion of others; and outside interference. Also, the specific trigger or triggers differ from conflict to conflict.

In terms of the impact of civil wars, the chapter identified several adverse consequences: the loss of state authority fueled by the break down of "law and order;" the occasioning of death, displacement and destruction; the undermining of productive economic activities; the reduction of the labor force; and capital flight. In short, civil war makes it impossible for national development to take place. This is because stability and peace are essential preconditions for the formulation and implementation of a national development agenda.

Finally, the chapter suggests some ways in which conflict could be managed so they do not degenerate into violence and its attendant adverse consequences. Politically, a democratic polity with its associated institutions, processes, rules and policies need to be developed and implemented. This would include the respect for human rights; the sanctity of the rule of law; checks on presidential powers; and the establishment of systems of accountability and transparency in the conduct of public affairs. In the economic realm, steps need to be taken to address issues such as job creation, equity in the distribution of wealth and improving the living standards of citizens. In the social areas, education is very critical. Hence, African states need to invest in the development of their educational systems. Also, the state needs to provide quality public health, public housing and other basic social needs. Culturally, it would be important for the conditions to be created so that all ethnic groups can live together in peace based on mutual respect. Similarly, a "culture of respect for religious diversity" needs to be established.

Note

1. Finally, Africa needs a new generation of dedicated and nationalistic leaders, who would put the interests of their respective citizens above their own. Additionally, these leaders must respect the constitution and laws, and enforce them in a fair and transparent manner. In short, African states need visionaries and "bridge builders" who can shepherd a national agenda that would transform the state and build holistic democracy by appealing to and mobilizing citizens across the broad spectrum—ethnic, regional, religious, etc.

Refeerences

American Soldier (1992). *Remarks concerning the Somali War.*

Anyang-Nyango, Peter (1991). "Crisis and Conflict in the Upper Nile Valley." In Francis Deng and I. William Zartman. *Conflict Resolution in Africa.* Washington D.C.: Brookings Institution Press.

Baregu, Mwesiga (2006). "Congo in the Great Lakes Conflict." In Gilbert Khadiagala (ed.). *Security Dynamics in Africa's Great Lakes Region.* Boulder, CO: Lynne Rienner, pp. 59-80.

Boahen, Adu (1987). *African Perspectives on Colonialism.* Baltimore, MD: The Johns Hopkins University Press.

Cole, Roy and H. J. DeBloji (2007). *Survey of Sub-Saharan Africa: A Regional Geography.* New York and Oxford: Oxford University Press.

Deng, Francis and I. William Zartman (eds.) (1991). *Conflict Resolution in Africa.* Washington D.C.: The Brookings Institution.

Ellis, Stephen (1995). "Liberia, 1989-1996: A Study of Ethnic and Spiritual Violence." *African Affairs*. Vol. 94. No. 375, pp.165-197.

Foltz, William (1998)."Restructuring the State in Chad." In I. William Zartman. *Collapsed States*. Boulder, CO: Lynne Rienner Publishers, pp. 15-32.

Gibson, Mark (1994). Interview *with Augustine Konneh on the First Liberian Civil War.*

Gurr, Ted Robert (1993). *Minorities at Risk: A Global View of Ethnopolitical Conflict*. Washington D.C.: United States Institute of Peace Press.

Horowitz, Donald (1985). *Ethnic Groups in Conflict*. Berkley, CA: University of California Press.

Hume, Cameron (1994). *Ending Mozambique's War*. Washington D.C.: United States Institute of Peace Press.

Ihonvbere, Julius (1998). *Africa's Past and Present: The Challenges of Democratic Reconstruction*. Paper delivered at the Nigerian Association Conference, Canada, April 15-17.

Ihonvbere, Julius (1994). "Beyond Warlords and Clans: The African Crisis and the Somali Situation." *International Third World Studies Journal and Review*. Vol. 6. No.1, pp.

Kandeh, Jimmy (1992)."Politicization of Ethnic Identities in Sierra Leone." *African Studies Review*. Vol. 35. No. 1, pp. 81-99.

Kieh, George Klay (2005). "State-Building in Post-Civil War Sierra Leone." *African and Asian Studies*. Vol. 4. Nos. 1 and 2, pp. 163-186.

Kieh, George Klay (1999). "Combatants, Patrons, Peacemakers and the Liberian Civil Conflict." *Studies in Conflict and Terrorism*. Vol. 15. No.2, pp. 125-143.

Kieh, George Klay (1996a). "The Political and Economic Roots of Civil Conflicts in Africa: Implications for American Foreign Policy." *Small Wars and Insurgencies*. Vol. 7. No.1, pp. 41-54.

Kieh, George Klay (1996b). "The Taproots of the Liberian Civil War." *Twenty-First Century Afro-Review*." Vol. 2, No.3, pp.123-152.

Konneh, Augustine (1997). *Understanding Conflicts in Africa*. Paper Presented at the Conference on Liberia at Morehouse College, Atlanta, Georgia. March 26.

Kpundeh, Sahr John (1995). *Politics and Corruption in Africa: A Case Study of Sierra Leone*. Lanham, MD: University Press of America.

Liebenow, J. Gus (1987). *The Quest for Democracy in Liberia*. Bloomington, IN: Indiana University Press.

Liebenow, J. Gus (1986). *African Politics*. Bloomington, IN: Indiana University Press.

Lumumba-Kasongo, Tukumbi (2005). "International Intervention, Democracy, Peacebuilding in the Great Lakes of Africa: A Regional Perspective to the Challenges." *African and Asian Studies*. Vol.4. Nos. 1 and 2. 2005, pp. 21-50.

Mbaku, John Mukum (1998). "Africa After More Than Thirty Years of Independence: Still Poor and Deprived." *Journal of Third World Studies*. Vol. 21. No. 2, pp. 13-58.

Murunga, Godwin (2005). "Conflict in Somalia and Crime in Kenya." *African and Asian Studies*. Vol. 4. Nos. 1 and 2, pp. 137-162.

Nasong'o, Shadrach Wanjalo and Godwin Murunga (2005)."Lack of Consensus in Constitutive Fundamentals: Roots of the Sudanese Civil War and Prospects for Settlement." *African and Asian Studies*. Vol.4. Nos. 1 and 2. 2005, pp. 51-82.

Newbury, Catherine (1995). "Background to Genocide: Rwanda." *Issue: A Journal of Opinion*. Vol. 23. No. 2, pp. 12-17.

Obasanjo, Olusegun (1991). "Preface." In Francis Deng and I. William Zartman (eds.) (1991). *Conflict Resolution in Africa*. Washington D.C.: Brookings Institution.

Reno, William (1997). "Privatizing War in Sierra Leone." *Current History*. Vol. 96. No. 601, pp.211-215.

Reyntjens, Flip (2006). "Governance and Security in Rwanda." In Gilbert Khadiagala (ed.). *Security Dynamics in Africa's Great Lakes Region*. Boulder, CO: Lynne Rienner Publishers, pp. 15-40.

Rosenblum, Peter (1997). "Endgame in Zaire." *Current History*. Vol. 96. No. 601, pp.200-205.

Rothchild, Donald (1991). "Interactive Model for State-Ethnic Relations." In Francis Deng and I. William Zartman (eds.). *Conflict Resolution in Africa*. Washington D.C.: Brookings Institution Press.

PART III

INSIGHTS AND PROSPECTS

Chapter 9

Beyond the Pantomimes of the Old Millennia: The Lessons

George Klay Kieh, Jr.

INTRODUCTION

What lessons can African states learned from the continent's predicament during the previous two millennia, in order to remove the albatross of underdevelopment? Given the multidimensionality of the crises of underdevelopment that has bedeviled the continent, the modalities that are designed and implemented would need to be comprehensive. Also, they must take cognizance of the objective conditions of the various states and formulate and implement measures that seek to address these realities. This is indispensable to addressing the continent's unending development crises. Although assistance from various sectors in the international community would be helpful, the continual practice of following prescriptions that are designed by external actors devoid of an understanding of the prevailing conditions in African states and the participation and input of Africans would continue to only exacerbate the crises of underdevelopment.

Against this background, this chapter has two major objectives. First, it will summarize the lessons the African continent should learn from the effects of the two previous millennia. These insights are drawn from the various chapters that constitute this volume. Second, the chapter will then suggest some ways in which Africa could transcend the pantomimes of the old millennia.

THE LESSONS

The Neo-Colonial State

After more than four decades, it is now abundantly clear that the neo-colonial state, which was bequeathed to African countries during independence, has failed to shepherd the process of building democratic and developed states. Hence, this genre of the state has become irrelevant to the lives of the subaltern classes on the continent. Samatar and Samatar (2002, p.5) provide put the case this way:

> Critical thinkers have certainly written off the African state in its post-colonial form, a stance that emits a degree of pessimism. However, one must acknowledge that their analytical animus is focused on the incapacity of the post-colonial state in history rather than the state per se. In other words, African development has stalled because the state is of the wrong kind, and therefore, a rethinking of its form seems to be of utmost necessity.

Similarly, Hadjor (1987, p. 68) asserts that "For most Africans, the state is an alien and hostile institution. The state never gives—it always takes. It never inquires or asks—the state demands and gives orders."

So, what attributes have made the post-colonial state a hindrance to people-centered development and holistic democracy in Africa? The foundational attribute is the nature of the state. The post-colonial state was not designed based on the historical and cultural experiences of the various African peoples. Instead, it is an alien construct that was fashioned to serve the interests of the metropolitan states and their ruling classes. Additionally, as the overarching architecture in a peripheral capitalist political economy, the neo-colonial African state lacks autonomy—relative or otherwise. So, the neo-colonial state is a partial and partisan construct that serves both the general interests of the metropolitan states and their dominant classes and the specific interests of the faction or fraction of the local African compradorial classes that has control of state power at given time intervals. As Ake (1985, p.10) notes,

> The state in Africa is not impartial. It means that the rules, whatever they are, which govern political competition and other aspects of social life do not have adequate institutional guarantee of their impartiality. Thus, political and economic competition becomes essentially "normless."

In short, because the neo-colonial state is a non-hegemonic, weak and dependent construct, it therefore lacks the capacity to be independent of the control of a particular faction or fraction of the African compradorial classes. Also, because the African compradorial classes lack independent economic bases, the capture and subsequent control of the state has become the dominant way for them to accumulate wealth. In other words, the control of political power equals the control of economic power. That is, the faction or fraction of the compradorial classes that has control of state power at a particular juncture uses it as a vehicle for predatory accumulation—the plundering and pillaging of the state's financial resources for private and personal enrichment.

Another feature that has made the neo-colonial state anti-people, anti-democracy and anti-development is its mission. The state has two major tasks. First, it superintends the process of the exploitation of African resources and the consequent transfer of wealth to the metropolis. The state does this by, *inter alia*, creating and maintaining a condusive environment in which metropolitan-based multinational corporations and other businesses can accumulate and siphon off profits by exploiting African workers and natural resources. When the African workers raise protests, the neo-colonial state then mobilizes the full battery of its repressive arsenal to "keep them in line." As Gana (1985, p. 116) observes, " The state in contemporary Africa...remains primarily the instrument of the metropolitan bourgeoisie for the reason that the internal process of capital accumulation is subordinated to the requirements of external, primarily metropolitan interests."The second and related dimension of the neo-colonial state's mission is to facilitate compradorial private accumulation of capital. As I have argued, the neo-colonial African state serves as an instrument in the hands of whatever faction or fraction of the local ruling class that has control of state power in an African country. The ruling compradors then use the power of the state to foster private wealth generation for them and their relations through the process of stealing from the public coffers. The mission of the neo-colonial state in Africa reflects the "Janus-faced" orientation of the construct: on the one hand, the neo-colonial state facilitates private wealth creation for the metropolitan ruling classes and their African compradors. But, on the other hand, the neo-colonial state generates mass and abject poverty and socio-economic malaise for the members of the various states' subaltern classes.

Also, the character of the neo-colonial African state constitutes an impediment as well. This is because it is the neo-colonial state's character that serves as the compass for guiding its actions in the various African polities. It is important to take cognizance of the fact that the construct's character is multidimensional—absolutist, criminalized, exploitative, neo-patrimonial, prebendal, predatory, privatized, repressive and vampirish. As Agbese (2007, p.36) argues, "The typical African state is a composite of several tendencies or characteristics." Importantly, the ascendancy of any particular tendency is a function of numerous conjunctural factors (Agbese, 2007, p.36). Thus, at several historical moments, some tendencies are clearly more dominant, while at other times, those same tendencies, while far from the political surface, do not completely disappear from the political arena (Agbese, 2007, p.36). For example, the repressive dimension of the neo-colonial state's character is often reflected in the way in which the construct responds to popular pressures. The dominant response is the use of violence as a vehicle for silencing the masses and other critics of state policies. The negligent aspect of the state's character is shown in the formation's lack of interest in addressing the basic human needs—education, health care, etc. —of the members of the subaltern classes. Consequently, as the various annual human development reports show, the vast majority of Africans are living precariously at the margins.[1]

The other characteristics of the neo-colonial state—values, institutions, rules, processes and policies—are designed and intended to foster the formation's twin mission of serving the interests of the metropolitan dominant classes and the African compradorial classes. For example, the state's investment policies generally give metropolitan-based multinational corporations and other businesses several perks, including duty-free privileges, tax breaks and the right to repatriate profits. Similarly, the lack of the enforcement of environmental policies allows multinational corporations and other foreign-owned businesses to degrade the continent's constituent states' ecosystems through, among other things, pollution.

Thus, the neo-colonial African state is intrinsically anti-people, anti-development and anti-democracy. Accordingly, it is virtually impossible to sustain even the modicum of reforms under such a tapestry. This is why, for example, it is difficult to consolidate political democratization in the various neo-colonial African state constructs. Over time, the neo-colonial state has undermined and eventually reversed whatever little gains that have been made in liberalizing the political space in several African countries. The intransigence of the "presidential monarchy," fraud-plagued elections and the "third term phenomenon" are manifestations of the neo-colonial African state's natural aversion to democratization—political or otherwise.

Economic Development

African states are confronted by myriad economic problems, including inadequate domestic capital formation, unfair trade, the debt crisis, unemployment and under employment, inequities in income and wealth and low standard of living. The locus of the domestic capital formation problem is that the African ruling classes have failed to make the internal creation of wealth the cornerstone of economic development. One of the major manifestations of this failure is the absence of major indigenous corporations in the various African states. To make matters worse, the managers of the neo-colonial African states are primarily interested in using state power to help facilitate wealth creation for metropolitan-based corporations and businesses.

Another problem is the unfairness of the international trading system. At the heart of the problem is the fact that the prices of the raw materials that constitute the kernels of African states' exports fluctuate based on the whims and caprices of the metropolis. Beyond the mythology of the so-called "laws of the market," it is actually the metropolis that determines the prices of Africa's agricultural, mineral and oil exports. So, in effect, the life blood of the economy of each African state is dependent upon the decisions of the metropolitan powers that control the international capitalist system. Within the resultant context of price fluctuations, the exports of African states experience various cycles of "boom" and "bust." The cyclical nature of the pricing of the exports of African states is worsen by the steady trend of the ever increasing prices of the manufactured goods produced mainly by the metropolis. Again, the prices for the metropolitan-produced manufactured goods are solely determined by the metropolitan powers. The resultant disparities between the prices of African states' primary products and the metropolitan powers' manufactured goods have regularly occasioned terms of trade problems for the former (with the exception of the oil producing African states, given the product's strategic nature).

Faced with low domestic capital formation and dwindling export earnings coupled with the effects of the "oil crisis" of the 1970s, most African states turned to external borrowing as a panacea—various loans were contracted from metropolitan powers, the metropolitan-dominated International Monetary Fund and the World Bank and metropolitan-based commercial banks. However, because the loans were not invested in productive economic activities that would have helped to generate domestic capital and wealth, African became engulfed in a "crisis." Characteristically, the African ruling classes looked to the metropolis for relief. The principal response from the metropolitan powers was a combination of debt re-scheduling and the contraction of more loans under the supervision of the International Monetary Fund (IMF).

In order to perform its role as the suzerain of "economic development" in Africa, the IMF designed and imposed its notorious "one size fits all" "structural adjustment programs" (SAPs) on debt-plagued African states. The fundamental premise of SAP was that the causes of the economic problems confronting all African states were the same; hence, the "solutions" had to be uniformed. So, the IMF required that various African states adopt and implement the "conditionalities" embedded in SAP; these included, trade liberalization, currency devaluation, the reduction of the size of the public bureaucracy, increased favorable investment terms for metropolitan-based multinational corporations and other businesses and the dismantling of "social safety nets." Again, SAP failed to address African states' fundamental economic problems. In fact, SAP exacerbated the continent's economic and social problems, and even precipitated political instability in some cases. Mbaku (1999, p.133) provides an analysis of the SAPs' deleterious effects on various African states thus:

> Perhaps, more important is the fact that despite many years of adherence to the SAPs, many countries in the region have been unable to reverse the continuing deterioration in living standards, and increasing inequality in the distribution of income and wealth. In fact, the evidence shows that Africa is poorer today than it was during the early 1960s, despite nearly16 years of adjustment.

Yet, another major lacuna is unemployment. Although the continent-wide unemployment rate of 11.1% in 1999 (United Nations Economic Commission for Africa, 2005) appears relatively low, the statistic is deceiving for two major reasons. First, the statistic does not reflect the magnitude of the problem among the various age grades. For example, youth unemployment on the continent stood at 21.9 % during the same period. With no gainful employment, the continent's youth have become quite disillusioned. As solutions, several of them have resorted to the engagement in criminal activities such as armed robbery as source of livelihood. Also, Africa's large reservoir of unemployed youth provides fertile recruitment pools for warlords and other militarists, who recruit young people as soldiers in their various militias. Second, another hidden dimension of the unemployment conundrum is the phenomenon of underemployment. Thousands of Africans are virtually nominally employed, because their wages are inadequate for meeting their basic needs. In 1999, 56% of the people working on the continent were considered underemployed. So, when the sectoral and underemployment dimensions are factored into the continent's unemployment matrix, the picture becomes bleaker.

Inequalities in income and wealth underscore the wide gulf that exists between the upper and lower classes on the continent. In terms of income, there is generally a huge gap between the salaries of top government officials and civil servants in the lowest rung of the public sector. For instance, the Gini coefficient for Sub-Saharan Africa stood at a high 72.2 % (Columnists, 2005). Additionally, there are huge disparities in the distribution of wealth on the continent. For example, while the members of the ruling classes and their relations and surrogates are amassing wealth through the instrumentality of the state, the members of the subaltern classes are drowning in the bottomless pool of abject poverty.

Another major problem is the overall low standard of living of the preponderant majority of the members of the subaltern classes. For example, in 1999, over 500 million of the region's population lived on less than $1 per day (Harsch, 2006). The gravity of the problem reflects the fact that thousands of Africans are virtually living from day to day, without knowing where the next meal will come from. Children, women and the elderly are the most vulnerable groups in the pantheon of the continent's most disadvantaged and destitute age and gender categories.

Democratization

There is no doubt that the "third wave of democratization," which began sweeping cross the continent in the early 1990s has had some positive impact. One of the most important effects has been the liberalization and subsequent opening of the political space. In turn, this has precipitated the disintegration of one-partyism as the kernel of the political system. And this has enabled Africans to establish political parties and to compete for state power.

Prior to the onset of the new millennium, appreciable strides were made in the efforts to improve the state of political rights and civil liberties. According to Freedom House, the number of African states that made great strides in the aforementioned area increased from two in 1990 to nine in 1999 (Freedom House, 2002). Countries such as Benin, Cape Verde, Ghana, Malawi, Mali, Senegal and South Africa made concerted efforts and set into motion the process of democratization.

Also, the "third wave" occasioned the emergence of numerous interest groups that constitute civil society in the various African states. These civil society organizations, among other things, are engaged in various activities that are helping to promote democratization. For example, some of these civil society organizations have undertaken various educational projects designed to acquaint the citizens of various African states with the constitutions of their various states. Others have engaged in activities intended to help develop the expertise, skills and capacities of various parliaments so that the latter can effectively provide oversight of the security sector.

On the other hand, there have been drawbacks in the efforts to democratize African states. The project has focused primarily on the political aspects of democratization to the neglect of the other aspects such as the economic and social dimensions. This problem is reflected, for example, in a country like Mali that has made laudable strides in terms of the respect for political rights and civil liberties and related areas; however, the country has fared very poorly in the economic and social domain. In effect, there is a disconnect between the political and the other dimensions of democratization, especially the economic and social ones. Another adverse effect was the slow pace of political democratic institutionalization. That is, very little progress was made in terms of making political rules, procedures and processes to transcend the whims and caprices of the ruling classes. This challenge was a major contributing factor to the recurrent oscillation between progress toward political democratization and the reversal to authoritarianism. Yet another lacuna was the growing trend of electoral fraud, which undermined the cherished democratic tenet of free and fair elections in which the electorate's choices are respected. Linked to this problem is the phenomenon of "constitutional coup-making" through the imposition of the "third term agenda" by various incumbents. That is, some African leaders made concerted efforts in trying to amend their countries' constitutions so that they could stay in power beyond their legally stipulated tenure of office. Clearly, this helped to undermine the rule of law and the process of political democratic institutionalization.

Social Development

The sordid state of the human condition on the continent was vividly reflected in various variables. In the area of public education, there were myriad problems. One of the cardinal ones was the inadequacy of access. This was demonstrated by the fact that about 40% of the school age children in the region did not attend school in 1999 (Harsch, 2006). A related challenge was the disparity in the limited access. Generally, schools were concentrated in the urban areas. Another problem was the woeful inadequacy of instructional resources and logistics. Critical tools such as books and chairs for students were generally in short supply across the continent. Consequently, in countries like Liberia, students were required to purchase their own instructional materials and chairs. Moreover, students were required to purchase lecture notes from their instructors. The failure to have done so adversely affected the academic success of students in many cases.

As the 20th century came to a close, Africa lagged behind the rest of the world in the area of health care and related areas (United Nations Development Program, 2001). This can be gauged by examining various indices—the access to health care; the number of health professionals; the number of health facilities—hospitals, clinics, etc; and the access to safe drinking water and acceptable sanitation. The inadequacy and overall poor state of the health infrastructure on the continent, among other things, made Africans vulnerable to death from curable diseases.

Similarly, the continent was plagued by a housing crisis as evidenced by the serious shortage of livable dwelling places across the continent. The problem was more acute in the urban centers. For example, between 40-70% of the urban dwellers lived in slums (Mutume, 2004). The conditions in these slums were horrendous. For example, there was the lack of electricity and inside plumbing for the preponderant majority of the shacks that constituted the dwelling places. Accordingly, residents used streams and other waterways as well as abandoned buildings, dilapidated automobiles and opened spaces as lavatory facilities. This practice contributed to the hazardous health conditions that obtained in these slums. In addition, these ghettos were enveloped by piles of uncollected garbage, thereby creating an environment smothered by filth and rot. These conditions also contributed to the residents' vulnerability to rodents and diseases. Given the limited capacity of the slums, scores of others, including young people were forced to become "street people."

Another major problem was urbanization and its attendant battery of challenges. This phenomenon was occasioned by the tremendous population growth in the various cities around the continent. For example, by 1999, the population in Lagos, Nigeria stood at 12.8 million people (United Nations Population Division, 1999, p. 9). According to South African Cities Network (2003, p.2), by 2020, Africa will have 11 cities having more than 5 million inhabitants and more than 3,000 cities with populations in excess of 20,000 (an increase of almost 300% from 1990). The population explosion in the continent during the latter half of the previous millennium was caused by several problems. At the epicenter was migration. With limited economic opportunities in various African states, especially in the rural areas, people moved to the various urban cities in search of employment and other economic opportunities. This put increased pressures on the already limited social services. Nwaka (2005, p.119) describes the impact of urbanization on the human condition in the region thus:

> The rapid pace of urbanization and the enormous scale of unmet needs are taking a toll on the continental cities and urban populations, especially the urban poor who live and work in appalling conditions that threaten their health and undermine their productivity.

The Environment

By the end of the last century, the cumulative effects of colonial and neo-colonial exploitation and neglect had taken their collective toll on the environment in Africa as was reflected in the pantheon of problems. So, given the multiplicity of the problems, it would not be possible to examine all of them in this section of the chapter. Accordingly, some of the critical ones will be discussed. Like the rest of the world, Africa greeted the 21st century amid bourgeoning increases in the adverse effects of climate change. Although the continent's emission of greenhouse gases was quite low, this did not reduce its susceptibility to the vagaries of "global warming." The problem was caused by a confluence of factors, including the inappropriate use and management of the land.

Linked to the challenge of climate change was climate variability. That is, the climatic conditions in the region experienced various changes. At the heart of the problem was the vexing issue of deforestation. In turn, the variations in the climate occasioned various negative consequences ranging from soil erosion to floods.

Another pervasive problem was pollution—air, land and water. The air was polluted by a host of factors—spanning from the burning of coal to smog generated by the burning of bushes for faming. Generally, the poor quality of the air contributed to people being afflicted by a host of respiratory diseases. In terms of land pollution, the culprits included human waste and toxic refuse. Faced with the acute shortages of lavatory facilities throughout the continent, people used the land as a major depository for human excreta. Additionally, the continent's land became prime territory for the disposal of toxic wastes from the metropolitan powers.

Civil Conflicts

During the last two decades of the previous millennium, the various conflicts that had been plaguing the continent since the advent of the post-colonial era reached their crescendo in some of the states as evidenced by the outbreak of several new civil wars. Beginning with Chad, the civil war virus quickly affected Somalia, Liberia, Sierra Leone, Burundi, Rwanda, the Congo, Djibouti, Guinea-Bissau and the Democratic Republic of the Congo. Characteristically, various scholars, the media and policy-makers in the metropolis blamed the implosion on "intractable ethnic animosities." In other words, the affected African states degenerated into civil wars because their various ethnic groups were divided by *ancien* hatred. To the contrary, the principal cause of civil wars on the continent was the failure of the neo-colonial state to address the legitimate aspirations and needs—cultural, economic, political, religious, security and social— of the vast majority of Africans. In turn, state failure generated multifaceted crises of underdevelopment, which provided the context for the germination of conflict and eventually war in some cases.

Generally, the various civil wars that rocked the continent during the second millennium negatively impacted the affected countries in various ways. For example, in 1999, there were 11.5 million refugees in Africa (Crisp, 2000, p.1). During the same period, there were 9.5 million internally displaced persons in Africa (Crisp, 2000, p.1). Also, the various civil wars wrecked havoc on social, educational and health services (Amoako, 1999, p.3).

PUTTING THE LESSONS INTO PRACTICE: SOME SUGGESTIONS

So, what needs to be done in order for Africa to transcend the pantomimes of the old millennia? Clearly, given the depth and dimensions of the multifaceted crises of underdevelopment that plagued the continent during the last two millennia and have continued into the 21st century, no study can even attempt to provide a comprehensive response. Notwithstanding, the provision of some suggestions would contribute to the much needed larger project of rescuing

Africa from the shackles of underdevelopment. In this spirit, drawing from the various chapters in this volume, I suggest some steps that need to be taken. The overarching step that needs to be taken is the deconstruction, rethinking and democratic reconstitution of the neo-colonial state in Africa. Given the centrality of the state as the arena in which all societal activities occur, the creation of a holistically democratic state in Africa is indispensable to the cultural, economic, environmental, political, religious and social development of the continent and its constituent states. Specifically, the neo-colonial state must be expunged as the social formation on the continent. This can be done through a national conference, on going discussions at various levels of the society, legal-constitutional changes and above all praxis. The resultant democratic reconstitution process should focus on systemic transformation that is anchored on radically changing the nature, mission, character, values, institutions, rules, processes and policies of African states. The ultimate objective is the establishment of a pro-people, pro-democracy and pro-development state. One of the major derivatives from the democratic reconstitution of the state in Africa would be the formulation and implementation of an economic development plan that seeks, *inter alia*, to promote productivity, the internal creation of wealth, the promotion of equity in the distribution of income and wealth and ultimately the improvement of the living standards of all Africans.

Another would be the transcendence of liberal democratization and its attendant narrow focus on political procedures and rights. Alternatively, the path to democratization should be holistic: it should seek to combine political procedures and freedoms with economic, social and others. The rationale is that in order for democratization and ultimately democracy to be meaningful to the lives of the majority of the African peoples, they must cover the broad gamut.

Democratic social development must focus on the formulation and implementation of plans that seek to address the challenges of urbanization, education, healthcare, access to safe drinking water and acceptable sanitation, housing and transportation. In other words, an effective "social safety net" must be created that has the right of citizens to live fulfilling lives as its centerpiece. One of the major preconditions for successful social development is the total rejection of neo-liberal theology and its attendant thrust of transferring wealth from African states to the members of the ruling classes.

In order to arrest the rising tide of environmental degradation on the continent, several steps would need to be taken. First, African states need to design and implement robust and effective anti-poverty programs. The purpose would be to help reduce the necessity for the members of the subaltern classes to abuse the environment as the search for sources for survival. Second, effective environmental regimes need to be established throughout the continent. An integral element of these regimes should be the application of procedures and rules as the bulwark against the marauding and environmentally destructive practices of metropolitan-based multinational corporations. Third, the regimes should seek to tackle the root causes of climate variability, climate change, pollution, deforestation and land degradation, among others. The ultimate goal should be to address these lacunas, so that the health of the environment can be improved.

Concerning the issue of civil wars, efforts need to be made to tackle the root causes—the failed neo-colonial state and its multifaceted crises of underdevelopment. In order words, democratic development should be used as the principal instrument of preventive diplomacy. That is, although civil conflicts are the handmaids of all human societies, democratic development can militate against the degeneration of such conflicts into armed violence.

CONCLUSION

The chapter has attempted to address two interrelated issues. First, the chapter summarized the lessons learned from some of the various frontier issues—the travails of the state, economic development, democratization, urbanization and social development, the tragedy of the environment and civil conflicts— addressed. The core lesson is that the neo-colonial state in Africa has failed to address the aspirations and needs of Africa's subaltern classes. In terms of economic underdevelopment, the findings indicate that several factors account for this, including the lack of democratic institutions and rules. As for democratization, especially its "third wave," some progress has been made. Among them is the liberalization of the political space. However, the "third wave" has not, among other things, promoted social and economic development on the continent. Social development on the continent is handcuffed by myriad problems including urbanization and its retinue of challenges. In terms of the environment, there is an increasing rate of degradation caused by factors such as pollution and deforestation. The aforementioned problems have contributed to civil wars in various African countries.

Second, the volume proffers some suggestions for improving the African condition. At the epicenter is the imperative of deconstructing, rethinking and democratically reconstituting the neo-colonial state on the continent so that it can be relevant to the lives of the majority of Africans. Based on the new state construct, holistic democratization can be pursued, economic, social and environmental development can be promoted and peace and stability can be established and maintained.

Note

1. For detailed and comprehensive data on the state of human needs in Africa, see the United Nations Development Program,

Human Development Reports, 1990-2006, (New York: Oxford University Press).

References

Agbese, Pita Ogaba (2007). "The State in Africa: A Political Economy." In George Klay Kieh, Jr. (ed.). *Beyond State Failure and Collapse: Making the State Relevant in Africa.* Lanham, MD: Lexington Books.

Ake, Claude (1985). "The Nigerian State: Antinomies of a Periphery Formation." In Claude Ake (ed.). *The Political Economy of Nigeria.* London and Lagos: Longman.

Gana, Aaron (1985). "The State in Africa: Yesterday, Today and Tomorrow." *International Political Science Review.* Vol. 6. No. 1, pp. 115-132.

Amoako, K.Y (1999). *The Economic Causes of Civil Wars and Unrest in Africa.* Address By the Under Secretary-General and Executive Secretary of the United Nations Economic Commission of Africa to the 70th Ordinary Session of the Council of Ministers of the Organization of African Unity. Held in Algiers, Algeria on July 8, p.3.

Columnists (2005). "Africa's Elite Enriched at the Expense of the Poor." September 9, p.1.

Crisp, Jeff (2000). *Africa's Refugees: Patterns, Problems and Policy Challenges.* New Issues in Refugee Research, Working Paper No. 28. Geneva: United Nations High Commissioner for Refugees.

Freedom House (2002). *Freedom in the World, 1972-2002.* New York: Freedom House.

Hadjor, Kofi Buenor (1987). *On Transforming Africa.* Trenton, NJ: Africa World Press.

Harsch, Ernest (2006). "Combating Inequality in Africa." *Africa Renewal.* Vol. 20. No. 2, pp. 16-30.

Mutume, Gumisai (2004). "Rough Road to Sustainable Development." *Africa Renewal.* Vol. 18. No. 2, pp. 19-20.

Nwaka, Geoffrey (2005). "Planning Sustainable Cities in Africa." In Okechuku Ukaga and Osita Afoaku (eds.). *Sustainable*

Development in Africa: A Multifaceted Challenge. Trenton, NJ: Africa World Press.

Samatar, Abdi and Ahmed Samatar (eds.) (2002). *The African State: Reconsiderations*. Portsmouth, NH: Heiniemann.

South African CitiesNetwork (2003). *Trends and Challenges in Sub-Saharan African Cities*. Cape Town: CitiesNetwork.

United Nations Development Program (2001). *Human Development Report*. New York: Oxford University Press.

United Nations Economic Commission for Africa (2005). *Economic Report on Africa, 2005*. Addis Ababa, Ethiopia: UNECA.

United Nations Population Division (1999). *World Urbanization Prospects: The 1999 Revisions*. New York: Population Division.

ABOUT THE CONTRIBUTORS

Ebenerzer O. Aka, Jr. is Professor of Urban Studies and Planning and Director of the Urban Studies Program at Morehouse College, Atlanta, Georgia, USA. His major research interests are in the areas of urban economic development, regional disparities and comparative urbanization. His works have been published in various scholarly journals, including International Journal of Urban Policy and Planning, African Urban Quarterly, International Journal of Public Sector Management, Review of Urban and Regional Development Studies and the Journal of Social Development in Africa. His most recent book is *Regional Disparities in Nigeria's Development: Lessons and Challenges for the 21st Century*, University Press of America.

Julius Ihonvbere served as the Special Advisor to President Olusegun Obasanjo of Nigeria on Policy and Project Monitoring from 2003-2007. Prior to that, he was Program Officer in the Civil Society and Social Justice Division of the Ford Foundation. Prior to joining the Ford Foundation, he served as Professor of Government at the University of Texas at Austin. He has published quite widely on several issues pertaining to Africa and the Third World. His most recent book is an edited volume (co-edited with John Mukum Mbaku on *Political Liberalization and Democratization in Africa: The Continuing Struggle*, Greenwood Press.

George Klay Kieh, Jr. is Professor of Political Science and African and African Amerian Studies at Grand Valley State University and Senior Research Fellow in the Program in Ethnic and Federal Studies at the University of Ibadan, Nigeria. Previously, he served as Dean of International Affairs at Grand Valley State University and Professor and Chair of the Department Science at Morehouse College, Atlanta, Georgia. He has published quite widely on various issues including peace and conflict, security studies, democratization, elections, foreign policy, political economy and international cooperation. His most recent book is *Liberia's First Civil War: The Crises of Underdevelopment*, Peter Lang Publishing.

Augustine Konneh is former Professor of History at Morehouse College. He previously served as Chair of the Department of History at Morehouse College. His research areas include African economic history, African American history and the history of civil conflicts. His publications have appeared in various journals, including the African Studies Review and the Liberian Studies Journal.

John Mukum Mbaku is the William Eccles Professor of Economics and John Hinkley Fellow at Weber State University, Utah. His research interests are in the areas of corruption, sustainable development, constitutional political economy and public choice theory. He has published quite prodigiously in the aforementioned areas in the forms of books, book chapters and journal articles. His most recent books are *Culture* and *Customs of Cameroon*, Greenwood

Press, and *Corruption in Africa: Causes, Consequences and Clean-ups*, Lexington Books.

F. Wafula Okumu is Head of the African Security Analysis Program at the Institute for Security Studies, Pretoria, South Africa. He has published on various issues, including democratization, governance and security in Africa. His most recent book (co-authored) is the African Union: Challenges of Globalization, Security and Governance (Routledge).

INDEX